4,-
LA
W29

FGF Studies in Small Business and Entrepreneurship

Editor-in-Chief
Joern H. Block
University of Trier, Heide, Germany

Andreas Kuckertz
University of Hohenheim, Stuttgart, Germany

Editorial Board
Dietmar Grichnik
University of St. Gallen, St. Gallen, Switzerland

Friederike Welter
University of Siegen, Siegen, Germany

Peter Witt
University of Wuppertal, Wuppertal, Germany

More information about this series at http://www.springer.com/series/13382

Stephanie Birkner • Kerstin Ettl •
Friederike Welter • Ilona Ebbers
Editors

Women's Entrepreneurship in Europe

Multidimensional Research and Case Study Insights

Editors
Stephanie Birkner
Carl von Ossietzky University of
Oldenburg
Oldenburg, Germany

Kerstin Ettl
University of Siegen
Siegen, Germany

Friederike Welter
University of Siegen/Institut für
Mittelstandsforschung Bonn
Siegen, Germany

Ilona Ebbers
European University of Flensburg
Flensburg, Germany

ISSN 2364-6918   ISSN 2364-6926 (electronic)
FGF Studies in Small Business and Entrepreneurship
ISBN 978-3-319-96372-3   ISBN 978-3-319-96373-0 (eBook)
https://doi.org/10.1007/978-3-319-96373-0

Library of Congress Control Number: 2018954501

© Springer International Publishing AG, part of Springer Nature 2018
This work is subject to copyright. All rights are reserved by the Publisher, whether the whole or part of the material is concerned, specifically the rights of translation, reprinting, reuse of illustrations, recitation, broadcasting, reproduction on microfilms or in any other physical way, and transmission or information storage and retrieval, electronic adaptation, computer software, or by similar or dissimilar methodology now known or hereafter developed.
The use of general descriptive names, registered names, trademarks, service marks, etc. in this publication does not imply, even in the absence of a specific statement, that such names are exempt from the relevant protective laws and regulations and therefore free for general use.
The publisher, the authors and the editors are safe to assume that the advice and information in this book are believed to be true and accurate at the date of publication. Neither the publisher nor the authors or the editors give a warranty, express or implied, with respect to the material contained herein or for any errors or omissions that may have been made. The publisher remains neutral with regard to jurisdictional claims in published maps and institutional affiliations.

This Springer imprint is published by the registered company Springer Nature Switzerland AG
The registered company address is: Gewerbestrasse 11, 6330 Cham, Switzerland

Preface

The internationally oriented German-based research association FGF (*Förderkreis Gründungsforschung e.V.*) has been partnering with Springer to showcase scholarly work in small business and entrepreneurship research since 2016. Titles in this series are by no means restricted to German-speaking countries, and this volume features research insights focusing on Germany with additional European perspectives. The aim of the *FGF studies in small business and entrepreneurship* is to acknowledge that small business and entrepreneurship phenomena occur on diverse levels of analysis. This is why the series addresses a plethora of research levels, has an interdisciplinary focus, and reflects on a wide range of methodological approaches. It aims to serve academics, educators, professionals, and policy makers as they disseminate and obtain new scientific insights and practical implications. The volume at hand is motivated by the discussions of a transdisciplinary group of researchers collaborating in the FGF standing working group "Gender & Entrepreneurship." Their joint target is to follow a twofold strategy to foster the academic focus on women's entrepreneurship. The first target is to offer researchers a portfolio of research approaches addressing current challenges and future perspectives of research on women's entrepreneurship. The second target is to provide entrepreneurship educators with a contemporary reference and essential reading material for students interested in questions addressing the challenges of and future academic and practical perspectives on gender and entrepreneurship. The ultimate objective of this volume is to combine theoretical as well as empirical research papers with teaching cases to deepen the reflections on women's entrepreneurship in research as well as in the educational field of the academic realm. Through this, the volume aims to serve as a vehicle to help researchers, educators, and professionals obtain multifaceted insights into women's entrepreneurship in Europe as a further basis to inform their actions in fostering future women's entrepreneurship. We would like to thank the FGF for the opportunity to shed this additional light on research and education about women's entrepreneurship from a European perspective. A particular word of thanks and credit belongs to everyone who served as reviewers supporting the double-blind peer review process of the volume: Elisabeth Berger, Nora Block, Siegrun Brink, Alexander Göbel,

Brigitte Halbfas, Sebastian Händschke, Lisa Heinrichs, Vivien Iffländer, Rosemarie Kay, Frauke Lange, Anna Müller, Kirsten Mikkelsen, André Pahnke, Ralf Philipp, Kathrin Rössler, Sanita Rugina, Katharina Schilling, Susanne Schlepphorst, Julia Schnittker, Demet Tuncer, Davy Vercruysse, Regina Wallner, and Claire Zerwas. Their critical and at the same time respectful feedback has been a major contribution. Furthermore, we would like to thank Elisabeth Berger who shared valuable insights from her experiences as an FGF series guest editor. Last but not least, we would like to thank Stephanie Weiss for providing patient and accurate assistance with the editing of the chapters.

Oldenburg, Germany	Stephanie Birkner
Siegen, Germany	Kerstin Ettl
Siegen, Germany	Friederike Welter
Flensburg, Germany	Ilona Ebbers

Contents

Part I Research Studies

Women's Entrepreneurship in Europe: Research Facets
and Educational Foci 3
Stephanie Birkner, Kerstin Ettl, Friederike Welter, and Ilona Ebbers

Female Migrant Entrepreneurship in Germany: Determinants
and Recent Developments 15
Nora Zybura, Katharina Schilling, Ralf Philipp, and Michael Woywode

Business Transferability Chances: Does the Gender
of the Owner-Manager Matter? 39
Rosemarie Kay, André Pahnke, and Susanne Schlepphorst

Does Gender Make a Difference? Gender Differences
in the Motivations and Strategies of Female and Male Academic
Entrepreneurs 65
Vivien Iffländer, Anna Sinell, and Martina Schraudner

Towards Emancipatory Aspects of Women's Entrepreneurship:
An Alternative Model of Women's Entrepreneurial Self-Efficacy
in Patriarchal Societies 83
Kirsten Mikkelsen

Women Entrepreneurship in Estonia: Formal and Informal
Institutional Context 105
Sanita Rugina

Entrepreneurship Education and Gender in Europe 137
Davy Vercruysse

Part II Case Studies

Coming to Entrepreneurial Berlin and Making Their Way in Silicon Allee: The Ups and Downs of Two Women Entrepreneurs 169
Alexander Goebel and Sebastian G. M. Händschke

Allure and Reality in FemTec Entrepreneurship 183
Frauke Lange

The Female Hunting Instinct: Entrepreneurial Life in Germany 197
Juliane Mueller

About the Editors and List of Contributors

About the Editors

Stephanie Birkner is junior professor in the field of female entrepreneurship at the Carl von Ossietzky University Oldenburg in Germany. Prior to this, she was appointed as acting professor with a focus on business simulations at the Jade University of Applied Sciences in Germany. She graduated in business administration (University of Applied Sciences Emden/Leer, also in Germany) and received her doctorate in consulting research from the Carl von Ossietzky University Oldenburg. Dr. Birkner is an active member of the scholarly associations ECSB (European Council for Small Business) and the FGF (*Förderkreis Gründungsforschung e.V.*), initiating and leading the FGF "Gender & Entrepreneurship" standing working group. In addition to social science approaches in the context of digital transformation with a focus on topics such as entrepreneurial identity and talent profiling, she is particularly interested in engineering and natural science (public) health perspectives on gendered innovation. As a certified personal coach and LSP facilitator, she supports academic start-ups. Since 2015, she has been gaining her own practical entrepreneurship experiences as co-founder of GREP: German Real Estate Pioneers GmbH. Her experiences here inform her lectures at the IREBS (University of Regensburg, Germany) in places such as the "Digital Real Estate Manager" study program.

Kerstin Ettl is junior professor in the field of entrepreneurial diversity and SME management at the University of Siegen's Department of Business in Germany. She holds a graduate and doctoral degree in business administration from the University of Siegen. She is country vice president for Germany of the European Council for Small Business (ECSB), active member of the FGF e.V. (the leading and most important scientific association for entrepreneurship, innovation, and SMEs in the German-speaking realm), and active member of the Women's & Gender Research Network NRW. Her current research interests include diversity, entrepreneurship, and SME management from individual and contextual points of view. Recurring topics in her research agenda are gender aspects, strategic and SME management, and innovation and technology. She also teaches bachelor's and master's classes, mainly in business administration, entrepreneurship, SME management, and plural economics.

Friederike Welter leads the *Institut für Mittelstandsforschung*(IfM) Bonn in Germany and is a professor of entrepreneurship and small business management at the University of Siegen in Germany. Prior to this, she was a professor and associate dean of research at the Jönköping International Business School in Sweden, professor at the University of Siegen, and senior researcher/deputy head of the research group "Craft enterprises, SME and entrepreneurship development" at RWI Essen in Germany. She has also served as president of the European Council for Small Business and Entrepreneurship. For her entrepreneurship and SME research, she has been honored as an ECSB fellow, as a Wilford L. White fellow of the International Council of Small Business, and received the Greif Research Impact Award. The *Frankfurter Allgemeine Zeitung* regularly lists her among the most influential economists in Germany. She has published extensively on entrepreneurship in different contexts, women's entrepreneurship, and entrepreneurship policies. Dr. Welter is also senior editor of the leading journal *Entrepreneurship Theory and Practice*.

Ilona Ebbers is a professor of economics and its didactics at the Department of International Management and Economic Literacy at the European University of Flensburg in Germany. Before this, she was professor of economics and its didactics at the Department of Business at the University of Siegen in Germany and the Center for Economic Literacy in Siegen. Prior to this, she was an assistant professor for SME management at the Department of Business at the University of Hildesheim in Germany. She holds a graduate and doctoral degree in economics and business administration from the Bergische University of Wuppertal in Germany. She is an academic officer of the German Council for Economic Literacy and member of the FGF e.V. Her research interests are in the field of entrepreneurship education, women's entrepreneurship, the transition from school to work, and gender as a didactical category. She teaches bachelor's and master's classes for future teachers of economics and politics.

List of Contributors

Stephanie Birkner Carl von Ossietzky University of Oldenburg, Oldenburg, Germany

Ilona Ebbers Abteilung Wirtschaftswissenschaften und ihre Didaktik, Europa Universität Flensburg, Flensburg, Germany

Kerstin Ettl University of Siegen, Siegen, Germany

Alexander Goebel Lehrstuhl für Arbeits-, Betriebs- und Organisationspsychologie, Friedrich Schiller University Jena, Jena, Germany

Sebastian G. M. Händschke Lehrstuhl für ABWL/Organisation, Führung und HRM, Friedrich Schiller University Jena, Jena, Germany

Vivien Iffländer Technical University of Berlin, Berlin, Germany

Rosemarie Kay Institut für Mittelstandsforschung (IfM) Bonn, Bonn, Germany

Frauke Lange Female Entrepreneurship, University of Oldenburg, Oldenburg, Germany

Kirsten Mikkelsen Europa-Universität Flensburg, Flensburg, Germany

Juliane Mueller Martin Luther University Halle-Wittenberg, Halle (Saale), Germany

André Pahnke Institut für Mittelstandsforschung (IfM) Bonn, Bonn, Germany

Ralf Philipp University of Mannheim, Mannheim, Germany

Sanita Rugina Kingston University, Kingston upon Thames, UK

Katharina Schilling University of Mannheim, Mannheim, Germany

Susanne Schlepphorst Institut für Mittelstandsforschung (IfM) Bonn, Bonn, Germany

Martina Schraudner Fraunhofer Center for Responsible Research and Innovation (CeRRI), Berlin, Germany

Anna Sinell Fraunhofer Center for Responsible Research and Innovation (CeRRI), Berlin, Germany

Davy Vercruysse Faculty of Economics and Business Administration, Ghent University, Ghent, Belgium

Friederike Welter University of Siegen, Siegen, Germany

Institut für Mittelstandsforschung (IfM) Bonn, Bonn, Germany

Michael Woywode University of Mannheim, Mannheim, Germany

Nora Zybura University of Mannheim, Mannheim, Germany

Part I
Research Studies

Women's Entrepreneurship in Europe: Research Facets and Educational Foci

Stephanie Birkner, Kerstin Ettl, Friederike Welter, and Ilona Ebbers

Abstract Women entrepreneurs currently enjoy their ascent as one of the fastest growing entrepreneurial populations worldwide. Nevertheless, they differ in both practice and in research from what is seen as "the norm." This introductory chapter aims to outline previous research facets of women's entrepreneurship by briefly mapping the status of the scientific field. In doing so, we lay the groundwork for presenting the scopes and foci of the articles in this volume which investigate different facets of women's entrepreneurship across Europe. Fostering women's entrepreneurship simultaneously implies including it in academic teaching. So in the second part of this introduction, we briefly talk about case studies as effective tools for teaching women's entrepreneurship. We conclude by introducing the cases provided in this volume.

S. Birkner (✉)
Carl von Ossietzky University of Oldenburg, Oldenburg, Germany
e-mail: stephanie.birkner@uol.de

K. Ettl
University of Siegen, Siegen, Germany
e-mail: kerstin.ettl@uni-siegen.de

F. Welter
University of Siegen, Siegen, Germany

Institut für Mittelstandsforschung (IfM) Bonn, Bonn, Germany
e-mail: welter@uni-siegen.de

I. Ebbers
European University of Flensburg, Flensburg, Germany
e-mail: ilona.ebbers@uni-flensburg.de

1 Research Facets of Women's Entrepreneurship

1.1 Mapping the Current Status of the Scientific Field of Women's Entrepreneurship

Almost every article on women's entrepreneurship starts with the notion that one of the fastest growing entrepreneurial populations are women, and that they significantly contribute to the innovativeness and development of economies and societies. These articles often end with the plea to better understand how to foster and make use of this potential. The short version of all of this is: A lot has happened in politics, academia and education in the last two decades—a lot still needs to be done!

Although the gender gap (the ratio of women to men participating in entrepreneurship) of 63 (out of 74) GEM-profiled economies narrowed by 5% in the year 2016 (GEM 2017), women are still more likely to start a business out of necessity rather than opportunity. Their businesses furthermore expect lower growth rates. A similar picture emerges for Europe, as seen in a recent policy brief on women's entrepreneurship. Here, women are less likely to be owners of new businesses: over the period of 2010–2014, only 2% of women indicated that they own and operate a business, while the number of men was 4% (OECD/European Commission 2017). Within the European Union (EU), several policy attempts have been made during the last decade to foster entrepreneurial opportunities for entrepreneurial women, e.g. by providing dedicated incubator and accelerator programs. However, comparing the positioning of women entrepreneurs in Sweden and the United States through the lens of public policy, Ahl and Nelson (2015) found that women are still seen as the "others," being inadequate and/or extraordinary without taking into account the social and structural conditions that shape their work experience. Henry et al. (2017) illustrate that only few governments pay attention to normative institutions when designing and implementing women entrepreneurship policies. This is one of the reasons we see the need to gain more insight into women's entrepreneurship in Europe to address and evaluate not only the design of European policies to foster women's entrepreneurship, but also to assess and address the impact of the overall position of women in the context of entrepreneurial equality.

Concepts in entrepreneurship theory and practice have long been either dominated by a supposedly gender-neutral perspective (Marlow et al. 2009), or mainly eulogized as part of a dominant male discourse lacking the complexity of theories on gender aspects (Lansky 2000). To overcome the subordination of female founders and funders, an understanding of the "genderedness" of entrepreneurship research and practice is needed (De Bruin et al. 2006, 2007). A women's perspective on entrepreneurship has become increasingly prevalent since the early 1980s, with a distinct rise since the mid-1990s. Greene et al. (2006) illustrate how research traditions shifted from analyzing gender through the variable of sex (1970s–1980s) towards applying more of a gender "lens" (1990s–2000s).

The plea by Ahl (2006) to capture a richer perspective on women's entrepreneurship (research) in the first special issues on women's entrepreneurship in the renowned journal *Entrepreneurship Theory and Practice* (De Bruin et al. 2006) found particular resonance in further special issues in the same journal (De Bruin et al. 2007; Hughes et al. 2012) as well as in special issues of *Small Business Economics* (Brush et al. 2018) or *Venture Capital* (Leitch and Hill 2006; Leitch et al. 2017). Since 2003, women entrepreneurship research has gained stronger visibility in the scientific community through its own international DIANA conference. Additionally, leading international scientific associations advocate focus groups and conference tracks on gender aspects in entrepreneurship. Another step forward in women's entrepreneurship research was the launch of the *International Journal of Gender and Entrepreneurship* (IJGE) in 2009. The regular anthologies published from the DIANA conferences, e.g. on entrepreneurial ecosystems and the growth of women's entrepreneurship (Manolova et al. 2017); women's entrepreneurship in different contexts (Díaz-García et al. 2016); research agendas regarding women entrepreneurship and entrepreneurial identity (Greene and Brush 2018); and research handbooks e.g. on gender and innovation (Alsos et al. 2016); on the performance of women-owned businesses (Yousafzai et al. 2018); or on the contextual embeddedness of women entrepreneurship (Yousafzai et al. 2018) inform and form the scientific community of women's entrepreneurship.

Along with a growing number of empirical surveys from a multitude of perspectives that span different cultures and countries, theoretical attempts to study women's entrepreneurship are increasing as well. However, following Brush et al. (2009, p. 18) "a separate theory on women's entrepreneurship may not be required if existing theoretical concepts are expanded to incorporate explanations for the distinctiveness of women's entrepreneurship."

So from an original paucity of research on women's entrepreneurship (Gatewood et al. 2003), this topic has now spawned into an actual field of research, characterized by Hughes et al. (2012, p. 429) 5 years ago as being "at the brink of adolescence." The field now seems to be in its "teens," challenged by a liminal state of its own reaching for broader acceptance in the "adult world" of entrepreneurship research. More and more researchers focusing on women's entrepreneurship consider gender as socially constructed (Tedmanson et al. 2012). Related studies have for example analyzed how identities are gendered and practiced (Díaz-García and Welter 2013). Other studies argue for considering gender in a more integrated and sophisticated way to analyze its many different effects on entrepreneurial activity (Marlow and Martinez Dy 2018), or focus on gender aspects of learning and opportunity recognition (Ettl and Welter 2010a, b). Further recurring topics include gendered contexts and institutions (Brush et al. 2009, 2014, 2018; Welter et al. 2014).

In spite of this progress, most research on women's entrepreneurship has taken place outside mainstream entrepreneurship debates (Jennings and Brush 2013). This is quite unfortunate, and not only from the point of view of women entrepreneurship. Entrepreneurship research in general would benefit from a gendered perspective because it would allow us to clearly articulate the full impact of entrepreneurship on societies and economies. It would also assist us in revising our assumptions about what constitutes success and performance as brought forth by Jennings and Brush (2013) and Baker and Welter (2017). For example, Calás et al. (2009) have used feminist theoretical perspectives to call for a broader focus on entrepreneurship (i.e. critical entrepreneurship studies (CES)). Ahl and Marlow (2012) introduced the post-structural feminist analysis to inform entrepreneurship theory. Rouse et al. (2013) edited a special issue of the *International Journal of Entrepreneurial Behaviour and Research* which brought together authors that employed existing gender theories to explore entrepreneurship. By way of example, Pathak et al. (2013) base their research on the sociological model of gender stratification to examine the effects of gendered institutions on women's entrepreneurship.

1.2 Landmarks of Women's Entrepreneurship Research in This Volume

To illustrate the multifaceted picture of women's entrepreneurship, the chapters in this volume address scientific as well as didactical fields of interest from various perspectives.

In chapter "Female Migrant Entrepreneurship in Germany: Determinants and Recent Developments", Nora Zybura, Katharina Schilling, Ralf Philipp and Michael Woywode investigate the growing group of female migrant entrepreneurs in Germany who have so far gained only limited scholarly attention. Migrant entrepreneurship is of increasing socio-economic significance in light of the current refugee crisis occurring in various parts of the world. Based on the German microcensus, the authors provide an overview of the structural characteristics of female migrant entrepreneurs. Looking at selective determinants such as qualification, occupational segregation and family responsibilities, they draw a detailed picture of female migrant entrepreneurship and its development in Germany between 2005 and 2016. Investigating a sub-group of women entrepreneurs under specific contextual conditions, Zybura et al. reveal the inherent, multifaceted nature of women entrepreneurship itself, emphasizing the intersectionality of gender and migration. Their results show for example that female migrant entrepreneurs often make career choices that lead to dependent occupations rather than entrepreneurship, and that a high qualification level is most favorable for female migrants in terms of entrepreneurial activities. Summing up, with a look at entrepreneurial activities and determinants of female migrants compared to women of German origin, the authors emphasize that it cannot clearly be stated that self-employed female migrants face a dual disadvantage per se.

In chapter "Business Transferability Chances: Does the Gender of the Owner-Manager Matter?", Rosemarie Kay, André Pahnke and Susanne Schlepphorst concentrate on the business transferability opportunities of female- vs. male-led family enterprises. Using large-scale panel data provided by the German Institute for Employment Research (IAB), the authors focus on the question of whether the sex of the owner-manager has an influence on the chances of business transferability. Their results support the findings on business successions and gender that highlight gender differences in general investment behavior, risk preferences, and business performance of companies. Drawing a detailed picture of enterprises, and especially those with business succession plans, their data show structural differences between women- and men-led enterprises, for example with the tendency of women-led businesses to invest less. The authors were however not able to confirm general gender-specific differences in the economic behavior of companies in their pre-transfer phase. Apparently, it's less the sex of the owner-manager than structural differences such as company size or industry that influence the business transfer process. This highlights the importance of the contextual embeddedness of entrepreneurship and entrepreneurial behavior where gender aspects are just one facet among many others.

The chapters authored by Zybura et al. and Kay et al. are complemented by chapter "Does Gender Make a Difference? Gender Differences in the Motivations and Strategies of Female and Male Academic Entrepreneurs", co-authored by Vivien Iffländer, Anna Sinell and Martina Schraudner. These authors focus on the gender differences in the motivations and strategies of female and male academic entrepreneurs. Using an exploratory case study method, Iffländer et al. draw on 40 interviews with academic entrepreneurs in Germany. In their sample, female academic entrepreneurs were often motivated to make a social difference through their ideas and products. Male academic entrepreneurs more frequently aimed to achieve goals like financial success and recognition, placing strong focus on product values and technological advantages. The authors conclude that the motivations of women, although important for societal development, are rarely addressed in government initiatives and policies. Their study enriches the debate about the exclusion and "othering" of women entrepreneurs, pointing once again to the need for policymakers and academics to be aware of hidden assumptions underlying policy initiatives and entrepreneurship support.

In chapter "Towards Emancipatory Aspects of Women's Entrepreneurship: An Alternative Model of Women's Entrepreneurial Self-Efficacy in Patriarchal Societies", Kirsten Mikkelsen offers a bi-national study, looking at both Germany and Denmark as patriarchal societies, and social mechanisms as a result of national cultural attitudes. She analyzes the emancipatory aspects of women's entrepreneurship and discusses an alternative model of women's entrepreneurial self-efficacy (ESE). In doing this, she addresses calls for more nuanced attempts at research on women's entrepreneurship, in particular arguing for the inclusion of gender into existing theories and concepts in entrepreneurship research. Her findings are based on 16 biographical narrative interviews with women entrepreneurs from diverse industries where women are underrepresented. Most studies on ESE treat gender as an external variable. However, Mikkelsen's approach stresses the value of inductive interpretative methods which enable researchers to find new concepts for understanding women's entrepreneurship as an alternative to what she calls "male-mainstream models and rationalities," and that are closer to the reality of women entrepreneurs.

Whereas Denmark has been in the top ranks of entrepreneurship rankings within Europe for years, in chapter "Women Entrepreneurship in Estonia: Formal and Informal Institutional Context", Sanita Rugina provides insights into Estonia, a former socialist republic and a country in which the women entrepreneurship rate is lower than the EU-28 average, and among the lowest in Europe. Looking at formal and informal institutional contexts and based on 20 interviews with women entrepreneurs in some of Estonia's major cities, Rugina highlights the embeddedness of (women's) entrepreneurship in its social and societal contexts. Her results indicate that gender stereotypes within Estonian society restrict women on their way towards self-employment—although these women are in fact motivated and have the required qualifications and skills to set up a business. The author concludes that Estonian government and policymakers need to urgently pay attention to women entrepreneurs and their support needs to foster a more enterprising attitude in the country. This chapter also highlights and illustrates the contextual embeddedness of women's entrepreneurship, calling for increased attention to it in policymaking.

As a perfect bridge to the second part of this volume, Davy Vercruysse provides in chapter "Entrepreneurship Education and Gender in Europe" insights into entrepreneurship education in Europe, with special emphasis on gender aspects. His results are based on a systematic literature review of studies about higher education, presenting the state of entrepreneurship education and gender within the last decade. Vercruysse develops a European map of research to identify implications for European educators and policymakers attempting to foster entrepreneurial ecosystems that also support women entrepreneurs. He concludes from his review that more customized, women-centered and diversified educational programs could allow female students to become more interested in entrepreneurial careers and have higher entrepreneurial intentions. He mentions promising elements within these programs such as networking events, tutoring sessions, testimonials of successful women entrepreneurs and female role models. Additionally, he discusses structural support from European and national governments as a key factor for stimulating women's entrepreneurship.

2 Teaching Women's Entrepreneurship Using Case Studies

Interestingly enough, the recognition of male dominance in the practical realm of entrepreneurship (Hamilton 2013), although repeatedly discussed in women entrepreneurship research, has not yet led to a shift that expands upon the entrepreneurial gender bias in teaching cases.

Empirically grounded teaching cases that include gender perspectives in entrepreneurship education continue to lack. So the second section of this volume attempts to do something about this deficit. It consists of three case studies that are accompanied by detailed teaching instructions. All of them are based on the actual life stories of women entrepreneurs; these case studies originated from empirical research projects on entrepreneurship issues.

But first things first: Why do we need (more) case studies about women entrepreneurs? Providing such cases in entrepreneurship courses aims to enhance women's visibility in entrepreneurship and sensitize (female) students towards starting their own business. By facing the cases and working through their inherent problems and challenges, students can experience societal realities via real case scenarios (Kaiser

1983) and holistically act, learn, and make decisions in situations that are drawn from actual business reality (Weitz 2011). Real cases offer the opportunity to reflect on one's own actions by diving into real scenarios and challenges (Kaiser and Kaminski 1997). The case study method requires an action- and decision-making orientation, and supports the development of key competencies such as systematic thinking, creativity, communication skills, cooperation competencies, decisiveness, and problem-solving skills (Wolf 1992). In general, case study didactics are guided by the students' living environment/realities, and thus corroborate the situation-theoretical approach of didactics. Utilizing cases in teaching facilitates individuals to mature and develop into autonomous decision makers who are able to take responsibility for their own decisions and actions (Kaiser 1983).

Successful teaching with cases is only possible if the teacher considers the specific background of the target group. This makes a horizontal internal differentiation within this group necessary. A division into two groups could be a viable didactical step in supporting internal differentiation, helping to underpin the multiple opportunities of using case studies to get individuals with different backgrounds interested in and motivated to work with or within the topic. This specifically means:

1. Students who want to discuss the discourse related to the cases presented
2. Students who already have (start-up) experience and use the cases to enrich their own experience with second-hand experience (Rebetja and Villnow 1994).

The cases presented in this book follow the principles of exemplarity, clarity and action orientation (Weitz 2011). They combine case study methods and case- problem methods. A case study method provides students with information, inviting them to identify challenges and find solutions for them. By contrast, the case problem method offers a more detailed description of an existing problem where students are invited to elaborate upon solutions (Kaiser and Kaminski 1997). Consequently, different levels of knowledge and experience on behalf of the students can be taken into account. In sum, the case studies presented in this book support the internal differentiation in (academic) entrepreneurship education and are a promising way of sensitizing and motivating students to get involved with the topic of women's entrepreneurship as both a field of research as well as an exciting career path. And who knows? They may even play a part in developing future knowledge in entrepreneurial intentions and actions.

The first case (chapter "Coming to Entrepreneurial Berlin and Making Their Way in Silicon Allee: The Ups and Downs of Two Women Entrepreneurs") describes and recounts the "ups and downs" of two female entrepreneurs from their early childhood experiences to reflections about recent entrepreneurial activity. The authors Alexander Goebel and Sebastian Händschke especially focus on how both women entrepreneurs coped with failure, allowing students to analyze an often neglected facet of (women's) entrepreneurship.

A female entrepreneur struggling in the mechanical engineering entrepreneurial ecosystem is the protagonist of the second case presented by Frauke Lange (chapter "Allure and Reality in FemTec Entrepreneurship"). Similar to the first case, the topic of failure is here handled as the "allure and reality" together with aspects of the contextual embeddedness of entrepreneurial paths.

Juliane Müller authored the third case (chapter "The Female Hunting Instinct: Entrepreneurial Life in Germany") which introduces a woman entrepreneur who founded a knowledge-intensive business service while also trying to successfully balance work and life as the mother of two children. The motivational factors—"the female hunting instinct"—of founding and running an own business are a main topic in this case. The additional teaching material accompanying this case study outlines an effective use of the jigsaw method, a cooperative learning approach encouraging the participation of learners by making their learning outcomes dependent on and interactive with each other.

3 Guideposts for Advancing Women's Entrepreneurship Research

This volume achieves advances in terms of the questions raised, methods used, and explanations proposed in the field of women's entrepreneurship research. With its teaching cases, it offers an additional element that raises the awareness and stimulates the appreciation of women-specific aspects of entrepreneurial intention and activity among future entrepreneurship researchers and educators, as well as (soon-to-be) start-up founders, funders, and supporters.

Nevertheless, and as stated in the first paragraph above, a lot remains to be done to further the frontiers of women's entrepreneurship research. One critical aspect lies in the fact that women's entrepreneurship research tends to fall into the trap of affirmative action. The growing breadth of scholarly, educational, and political activity is encouraging in how it continues to correct the historical inattention paid to the perspectives of female entrepreneurship (Hughes et al. 2012). But research on women's entrepreneurship still in fact has its own blind spots: It takes women as the proxy for gender perspectives in entrepreneurship research, while simultaneously criticizing entrepreneurship research for positioning women as "the other" (Ahl 2002). We concur with Marlow and Martinez Dy (2018) that it is time to open up the gender agenda in entrepreneurship research to generate a richer and more robust understanding of the impact of gender upon entrepreneurial intention, propensity, and activity. This also implies that we need to rethink our label for this strand of research. When we study entrepreneurship from a woman's perspective, why is this automatically gender research? Can't it also be women's entrepreneurship research with a focus on gender aspects, or maybe just plain old entrepreneurship research, period? Challenging ontological as well as epistemological assumptions from a woman's perspective have been vital in revealing the masculine bias and the masculine norm in entrepreneurship research. Therefore, in order to further the field of women's entrepreneurship research, we suggest better distinguishing between research on women's entrepreneurship and gender research on women and men entrepreneurs.

So what is left to do? A further step in acknowledging the complexity and diversity of gendered ascription in the context, processes, and interaction inherent to entrepreneurship would be a good idea that would open up promising avenues for future research. For example, gender studies have emphasized gender as something that we "do," not as something that we "are" (West and Zimmermann 1987; Bruni et al. 2004; Butler 2004; Deutsch 2007). We encourage more studies that draw attention to "doing gender" and "undoing gender" (e.g. Bianco et al. 2017; Díaz-García and Welter 2013; Pecis 2016); also in relation to gendered contexts (Baker and Welter 2017). Moreover, with the need for enhanced transnational exchange in women's entrepreneurship research, especially in accordance with the powerful role of globalization as an economic, social, and cultural force (Hughes et al. 2012), gender is one of the aspects that needs to be studied when conceptualizing intersectionality in entrepreneurship: How for example do gender, demographic and structural characteristics interact and influence entrepreneurship? Interesting research impulses are currently coming from studies on ethnic, migrant and refugee entrepreneurship (see e.g. the special issue of *Ethnic and Racial Studies* edited by Romero and Valdez (2016); Barrett and Vershinina (2017). Another signpost for future research points to the role of gender in digital transformation and digital entrepreneurship. Here we need interdisciplinary research approaches that broaden the scope of gender capture to include human-digital interactions of all kinds in entrepreneurship to better understand the extent to which technologies change gender positions, create or destroy gendered institutions and gendered contexts, and any (dis)advantages that result.

From a historically ignored issue to a road less travelled, gender has emerged to become a construct of its own with the potential to enrich the collective work of entrepreneurship research. Some promising strands have been identified and continue to develop, and many are still untapped.

References

Ahl, H. (2002). The construction of the female entrepreneur as the other. In B. Czarniawska & H. Höpfl (Eds.), *Casting the other* (pp. 64–71). London: Routledge.

Ahl, H. (2006). Why research on women entrepreneurs needs new directions. *Entrepreneurship Theory and Practice, 30*(5), 595–621. https://doi.org/10.1111/j.1540-6520.2006.00138.x

Ahl, H., & Marlow, S. (2012). Exploring the dynamics of gender, feminism and entrepreneurship: Advancing debate to escape a dead end? *Organization, 19*(5), 543–562. https://doi.org/10.1177/1350508412448695

Ahl, H., & Nelson, T. (2015). How policy positions women entrepreneurs: A comparative analysis of state discourse in Sweden and the United States. *Journal of Business Venturing, 30*(2), 273–291. https://doi.org/10.1016/j.jbusvent.2014.08.002

Alsos, G. A., Hytti, U., & Ljunggren, E. (2016). *Research handbook on gender and innovation*. Cheltenkam: Edward Elgar.

Baker, T., & Welter, F. (2017). Come on out of the ghetto, please! – Building the future of entrepreneurship research. *International Journal of Entrepreneurial Behavior & Research, 23*(2), 170–184. https://doi.org/10.1108/ijebr-02-2016-0065

Barrett, R., & Vershinina, N. (2017). Intersectionality of ethnic and entrepreneurial identities: A study of post-war polish entrepreneurs in an English city. *Journal of Small Business Management, 55*(3), 430–443.

Bianco, M. E., Lombe, M., & Bolis, M. (2017). Challenging gender norms and practices through women's entrepreneurship. *International Journal of Gender and Entrepreneurship, 9*(4), 338–358. https://doi.org/10.1108/IJGE-10-2017-0060

Bruni, A., Gherardi, S., & Poggio, B. (2004). Doing gender, doing entrepreneurship: An ethnographic account of intertwined practices. *Gender, Work & Organization, 11*(4), 406–429.

Brush, C. G., de Bruin, A., & Welter, F. (2009). A gender-aware framework for women's entrepreneurship. *International Journal of Gender and Entrepreneurship, 1*(1), 8–24. https://doi.org/10.1108/17566260910942318

Brush, C. G., de Bruin, A., & Welter, F. (2014). Women's entrepreneurship in the 21st century – An international multi-level research analysis. In K. Lewis, C. Herny, E. J. Gatewood, & J. Watson (Eds.), *Advancing theory development in venture creation: Signposts for understanding gender* (pp. 11–31). Cheltenham: Eward Elgar.

Brush, C. G., Edelman, L. F., Manolova, T. S., & Welter, F. (2018). A gendered look at entrepreneurship ecosystems. *Small Business Economics*, 1–16. https://doi.org/10.1007/s11187-018-9992-9

Butler, J. (2004). *Undoing gender.* Psychology.

Calás, M. B., Smircich, L., & Bourne, K. A. (2009). Extending the boundaries: Reframing "entrepreneurship as social change" through feminist perspectives. *The Academy of Management Review, 34*(3), 552–569.

De Bruin, A., Brush, C. G., & Welter, F. (2006). Introduction to the special issue: Towards building cumulative knowledge on Women's entrepreneurship. *Entrepreneurship Theory and Practice, 30*(5), 585–593. https://doi.org/10.1111/j.1540-6520.2006.00137.x

De Bruin, A., Brush, C. G., & Welter, F. (2007). Advancing a framework for coherent research on women's entrepreneurship. *Entrepreneurship Theory and Practice, 31*(3), 323–339. https://doi.org/10.1111/j.1540-6520.2007.00176.x

Deutsch, F. M. (2007). Undoing gender. *Gender & Society, 21*(1), 106–127.

Díaz-García, C., Brush, C., Gatewood, E., & Welter, F. (2016). *Women's entrepreneurship in global and local contexts.* Cheltenkam: Edward Elgar.

Díaz-García, C., & Welter, F. (2013). Gender identities and practices: Interpreting women entrepreneur's narratives. *International Small Business Journal, 31*(4), 384–404.

Ettl, K., & Welter, F. (2010a). Gender, context and entrepreneurial learning. *International Journal of Gender and Entrepreneurship, 2*(2), 108–129.

Ettl, K., & Welter, F. (2010b). How female entrepreneurs learn and acquire (business-relevant) knowledge. *International Journal of Entrepreneurship and Small Business, 10*(1), 65–82. https://doi.org/10.1504/ijesb.2010.033049

Gatewood, E. J., Brush, C. G., Carter, N. M., Greene, P. G., & Hart, M. M. (2003). *Women entrepreneurs, their ventures, and the venture capital industry: An annotated bibliography.* Stockholm: Entrepreneurship and Small Business Research Institute (ESBRI).

GEM. (2017). Global Entrepreneurship monitor – Women's entrepreneurship 2016/2017 report. In D. J. Kelley, B. S. Baumer, C. Brush, P. G. Greene, M. Mahdavi, M. M. M. Cole, M. Dean, & R. Heavlow (Eds.), *Global entrepreneurship monitor.*

Greene, P. G., & Brush, C. G. (Eds.). (2018). *A research agenda for women and entrepreneurship: Identity through aspirations, behaviors and confidence.* Cheltenham: Edward Elgar.

Greene, P. G., Brush, C., & Gatewood, E. J. (2006). Perspectives on women entrepreneurs: Past findings and new directions. In M. Minitti (Ed.), *Entrepreneurship: The engine of growth* (Vol. 1). New York: Praeger.

Hamilton, E. (2013). The discourse of entrepreneurial masculinities (and femininities). *Entrepreneurship & Regional Development, 25*(1–2), 90–99. https://doi.org/10.1080/08985626.2012.746879

Henry, C., Orser, B., Coleman, S., & Foss, L. (2017). Women's entrepreneurship policy: A 13 nation cross-country comparison. In T. S. Manolova, C. G. Brush, L. F. Edelman, A. Robb, & F. Welter (Eds.), *Entrepreneurial ecosystems and growth of women's entrepreneurship: A comparative analysis* (pp. 244–278). Cheltenham: Edward Elgar.

Hughes, K. D., Jennings, J. E., Brush, C., Carter, S., & Welter, F. (2012). Extending women's entrepreneurship research in new directions. *Entrepreneurship Theory and Practice, 36*(3), 429–442. https://doi.org/10.1111/j.1540-6520.2012.00504.x

Jennings, J. E., & Brush, C. G. (2013). Research on women entrepreneurs: Challenges to (and from) the broader entrepreneurship literature? *The Academy of Management Annals, 7*(1), 663–715. https://doi.org/10.1080/19416520.2013.782190

Kaiser, F.-J. (1983). Grundlagen der Fallstudiendidaktik. Historische Entwicklung, Theoretische Grundlagen, Unterrichtliche Praxis. In F.-J. Kaiser (Ed.), *Die Fallstudie – Theorie und Praxis der Fallstudiendidaktik* (pp. 9–34). Bad Heilbrunn: Klinkhardt.

Kaiser, F.-J., & Kaminski, H. (1997). *Methodik des Ökonomie-Unterrichts*. Bad Heilbrunn: Klinkhardt.

Lansky, M. (2000). Gender, women and all the rest (Part I). *International Labour Review, 139*(4), 481–504. https://doi.org/10.1111/j.1564-913X.2000.tb00529.x

Leitch, C., & Hill, F. (2006). Women and the financing of entrepreneurial ventures: More pieces for the jigsaw puzzle. *Venture Capital, 8*(2), 159–182.

Leitch, C., Welter, F., & Henry, C. (2017). Women entrepreneurs' financing revisited: Taking stock and looking forward. New perspectives on women entrepreneurs and finance. *Venture Capital, 20*(2), 103–114.

Manolova, T. S., Brush, C. G., Edelman, L. F., Robb, A., & Welter, F. (2017). *Entrepreneurial ecosystems and growth of women's entrepreneurship*. Cheltenham; Northhampton: Edward Elgar.

Marlow, S., Henry, C., & Carter, S. (2009). Exploring the impact of gender upon women's business ownership: Introduction. *International Small Business Journal, 27*(2), 139–148. https://doi.org/10.1177/0266242608100487

Marlow, S., & Martinez Dy, A. (2018). Annual review article: Is it time to rethink the gender agenda in entrepreneurship research? *International Small Business Journal, 36*(1), 3–22. https://doi.org/10.1177/0266242617738321

OECD/European Commission. (2017). *Policy brief on women's entrepreneurship*. Luxembourg: Office of the European Union.

Pathak, S., Goltz, S., & Buche, M. W. (2013). Influences of gendered institutions on women's entry into entrepreneurship. *International Journal of Entrepreneurial Behavior & Research, 19*(5), 478–502. https://doi.org/10.1108/IJEBR-09-2011-0115

Pecis, L. (2016). Doing and undoing gender in innovation: Femininities and masculinities in innovation processes. *Human Relations, 69*(11), 2117–2140.

Rebetja, M., & Villnow, M. (1994). Pädagogik-Studentinnen berichten: Von der Lust und von der Last, feministische Wissenschaft zu studieren. In H. Kahlert & E. Kleinau (Eds.), *Feministische Erbschaften – Feministische Erblasten* (pp. 132–140). Hamburg: Interdisziplinäres Zentrum für Hochschuldidaktik der Universität Hamburg.

Romero, M., & Valdez, Z. (2016). Introduction to the special issue: Intersectionality and entrepreneurship. *Ethnic and Racial Studies, 39*(9), 1553–1565.

Rouse, J., Treanor, L., & Fleck, E. (2013). The gendering of entrepreneurship: Theoretical and empirical insights. *International Journal of Entrepreneurial Behavior & Research, 19*(5), 452–459. https://doi.org/10.1108/IJEBR-06-2013-0083

Tedmanson, D., Verduyn, K., Essers, C., & Gartner, W. B. (2012). Critical perspectives in entrepreneurship research. *Organization, 19*(5), 531–541. https://doi.org/10.1177/1350508412458495

Weitz, B. O. (2011). Fallstudien im Ökonomieunterricht. In T. Retzmann (Ed.), *Methodentraining für den Ökonomieunterricht* (pp. 101–119). Schwalbach: Wochenschau Verlag.

Welter, F., Brush, C., & de Bruin, A. (2014). *The gendering of entrepreneurship context, working paper 01/14*. Bonn: IfM Bonn.

West, C., & Zimmerman, D. (1987). Doing gender. *Gender and Society, 1*(2), 125–151.

Wolf, K. (1992). Die Fallstudie als Unterrichtsmethode, ein Plädoyer. *Wirtschaft und Erziehung, 44*(5), 158–159.

Yousafzai, S., Fayolle, A., Lindgreen, A., Henry, C., Saeed, S., & Sheikh, S. (Eds.). (2018). *Women Entrepreneurs and the Myth of 'Underperformance'*. Cheltenham: Edward Elgar.

Yousafzai, S. Y., Lindgreen, A., Saeed, S., & Henry, C. (Eds.). (2018). *Contextual embeddedness of women's entrepreneurship: Going beyond a gender neutral approach*. Abingdon: Routledge.

Female Migrant Entrepreneurship in Germany: Determinants and Recent Developments

Nora Zybura, Katharina Schilling, Ralf Philipp, and Michael Woywode

Abstract Although female migrant entrepreneurship has gained some momentum during the last decade, research on it is limited, and empirical findings in the German context remain scarce. The entrepreneurial activities of female migrants have long been ascribed to certain industries. Their businesses often remain small with limited prospects for revenue. However, recent developments indicate some emerging changes in terms of female migrant entrepreneurship. Based on the empirical data of the German microcensus, we analyze structural characteristics of female migrant entrepreneurship and its development in Germany between 2005 and 2016. We further examine how selected determinants (qualification, occupational segregation, family responsibilities) can explain these developments, and how these determinants affect the propensity of female migrants to become self-employed. Our findings cast new light on country-specific aspects of female migrant entrepreneurship and how entrepreneurial activities of female migrants and selected determinants differ from their native counterparts.

1 Introduction

Entrepreneurial activities of female migrants have long been perceived in light of their subordinate position or patriarchal control mechanisms (e.g. unpaid or underpaid workers in their husbands' businesses) (Baycan-Levent 2010). Previous literature indicates that female migrants in Germany and other OECD countries tend to become self-employed[1] in specific industries (e.g. cosmetics, fashion, office services)

---

[1]Because previous literature has not been able to accurately separate the two, we use the terms *entrepreneurship* and *self-employment* in our literature review synonymously. *Entrepreneurship* is commonly used in international literature, whereas *self-employment* is predominantly used in studies relying on the German context. This also accounts for the terms *immigrant* (international

N. Zybura (✉) · K. Schilling · R. Philipp · M. Woywode
University of Mannheim, Mannheim, Germany
e-mail: norazybura@ifm.uni-mannheim.de; schilling@ifm.uni-mannheim.de; philipp@ifm.uni-mannheim.de; woywode@ifm.uni-mannheim.de

where their businesses often remain small and revenue prospects are limited (Baycan-Levent 2010; Leicht et al. 2017). The overrepresentation of female migrants in certain sectors is possibly the result of educational and occupational choices/opportunities (Leicht and Lauxen-Ulbrich 2005). The entrepreneurial activities of female migrants are further shaped by ethnic as well as gender-based barriers and opportunities (Azmat 2013; Bührmann et al. 2010a). Female migrants might be able to combine these opportunities, which can foster their entrepreneurial activities. Or, they are doubly impacted by barriers, placing them at a disadvantage when starting their own business. International literature on migrant entrepreneurship recently stated that female migrant entrepreneurship has been subject to significant changes (e.g. the number of female migrant entrepreneurs is rising and their entrepreneurial activities in knowledge-intensive services are increasing). These changes indicate a slightly different positioning of entrepreneurial activities of female migrants that is related to strong potential in terms of socio-economic cohesion and integration (Baycan-Levent 2010).

Research on the entrepreneurial activities of female migrants gained its initial momentum during the last decade. It still however cannot be considered comprehensive. Extant literature focuses on the motivations, enablers and barriers of female migrant entrepreneurship (e.g. Bührmann 2010; Leicht et al. 2009; Pio 2007). A multitude of studies use a qualitative research design (e.g. Dannecker and Cakir 2016; Essers et al. 2013; Munkejord 2017) or aim at theorizing the phenomenon and/or conceptualizing the research field (e.g. Azmat 2013; Baycan-Levent 2010; Essers et al. 2010; Villares-Varela et al. 2017). Quantitative approaches remain scarce. From a European perspective, recent studies have predominantly focused on a particular country or migrant group from a specific country of origin (e.g. Baycan-Levent et al. 2003; Dhaliwal et al. 2010; part IV in Halkias et al. 2011). A comprehensive overview on the European level or cross-country comparisons are lacking. In addition, only very few studies focus on Germany (e.g. bga 2010; Bührmann et al. 2010b; Hillmann 1999; Leicht et al. 2009). Therefore, it is questionable whether existing findings and insights on an international level also apply to the German context.

In light of the above, our chapter relies on data from the German microcensus to focus on female migrant entrepreneurs in Germany. The chapter provides quantitative insights of female migrant entrepreneurship in Germany with a particular focus on recent developments and selected determinants. Following a quantitative approach and including the gender dimension of migrant entrepreneurship in Germany, we shed light on a topic that has received only limited scholarly attention. We position our chapter in the realm of migrant entrepreneurship, taking an intersectional approach combining gender and ethnicity.

---

literature) and *migrant/migration background* (German context). A consistent and generally accepted definition is missing for *migrant entrepreneurship* (Ram et al. 2017). We therefore base our definitions of migrants and self-employment on the German microcensus (see Sect. 3 for further details).

The objectives of our study are twofold. First, we aim at analyzing the structural characteristics of female migrant entrepreneurship and its development in Germany between 2005 and 2016. Second, we examine to what extent qualification, occupational segregation, and family responsibilities can explain these developments, and how these determinants influence the propensity of becoming self-employed among female migrants. By focusing on the differences between female migrant entrepreneurs and female entrepreneurs of German origin, we further consider whether female migrant entrepreneurs face other self-employment opportunities and barriers than their native counterparts. Thereby, our findings cast new light on country-specific aspects (Germany) of female migrant entrepreneurship and draw some initial attention to the debate of whether female migrant entrepreneurs face a double barrier of being both women and migrants.

After a brief review of the literature, we discuss selected determinants of female migrant entrepreneurship (qualification, occupational segregation, family responsibilities) followed by methods and descriptive as well as multivariate results. The chapter concludes with a brief discussion of the results, limitations and avenues for further research.

2 Female Migrant Entrepreneurship

2.1 Women's and Migrants' Entrepreneurship

From a European perspective, the underrepresentation of women in self-employment is a consistent finding (Hatfield 2015). This gender gap, although Europe-wide, is not necessarily a worldwide phenomenon. In some countries (e.g. Brazil, Indonesia, Mexico, the Philippines, Vietnam), entrepreneurial activities of women are on the same level of or even exceed those of men (GERA 2017). In Europe, the proportion of self-employed men (among all employed people) is considerably higher (2016: 17.5%) than that of self-employed women (2016: 9.9%) (OECD 2017). This gender difference also holds true for Germany. Here women continue to be less present in self-employment. Even though the number of female entrepreneurs has in fact increased over the past years, the self-employment rate of women has remained consistently low, and is still lower than for men. Nevertheless, a slight harmonization of the self-employment rate has occurred between men and women. This might be rather the result of a small decrease in the male self-employment rate than an increase in the female self-employment rate (bga 2015; Neuffer 2015). Overall, female and male entrepreneurial activities range among a lower level in Northern European countries (Germany included) than in Southern and Eastern Europe (Hatfield 2015). Comparing the ratio between male and female self-employment rates in different European countries, Germany ranks among those with a relatively small gap (ibid.).

Businesses owned by women are often found in traditionally female dominated industries (e.g. personal services, fashion, office services) and tend to be less innovative, smaller in size, less prone to grow, and less internationalized than businesses owned by men (Niefert and Gottschalk 2015; Strohmeyer et al. 2017).

Researchers have extensively examined these gender differences in self-employment. Various international studies describe the characteristics and performance aspects of women-led businesses (e.g. Bijedić et al. 2016; bga 2015; Brink et al. 2014; Niefert and Gottschalk 2015; Strohmeyer et al. 2017), while further studies focus on individual and contextual factors that determine the likelihood, entry points, and motives of women's self-employment (e.g. Hughes 2003; Lauxen-Ulbrich and Leicht 2003; Leoni and Falk 2010; Kay et al. 2014; McManus 2001; Neuffer 2015). Other scholars conceptualize women's entrepreneurship by drawing on theoretical perspectives derived from gender studies (e.g. Brush et al. 2014; Ettl and Welter 2010; Gupta et al. 2009; Henry et al. 2016; Marlow 2015).

Several factors and characteristics have been identified as influencing the entrepreneurial activities of women. These include human capital (i.e. qualification and education), gender-specific occupational choices, family responsibilities, and family-related employment interruptions (Kay et al. 2014; Leicht and Lauxen-Ulbrich 2005; Leoni and Falk 2010).

The influence of gendered socialization and education processes is also considered in some studies. Self-perceptions of desirability and feasibility of entrepreneurial activities are shaped by gendered self-conceptions and stereotypes, which essentially influence the "perceptions of and intentions to become an entrepreneur" (Gupta et al. 2009, p. 412f.).

Looking at the characteristics and determining factors of women's entrepreneurship, it becomes obvious that some apply to migrant entrepreneurs as well (see Baycan-Levent et al. 2003 for an extensive comparison). Similarities can be found regarding the characteristics of the business (e.g. service sector, small size, low capital) and the characteristics of entrepreneurs (e.g. lack of integration in the labor market, irregular career paths, fewer opportunities/resources) (Apitzsch and Kontos 2003; Baycan-Levent et al. 2003). Along with the relevant studies on migrant entrepreneurship in Germany (e.g. Bührmann et al. 2010b; Brüderl et al. 2009; Fertala 2006; Hillmann 2011; Leicht 2016; Leicht et al. 2015, 2017; Sachs et al. 2016; Schaland 2010), international migrant entrepreneurship research looks back on a long tradition. Its main theoretical frameworks include the middle man minorities approach (Bonacich 1973), the interaction model approach (Waldinger et al. 1990) and the mixed embeddedness approach (Kloosterman et al. 1999). However, these "classics" of ethnic economy theory have very "little consideration of gendered patterns of migration, labour [sic] incorporation or family relationships within the household" (Villares-Varela et al. 2017, p. 344f.).

But what about entrepreneurs who fit into both categories, i.e. those who are women *and* migrant entrepreneurs? Only very few studies focus in particular on female migrant entrepreneurs (Azmat 2013), and little is known about the ethnic aspects of female entrepreneurship in Germany (Leicht et al. 2017). The long-shared belief that the number of self-employed migrant women is negligibly small, and the assumption that women were "tag-alongs" in a migration dominated by men might explain this lack of scholarly attention (Baycan-Levent 2010).

It's relevant and essential to focus on female migrants as a particular group of entrepreneurs for at least two reasons. First, the percentage of self-employed female migrants in Germany and Europe has increased significantly in recent years (LFS, own calculations). In Germany, migrant women appear less underrepresented in self-employment than native women (Neuffer 2015). The question therefore arises of whether this growth relates to a change in structures and characteristics of female migrant entrepreneurship in Germany. Second, female migrant entrepreneurs have transformed from being (unpaid) helpers within their family's businesses to being entrepreneurs in their own right (Baycan-Levent 2010; Leicht et al. 2017).

Looking at some statistical trends and developments of (female) migrant self-employment in the EU, the following can be stated[2]: Overall, migrant entrepreneurship in Germany and other European countries has gained traction over the last decade, although the increase in entrepreneurial activities of migrants occurred in Germany on a lower level than in other EU-28 countries. Gender differences nevertheless exist. First, more migrant men than women are self-employed, also reflected in the 2016 self-employment rate in both Germany (male migrants: 12.1%, female migrants: 7.3%) and EU-28 countries (male migrants: 15.3%, female migrants: 9.2%). Second, in Germany (male migrant increase of about 25.1%, female migrant increase of about 31.1%) as well as in EU-28 countries (male migrant increase of about 66.2%, female migrant increase of about 90.2%) the number of female migrant entrepreneurs has risen more than the number of their male counterparts between 2005 and 2016.

2.2 *Literature on Female Migrant Entrepreneurship*

Female migrant entrepreneurs received some scholarly attention at the beginning of the 1990s (e.g. Hillmann 1999; Dallalfar 1994; Kermond et al. 1991; Morokvasic 1991). Research has however only gained real momentum during the last decade. It remains scarce, and female migrants are less visible as entrepreneurs than their male counterparts (Verduijn and Essers 2013).[3]

---

[2]Displayed trends rely on own calculations based on the Eurostat Labor Force Survey (LFS) (EU-28; years 2005–2016). Due to different classifications of nationals/foreigners in the LFS, the results of the LFS are only partially comparable to analyses based on the microcensus. See Sect. 3 for further details.

[3]Our literature review was conducted using the following keywords (and selected combinations): migrant, immigrant, women, female, entrepreneur, entrepreneurship, *Migrantin, selbständig, Selbständigkeit, Existenzgründung, Gründerinnen mit Migrationshintergrund*. These were done in the literature databases of Google Scholar, IBZ Online, Web of Science and WISO. Our strategy was twofold: (1) literature research for the German and international context (focusing on the latest publications in English or German), and (2) screening and selecting the available literature in terms of our research objectives.

Several studies focus on the motivation(s) of migrant women to become self-employed (e.g. Baycan-Levent et al. 2003; Baycan-Levent 2010; Leicht et al. 2009; Munkejord 2017; Pio 2007). Blocked career advancement in terms of dependent employment ("glass ceilings"), a desire for (financial) independence, entrepreneurship as an alternative to unemployment, and the individual intrinsic wish to become an entrepreneur are all seen as motives in these studies.

The factors fostering or impeding female migrant entrepreneurship form another stream of literature (e.g. Anthias and Mehta 2008; Azmat 2013; Baycan-Levent et al. 2003; bga 2010; Leicht et al. 2009). Baycan-Levent et al. (2003) introduce a useful framework for categorizing opportunities and barriers; these are also found in the studies referenced above. This framework distinguishes between ethnic-based and gender-based barriers, as well as opportunities to visualize effects that apply to migrants and women. It helps to conceptualize the question of whether female migrant entrepreneurs are able to combine opportunities, or are instead doubly affected by barriers. The existence of a special market or demand for female services, specific management styles, the existence of informal information networks, and potential competitive advantages offered by the ethnic community are included among the factors that can foster the entrepreneurial activities of migrant women. Inhibiting factors here include among other things a lack of capital and credit, a lack of financial and managerial knowledge, cultural and social values, lacking qualifications and language proficiency, family responsibilities, and exclusion from "non-ethnic" or "old-boys" business networks. Azmat (2013) introduces another theoretical framework. She considers social capital, human capital, culture, family, gender, and institutional factors which might serve as barriers and in some cases as enablers of female migrant entrepreneurship. Interestingly, both frameworks neglect occupational segregation as influential factors.

These frameworks pinpoint two questions related to female migrants: Is gender or ethnicity more relevant with regard to entrepreneurial activities? Or is there a dual disadvantage? Several studies emphasize that migrant women are affected by a dual disadvantage because of their gender and migration background (Baycan-Levent 2010; Bührmann et al. 2010a). Moreover, some authors criticize how research has so far failed to acknowledge the interplay between these two factors, separately focusing instead on one or the other. And "[l]acking is the understanding of the *interaction* between gender and ethnicity" (Villares-Varela et al. 2017, p. 344, emphasis in original). To conceptualize this idea, some studies use the approach of intersectionality to overcome the lack of a comprehensive argumentation that addresses gender, ethnicity, and entrepreneurship (e.g. Essers et al. 2010; Knight 2016).

2.3 Determinants of Female Migrant Entrepreneurship

Previous research has identified various determinants which might influence the entrepreneurial activities of individuals. Research on women's entrepreneurship emphasizes three sets of determinants: human capital, occupational segregation, and family responsibilities (see for example McManus 2001; Leicht and Lauxen-Ulbrich 2005). Determinants might have a different influence on entrepreneurial intentions and activities in various contexts. The importance of the contextual embeddedness of entrepreneurship is widely considered in the field of entrepreneurship research (e.g. Díaz-García et al. 2016; Welter and Gartner 2016a). It helps to understand "when, how, and why entrepreneurship happens and who becomes involved" (Welter 2011, p. 166).

Female migrant entrepreneurship occurs in various contexts and is shaped by several (intersectional) determinants that subjectively and objectively affect entrepreneurship in different ways depending on the social, spatial, institutional and temporal context (Welter 2011; Welter and Gartner 2016b). Drawing on the notions of intersectionality and context, we consider how gender and migration background shape the above-mentioned determinants of migrant women's entrepreneurial activities in Germany.

2.3.1 Qualification

Research on early ventures considers education and practical knowledge as key determinants of self-employment (Brüderl et al. 2009). Qualifications and managerial experiences are part of the individual human capital needed to start and run a business (Azmat 2013; Leicht et al. 2009). Any lack thereof is considered as one of the main obstacles to self-employment and business success. In their framework of obstacles and enablers, Baycan-Levent et al. (2003) consider a lack of education to be an ethnic-based obstacle. Migrant women often have fewer chances to acquire formal qualifications or job experience. They may face educational inequalities in their country of origin because of their gender, which might lead to fewer opportunities to gain additional (formal) human capital. Upon arriving in their host country, migrants often experience a certain devaluation of their human capital acquired abroad (Azmat 2013; Collins and Low 2010). The unique structure of the German vocational education system marks another challenge, because here, the formal recognition of foreign qualifications is quite difficult. Even so, some studies indicate that self-employment (in comparison to dependent employment) represents an opportunity to better utilize qualifications that are not formally recognized (e.g. Leicht et al. 2017).

Migrant women born in Germany often face disadvantages in the education system because educational opportunities and success (on both school and vocational levels) are highly influenced by social and ethnic backgrounds (Kristen et al. 2011; Schneider et al. 2014). Some studies point to further discrimination on the labor market, in particular for migrant women with foreign-sounding names or who wear head coverings (Weichselbaumer 2016), perhaps limiting their opportunity to attain work experience.

Unequal opportunities offer fewer possibilities for migrant women to acquire quality levels of human capital. This is why we consider qualification as a relevant determinant in our analyses.

2.3.2 Occupational Segregation

Although some integrated occupations do in fact exist, the majority of occupations worldwide are dominated by either men or women (Busch 2013). The occupational structure in Germany is highly segregated. This has not changed significantly, even though women's labor market participation has increased and a fundamental change in the structure of occupations has occurred (Hausmann and Kleinert 2014). Female dominated occupations are represented in the trade or personal service sectors as well as the social and health care sectors. Male dominated occupations are characterized by a stronger technical focus and often include manual labor (Busch 2013; Hausmann and Kleinert 2014).

Gender-specific occupational and industrial segregation is primarily related to the field of (migrant) female entrepreneurship. It is perceived as a main obstacle to self-employment access. The field of study or occupational choices determine the possibilities of becoming self-employed, with some industries being more suitable for entrepreneurship than others (Leicht and Lauxen-Ulbrich 2005). A high proportion of migrant women choose traditional women's professions/occupations, reducing their chances of founding a business because these professions are less suitable for self-employment (Leicht et al. 2017). Brink et al. (2014) emphasize how this also influences the innovativeness of a business venture (see also Leoni and Falk 2010). This gender-specific division is even mirrored among established firms led by migrant women which often operate in the service sector (Baycan-Levent 2010).

Occupational choices and specifications indicate different opportunities for self-employment. Accordingly, we consider occupational segregation as a significant determinant in our analyses.

2.3.3 Family Responsibilities

Recent literature discusses family responsibilities and professional entrepreneurial activities of women from two perspectives: as an obstacle and enabler of entrepreneurship (Leicht et al. 2017). Family care is still predominantly done by women, and this doesn't change when women are employed full-time. Family care is an addition to employment that increases the overall workload (Baycan-Levent 2010; Leicht et al. 2017). It is argued on the other hand that self-employment offers flexible working conditions (e.g. in terms of time management and workplace location) and is therefore more suitable for an effective work-family balance (Leicht and Lauxen-Ulbrich 2005). "Family balancing" is thus seen as a possible motivational factor for (migrant) women to consider self-employment as an attractive option for their professional careers (McManus 2001).

Having a family or partner can also be supportive when starting or running a business. This support can include moral encouragement and mentoring, financial contributions, or risk absorption (Dhaliwal et al. 2010). Lauxen-Ulbrich and Leicht (2003) find in their study on native women entrepreneurs that family responsibilities influence the professional activities of women as such but do not necessarily disadvantage entrepreneurial activities. Is this finding also valid for female migrant entrepreneurs in Germany, assuming that migrant women are more affected by family responsibilities than non-migrant women (Henkel et al. 2015)?

It is still not clear whether family obligations tend to foster or hinder the transition into self-employment. Therefore, we focus on the structure of the household and to what extent female migrants differ from women of German origin.

3 Methods

3.1 Sample and Definitions

We base our analyses on the German microcensus, an annual sample survey carried out by the Federal Statistical Office that covers 1% of the German population. The survey contains information on the population (i.e. socio-demographic data) and the labor market in Germany. Information on a person's migration background (*Migrationshintergrund*) has been available since 2005.

Our analyses rely on different sources of the microcensus. First, we use scientific use files (SUF) for the years 2005–2012. The SUF is a 70% anonymized sample of the microcensus and includes information on all employed people between the ages of 15 and 64. Analyses including the years 2005–2012 rely solely on the SUF. Since 2012, the microcensus has used an updated weighting. Consequently, the 2011 microcensus was revised, which is not included in the SUF. Most of our analyses also include the years 2013 and 2014. We completed the SUF for the years 2005–2010, with data for the years 2011–2014 of the research data center (FDZ) at the Federal Statistical Office in Wiesbaden, Germany (our second source of the microcensus). We furthermore use the microcensus subject matter series (*Fachserie*) to integreate the latest available data up to 2016. The microcensus subject matter series base on aggregated data. Therefore, it does not include an upper age limit for people in employment. Due to different sources of the microcensus, results differ regarding the last reported year.

Persons with a Migration Background We draw on the definition of the microcensus for persons with a migration background (*Migrationshintergrund*). The term "person with a migration background" is predominantly used in the German context. "The population group with a migration background consists of all persons who have immigrated into the territory of today's Federal Republic of Germany after 1949, and of all foreigners born in Germany and all persons born in Germany who have at least one parent who immigrated into the country or was born as a foreigner in Germany" (Statistisches Bundesamt 2018a). We do not differentiate between the first and second generation of migrants, nor their country of origin.

Self-Employment We follow the microcensus definition of self-employment. A self-employed person is someone who manages a business as owner, co-owner, tenant, self-employed craftsman or freelancer. The term self-employment excludes individuals who are in a work relationship/contract with an employer (Statistisches Bundesamt 2018b). We do not distinguish between solo self-employed people, those with their own employees, or between full-time and part-time self-employment.

3.2 Empirical Strategy

Our analyses focus on female migrant entrepreneurs while comparing results in relation to female entrepreneurs of German origin. A comparison with male migrant entrepreneurs as well as with dependent employed individuals is reported only for selected analyses.

We first provide a descriptive overview of the development of self-employment in Germany, focusing particularly on female migrant entrepreneurs. Further descriptive results refer to the level of qualification, industry structure, and occupational segregation as well as the household structure.

Second, we estimate a maximum likelihood regression (logit regression) regarding the propensity to become self-employed with a binary dependent variable (1 = self-employed, 0 = dependent employed). We estimate two separate models for migrant women (Model I) and native women (Model II). Two separate models allow us to depict the relevance of structures and determinants for both groups. The role of qualification, occupational segregation, and household structure is examined, while also controlling for age. We focus on female migrant entrepreneurs, and the results are contrasted to those of female entrepreneurs of German origin.

4 Results

4.1 Development of Self-Employment in Germany Since 2005

The total number of all employed persons and dependent employed individuals in Germany continuously increased during the last decade, whereas the rate of self-employed individuals declined (2005: 11.2%, 2016: 10.0%). A closer look from an origin and gender-specific perspective indicates a slightly different development (see Fig. 1).

Migrant entrepreneurship has gained traction in recent years. Since 2005, the number of self-employed migrants has risen by about 33.3% (increase of about 189,000) while the number of self-employed of German origin has slightly declined (about 3.6% between 2005 and 2016). However, the increasing number of self-employed migrants is not necessarily reflected in their self-employment rate (see Table 1), which has remained stable over time (2005: 9.7%, 2016: 9.0%). It is lower than that of their native counterparts, which has slightly declined since 2005 (2005: 11.5%, 2016: 10.3%).

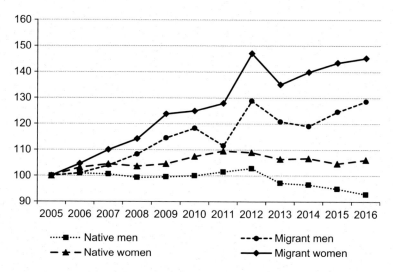

Fig. 1 Self-employed trends by gender in Germany (index base year 2005 = 100%). Source: Federal Statistical Office (microcensus); own calculations

Table 1 Proportion of self-employed (SEP) and self-employment rate

	Migrant			Native		
Year	In 1000	PROP of SEP (%)	SEP rate (%)	In 1000	PROP of SEP (%)	SEP rate (%)
Women						
2005	167	29.5	6.8	1055	30.2	7.6
2016	243	32.1	6.7	1120	33.1	7.2
Men						
2005	399	70.5	11.7	2442	69.8	14.7
2016	513	67.5	10.8	2267	66.9	13.0

Source: Federal Statistical Office (microcensus); own calculations

The number of women in employment has risen about 17.0% since 2005 (increase of about 2,800,000). This is also reflected in the number of female entrepreneurs, which rose about 10.9% between 2005 and 2016 (increase of about 134,000), whereas the number of male entrepreneurs slightly declined in the same time period (decrease of about 73,000). Nevertheless, the self-employment rate of women remained stable over the last 10 years (2005: 7.5%, 2016: 7.1%), and the entrepreneurial gender gap still exists.

Since 2005, female migrants have shown the largest increase in self-employment. The number of female migrant entrepreneurs has risen significantly by about 45.3% between 2005 and 2016 (increase of about 76,000). This increase is higher than the rise of their male (28.6%) or native counterparts (6.1%). The tremendous development in the number of female migrant entrepreneurs might be explained by its comparatively low level over the past years (see Table 1). Moreover, the total number of female migrants in employment has risen constantly over the last years. Therefore, the increase of female migrant entrepreneurs is not necessarily related to a "boom" in female migrant entrepreneurs. The self-employment rate of female migrants—a better reflection of self-employment trends—rose slightly between 2005 and 2015 (from 6.8% to 7.1%), almost at the same level as for women of German origin (7.2%). While their self-employment rate remained at the same level (7.2%) in 2016, the rate for female migrants slightly decreased in 2016 (6.7%).

Nevertheless, the self-employment rate of male migrant entrepreneurs (2005: 11.7%, 2016: 10.8%) is considerably higher than the one of their female counterparts. Accordingly, gender-specific inequalities also apply for migrants, and the so-called gender gap regarding self-employment rates still exists for both migrant and native entrepreneurs.

4.2 Structural Characteristics of Female Migrant Self-Employed

4.2.1 Qualification

Qualification and (professional) experience are important resources for the transition into self-employment. Migrant women have a higher qualification level both in self-employment and dependent employment compared to their male counterparts. More than a third of female migrant entrepreneurs (36.4%) have a university degree or a degree from a university of applied science (see Fig. 2) which corresponds to the proportion of self-employed German women (35.2%). The proportion of self-employed male migrants with a university/university of applied science degree is considerably low (23.3%). In contrast, the proportion of female migrant entrepreneurs without a vocational qualification is lower than the one of their male counterparts (23.9% vs. 29.0%). Nevertheless, the proportion of female migrant entrepreneurs without a vocational qualification is quite high, which becomes particularly evident when compared to self-employed women of German origin (6.8%).

A closer look at the distribution of qualifications (see Fig. 2) and their development indicates that the proportion of female migrant entrepreneurs without a vocational qualification has slightly declined since 2005 (2005: 26.4%, 2014: 23.9%). In addition, the proportion of migrant women holding a university degree has increased (2005: 28.1%; 2014: 30.9%). This development also applies for self-employed women of German origin, with a slightly higher increase of individuals with a university degree (2005: 22.5%, 2014: 27.5%).

The level of qualification is also related to the self-employment rate, while a higher qualification level indicates a higher self-employment rate (not shown in Fig. 2). Self-employment rates of female migrants holding a university degree (15.0%) or master craftsman's/technician's qualification (21.8%) are quite high as

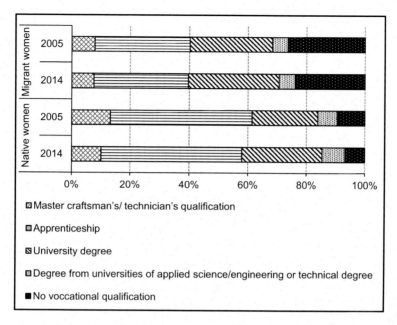

Fig. 2 Distribution of self-employed women (aged between 15 and 64) across qualifications. Source: Federal Statistical Office (microcensus); own calculations

opposed to lower qualification levels. Female migrants without vocational qualification show the lowest self-employment rate (5.4%).

Summing up, the level of qualification appears to be of significance for female migrant entrepreneurship. The role of qualification is further examined below under control of other influencing factors.

4.2.2 Industry Structure

The qualification level of female migrants corresponds to the allocation of female migrant businesses across various industries. In this regard, we might obtain more insight into how and to what extent female migrant entrepreneurs are able to use their (higher) qualifications, and how this is reflected in their distribution across industries.

Most self-employed female migrants work in non-knowledge-intensive services (40.5%) (see Fig. 3). The share of self-employed women of German origin in non-knowledge-intensive services is also on a relatively high level (31.6%), although most of them work in knowledge-intensive services (42.0%). The proportion of male migrant entrepreneurs in non-knowledge-intensive services is comparatively low (15.6%). Non-knowledge-intensive services are often comprised of traditionally female dominated professions (e.g. including household and personal services),

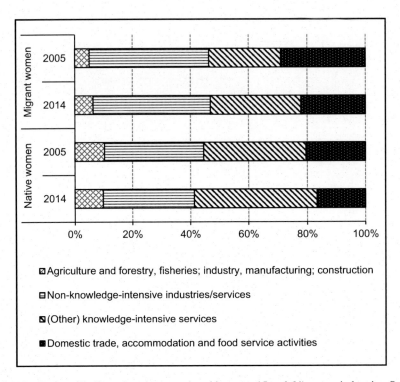

Fig. 3 Distribution of self-employed women (aged between 15 and 64) across industries. Source: Federal Statistical Office (microcensus); own calculations

which explains the overall high proportion of women in non-knowledge-intensive services.

Compared to their male counterparts, the higher qualification level of female migrants is reflected in their distribution across corresponding industries. Female migrant entrepreneurs work more frequently in knowledge-intensive services (31.0%) than their male counterparts (19.7%). Nevertheless, the share of female migrant entrepreneurs in knowledge-intensive services is significantly lower than that of their native counterparts (42.0%). Female migrant entrepreneurs (22.1%) are also quite active in the sectors of domestic trade, accommodation, and food service, while self-employed women of German origin are less represented in these industries (16.7%). Self-employed female migrants are rarely active in the sectors of construction, manufacturing, agriculture, forestry, and fishing (6.4%), while most male migrant entrepreneurs work in these industries (34.0%).

Two interesting observations can be made regarding the development of the industry structure. First, a stronger orientation of female migrant entrepreneurs is seen towards knowledge-intensive services (increase from 24.6% to 31.0% between 2005 and 2014). Second, a slight decline is seen in female migrant self-employment in traditionally migrant dominated industries such as domestic trade, accommodation, and food services (decrease from 29.0% to 22.1% between 2005 and 2014). These developments might be a first indicator of a modernization of female migrant entrepreneurship. In total, the distribution of female migrant entrepreneurs across non-knowledge-intensive services as well as agriculture and forestry, fisheries, manufacturing, and construction has remained quite stable.

4.2.3 Occupational Segregation

Various professions/occupations offer different opportunities regarding the transition into self-employment. The following considers occupational segregation and its implication for the self-employment opportunities of female migrants.[4]

Female and male dominated occupations are not equally distributed across the overall economy, which also applies to the distribution of occupations among female migrant entrepreneurs (see Table 2). They work most frequently in female dominated occupations (67.1%). This is also evident for female entrepreneurs of German origin on a slightly lower level (61.6%). One third of female migrants pursue their entrepreneurial activities in integrated occupations (29.6%), which is also true for self-employed native women (30.8%). The proportion of female migrant entrepreneurs in male dominated occupations is quite low (3.3%), and slightly higher for self-employed women of German origin (7.6%).[5]

Differences for female and male dominated as well as integrated occupations are also depicted in the self-employment rates of female migrants (see Table 2). Female dominated occupations do not offer favorable conditions for female migrants to found a business, which is mirrored in the low self-employment rate in these occupations (7.0%). The same holds true for women of German origin (6.4%). As opposed to this, integrated occupations seem more favorable in terms of self-employment because of their higher self-employment rate (9.9%). For women of German origin the self-employment rate in these occupations is slightly lower (9.2%). Male dominated occupations indicate a low self-employment rate for female migrants (2.7%). In contrast, the self-employment rate for women of German origin is much higher in male dominated occupations (7.0%).

Looking at the distribution of occupations by qualification, the following can be observed: The higher the level of qualification, the higher the proportion of integrated occupations. Female migrants with a university degree (among all qualifications)

---

[4]People in employment are allocated to around 400 occupations in the microcensus (KldB2010). Female dominated occupations are those with a corresponding gender share of more than 15% compared to the gender-specific share of all employees. Here we follow the definition of Hakim (1998) that is also used by Leicht and Lauxen-Ulbrich (2005). We apply KldB2010 based on two digits.

[5]Due to changes in the occupational classification in the microcensus (KldB92/KldB2010), it is not possible to present a consistent time series regarding the development of occupational segregation. The development can either be displayed for the years 2005–2012 (SUF data) or for the years 2011 to 2014 (FDZ microcensus), which is further related to a slightly different representation of results.

Table 2 Occupational segregation for self-employed (SEP)[a]

	Migrant women		Native women	
Occupations	SEP (%)	SEP rate (%)	SEP (%)	SEP rate (%)
Female dominated occupations	67.1	7.0	61.6	6.4
Integrated occupations	29.6	9.9	30.8	9.2
Male dominated occupations	3.3	2.7	7.6	7.0
Total	100.0	7.3	100.0	7.1

Source: Statistical Federal Office (microcensus 2014), own calculations based on KIdB2010, two digits
[a]Aged between 15 and 64

indicate the highest proportion of integrated occupations (49.0%). In contrast, those with an apprenticeship qualification display the highest proportion of female dominated occupations (79.0%).

In conclusion, the type of occupation appears decisive for the low level of self-employed female migrants. The role of occupational segregation is further examined under control of further influencing factors.

4.2.4 Household Structure and Family Responsibilities

Family responsibilities are discussed as both enablers and barriers for self-employment within existing research. The structure of the household is considered below.

More than half of self-employed female migrants (52.5%) live with at least one child in the household (couple household with children and single parents) (see Fig. 4). Self-employed female migrants are more likely to live in couple households with children than their native counterparts (41.4% vs. 37.1%). Further differences for couple households are stated in terms of the children's age. Self-employed female migrants live more often with younger children (<12 years: 23.2%) than with older children (≥12 years: 18.2%). For self-employed women of German origin, only a small difference regarding children's age (<12 years: 17.7%, ≥12 years: 19.4%) applies. Gender-specific differences are particularly evident for single parents. Self-employed female migrants are twice as often a single parent than their male counterparts (11.0% vs. 4.0%). The proportion of single parents among self-employed native women is nearly the same (10.0%) than among female migrant entrepreneurs.

A slight decline of couple households with children has been observed since 2005. This development applies to female migrant entrepreneurs (2005: 46.0%, 2014: 41.4%), female entrepreneurs of German origin (2005: 42.7%, 2014: 37.1%) as well as to male migrant entrepreneurs (2005: 53.5%, 2014: 46.5%). The share of self-employed female migrants living in single households with older children (≥12 years) slightly increased (2005: 4.3%, 2014: 6.7%) which applies to native women as well (2005: 5.4%, 2014: 6.4%).

In conclusion, female migrant entrepreneurs bear family responsibilities more frequently than self-employed women of German origin. The structure of the household as well as the role of children in the household will be further examined

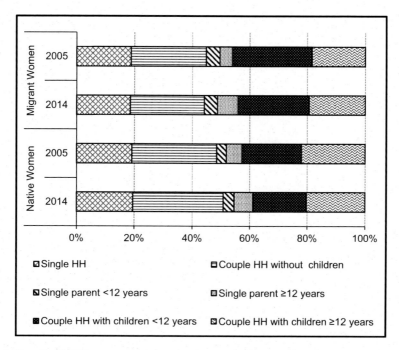

Fig. 4 Household (HH) structure of self-employed women (aged between 15 and 64). Source: Federal Statistical Office (microcensus); own calculations

under control of other influencing factors. Multivariate analyses also include the category "other types of households", which is available in the microcensus 2014, but not for 2005.

4.3 Multivariate Results

Descriptive results provide first insights about female migrant entrepreneurs in Germany along with various related structural characteristics. However, it is still questionable to what extent these determinants as well as further factors influence the propensity for female migrants to become self-employed. Accordingly, under control of other factors, we estimate a logistic regression with a binary variable as our dependent variable (1 = self-employed, 0 = dependent employed). The resulting coefficients, reflected as odds ratios (indicated as Exp(B)), are interpreted as the propensity to be self-employed. Moreover, we examine whether various determinants differ between female migrants and women of German origin.

In our regression model, we consider occupational segregation and the type of household (including children) as the most relevant determinants for female migrants' self-employment. Age and education are included as further factors of influence and control. The results of the binary logit models are displayed in Table 3 for female migrants (Model I) and for women of German origin (Model II).

Table 3 Influence of determinants on propensity for self-employment of women[a]

Dependent employed = 0 Self-employed = 1	Model I Migrant women Logit-coefficient	Model II Native women Logit-coefficient
Age	1.029***	1.041***
	(0.003)	(0.001)
Type of household		
Other (ref)		
Single HH	1.457***	1.077***
	(0.124)	(0.061)
Couple HH without children	1.181	0.979
	(0.121)	(0.060)
Couple HH with children <12 years	1.698***	1.478***
	(0.116)	(0.061)
Couple HH with children ≥12 years	1.226*	1.179
	(0.125)	(0.062)
Single HH with children <12 years	1.684***	1.769***
	(0.162)	(0.081)
Single HH with children ≥12 years	1.272*	1.097
	(0.145)	(0.071)
Qualification		
No formal qualification (ref)		
Apprenticeship	0.859**	0.975
	(0.068)	(0.045)
Master craftsman's/technician's qualification	4.325***	2.687***
	(0.113)	(0.056)
Degree from universities of applied science/engineering or technical degree	1.811***	2.087***
	(0.121)	(0.059)
University degree	2.877***	2.856***
	(0.072)	(0.049)
Occupational segregation		
Integrated occupation (ref)		
Female dominated occupation	0.866**	0.872***
	(0.058)	(0.026)
Male dominated occupation	0.280***	0.911**
	(0.144)	(0.046)
Constant	0.016***	0.009***
	(0.143)	(0.079)
Observations	23,926	122,595
R^2	0.081	0.071

Source: Federal Statistical Office (microcensus); own calculations
*$p < 0.1$; **$p < 0.05$; ***$p < 0.01$, standard errors are displayed in parentheses
[a]Aged between 15 and 64

Previous work experiences are partly reflected in one individual's age. Our results reveal that increasing age slightly increases the propensity for self-employment of both female migrants as well as women of German origin.

With household structure, having children under 12 years increases the propensity of becoming self-employed for female migrants and native women in both couple and single households. However, being a single parent with children younger than 12 years influences entrepreneurial activities for native more than for migrant women. This result might indicate that self-employment is related to a better reconciliation of family and work for female migrants living together with younger children (as well as for women of German origin).

Qualification has the strongest impact on female migrants' entrepreneurial activities. Controlling for type of household and age, holding a craftsman's/technician's qualification highly increases the propensity for female migrants to become self-employed, followed by a university degree. This also applies for women of German origin, with the effect being higher for female migrants. Having an apprenticeship decreases the propensity for entrepreneurial activities of female migrants (not significant for native women). Controlling for occupational segregation diminishes the influence of qualification. Compared to integrated professions, female dominated professions decrease the propensity of becoming self-employed for female migrants as well as for women of German origin. Male dominated professions also decrease the propensity of entrepreneurial activities for female migrants. This is even the case for women of German origin, although the difference regarding male and female dominated occupations appears stronger for female migrants. We find support that female and male dominated occupations (as well as integrated professions) indicate different opportunities regarding self-employment for female migrants. Integrated professions are most favorable in terms of the entrepreneurial activities of female migrants, while male dominated occupations bear the least opportunities for entrepreneurial activities.

5 Conclusion

Our chapter provides an overview of the development and structural characteristics of female migrant entrepreneurs in Germany, and displays how selected determinants affect entrepreneurial activities.

We show that the number of female migrant entrepreneurs has risen during the last decade—even more than for migrant men and women of German origin. The self-employment rate of female migrants reveals that they are less involved in entrepreneurial activities than their male counterparts (gender gap). Taking up the various structural characteristics and their development, we presented a more concise consideration of female migrant entrepreneurship in Germany, highlighting that qualification is the determinant that matters the most for female migrant entrepreneurs. A high qualification level is most favorable for female migrants in terms of entrepreneurial activities. Here we confirm previous findings on the relevance of qualification for founding a business (e.g. Brüderl et al. 2009; Azmat 2013).

The high proportion of female migrants holding a university degree (one third) is also reflected in the increasing entrepreneurial activities of female migrants in knowledge-intensive services during the last decade. Nevertheless, a large amount of female migrant entrepreneurs remain active in non-knowledge-intensive services that are often comprised of female dominated occupations. This essentially means that female dominated occupations decrease the propensity of becoming self-employed for female migrants, while integrated occupations increase it. A different pattern of career choices (including occupational choices) of female migrants may have a distinct effect on female migrants' gender gap regarding self-employment. Female migrants often choose occupations (i.e. female dominated occupations) which lead to dependent employment; this has been observed in previous studies as well (e.g. Baycan-Levent 2010; Leicht et al. 2017). This means that specific measures and programs regarding different career choices for female migrants need to be considered by policymakers. On a conceptual note, and because our results show its high relevance, occupational segregation could be included in theoretical models (e.g. Azmat 2013; Baycan-Levent et al. 2003) examining the barriers and enablers of female migrant entrepreneurship.

When looking at entrepreneurial activities and the determinants of female migrants and women of German origin, it cannot clearly be stated that self-employed female migrants face a dual disadvantage per se. Although the proportion of female migrant entrepreneurs without a qualification is higher than for their native counterparts, both native and migrant female entrepreneurs hold a university degree almost at the same level. In this regard, it is questionable to what extent the lack of vocational qualifications of female migrant entrepreneurs is related to the recognition of their qualification in Germany ("devaluation" described by Collins and Low 2010) or even their missing acquisition of qualifications. Moreover, female migrant entrepreneurship is changing in terms of its activities. For example, we emphasize a slight decline in female migrant businesses in traditionally migrant dominated industries such as domestic trade, accommodation, and food services. Living in a household with young children (single or couple) appears to be an enabler of entrepreneurial activities, not a barrier. This also holds true for both female migrants and women of German origin, a finding previously observed by Lauxen-Ulbrich and Leicht (2003).

Our results reveal that female migrants indicate an increasing growth potential regarding self-employment, which is furthermore related to increasing socio-economic potential in terms of greater social inclusion, revenue and employment opportunities, as well as technological innovation.

Our study relies on the German microcensus, so its results apply only to the German context. Other limitations are found with our data source. Several definitions and statistical classifications are predefined in the microcensus (e.g. self-employment, clustering of industries, qualifications) and do not allow an alternative operationalization of variables. We set our focus on female migrant entrepreneurs as one group, and do not differ between various generations (first/second) or country of origin. Further research should include these aspects because previous studies have emphasized considering migrant women as a heterogeneous group due to their considerable differences in entrepreneurial activities, socioeconomic characteristics, and qualifications (Azmat 2013; Dannecker and Cakir 2016; Leicht et al. 2017). Our results only indicate some initial insights on the debate of whether female migrant entrepreneurs face a double barrier of being both women and migrants. Further research should tackle this aspect more in depth.

The motives and obstacles (e.g. the role of necessity entrepreneurship) of female migrants to become self-employed could be included in future studies. Additional research avenues could add performance as well as other female migrant business aspects (e.g. innovation behavior, growth expectations, income prospects, ratio of part-time/full-time self-employed). Future research in this area might tackle the question of how changes in the labor market and in the nature of work (e.g. digital transformation related to an occupational shift, loss of significance of manual labor) affect the self-employment of female migrant entrepreneurs. There's no question that a more detailed Europe-wide comparative analysis would reveal new findings and perspectives. In addition, more effort is needed to develop theoretical models which take into account the fact that female migrant entrepreneurship is shaped by the individual experiences of women, migrants, and members of a social class or a certain religion (intersectional perspective).

References

Anthias, F., & Mehta, N. (2008). Gender, the family and self-employment: Is the family a resource for migrant women entrepreneurs? In U. Apitzsch & M. Kontos (Eds.), *Self-employment activities of women and minorities* (pp. 97–107). Wiesbaden: VS Verlag für Sozialwissenschaften.

Apitzsch, U., & Kontos, M. (2003). Self-employment, gender and migration. *International Review of Sociology, 13*, 67–76.

Azmat, F. (2013). Opportunities or obstacles? Understanding the challenges faced by migrant women entrepreneurs. *International Journal of Gender and Entrepreneurship, 5*(2), 198–215.

Baycan-Levent, T. (2010). Migrant women entrepreneurhip in OECD countries. In OECD (Ed.), *Open for business: Migrant entrepreneurship in OECD countries* (pp. 227–254). Paris: OECD.

Baycan-Levent, T., Masurel, E., & Nijkamp, P. (2003). Diversity in entrepreneurship: Ethnic and female roles in urban economic life. *International Journal of Social Economics, 30*(11), 1131–1161.

Bundesweite Gründerinnenagentur (bga). (2010). *Unternehmerische Selbständigkeit von Frauen mit Migrationshintergrund*. Stuttgart: bga.

Bundesweite Gründerinnenagentur (bga). (2015). *Gründerinnen und Unternehmerinnen in Deutschland-Daten und Fakten IV*. Stuttgart: bga.

Bijedić, T., Brink, S., Ettl, K., Kriwoluzky, S., & Welter, F. (2016). Innovation and women's entrepreneurship: (Why) are women entrepreneurs less innovative? In C. Díaz-García, C. G. Brush, E. J. Gatewood, & F. Welter (Eds.), *Women's entrepreneurship in global and local contexts* (pp. 63–80). Cheltenham: Edward Elgar.

Bonacich, E. (1973). A theory of middleman minorities. *American Sociological Review, 38*(5), 583–594.

Brink, S., Kriwoluzky, S., Bijedić, T., Ettl, K., & Welter, F. (2014). *Gender, Innovation und Unternehmensentwicklung. IfM-Materialien nr. 228*. Bonn: Institut für Mittelstandsforschung.

Brüderl, J., Preisendörfer, P., & Ziegler, R. (2009). *Der Erfolg neugegründeter Betriebe: Eine empirische Studie zu den Chancen und Risiken von Unternehmensgründungen* (3rd ed.). Berlin: Duncker & Humblot.

Brush, C. G., de Bruin, A., & Welter, F. (2014). Auf dem Weg zu genderspezifischen Modellen in der Gründungsforschung. In C. Gather, I. Biermann, L. Schürmann, S. Ulbricht, & H. Zipprian (Eds.), *Die Vielfalt der Selbständigkeit. Sozialwissenschaftliche Beiträge zu einer Erwerbsform im Wandel* (pp. 37–47). Berlin: Edition Sigma.

Bührmann, A. D. (2010). Wider die theoretischen Erwartungen: Empirische Befunde zur Motivation von Unternehmensgründungen durch Migrant/inn/en. In A. D. Bührmann & H. J. Pongratz (Eds.), *Prekäres Unternehmertum: Unsicherheiten von selbständiger Erwerbstätigkeit und Unternehmensgründungen* (pp. 270–293). Wiesbaden: Springer VS.

Bührmann, A. D., Fischer, U. L., & Jasper, G. (2010a). Einleitung. In A. D. Bührmann, U. L. Fischer, & G. Jasper (Eds.), *Migrantinnen gründen Unternehmen: Empirische Analysen und innovative Beratungskonzepte* (pp. 9–18). München: Hampp.

Bührmann, A. D., Fischer, U. L., & Jasper, G. (Eds.). (2010b). *Migrantinnen gründen Unternehmen: Empirische Analysen und innovative Beratungskonzepte*. München: Hampp.

Busch, A. (2013). *Die berufliche Geschlechtersegregation in Deutschland: Ursachen, Reproduktion, Folgen*. Wiesbaden: Springer VS.

Collins, J., & Low, A. (2010). Asian female immigrant entrepreneurs in small and medium-sized businesses in Australia. *Entrepreneurship & Regional Development, 22*(1), 97–111.

Dallalfar, A. (1994). Iranian women as immigrant entrepreneurs. *Gender & Society, 8*(4), 541–561.

Dannecker, P., & Cakir, A. (2016). Female migrant entrepreneurs in Vienna: Mobility and its embeddedness. *Österreichische Zeitschrift für Soziologie, 41*(1), 97–113.

Dhaliwal, S., Scott, J. M., & Hussain, J. (2010). Help or hindrance? South Asian women in the family firm. *Electronic Journal of Family Business Studies, 4*(1), 5–23.

Díaz-García, C., Brush, C. G., Gatewood, E. J., & Welter, F. (2016). Introduction: Women's entrepreneurship in global and local contexts. In C. Díaz-García, C. G. Brush, E. J. Gatewood, & F. Welter (Eds.), *Women's entrepreneurship in global and local contexts* (pp. 1–17). Cheltenham: Edward Elgar.

Essers, C., Benschop, Y., & Doorewaard, H. (2010). Female ethnicity: Understanding muslim immigrant businesswomen in the Netherlands. *Gender Work & Organization, 17*(3), 320–339.

Essers, C., Doorewaard, H., & Benschop, Y. (2013). Family ties: Migrant female business owners doing identity work on the public–private divide. *Human Relations, 66*(12), 1645–1665.

Ettl, K., & Welter, F. (2010). Gender, context and entrepreneurial learning. *International Journal of Gender and Entrepreneurship, 2*(2), 108–129.

Fertala, N. (2006). *Determinants of successful immigrant entrepreneurship in the Federal Republic of Germany*. Tübingen: Universität Tübingen.

Global Entrepreneurship Research Association (GERA). (2017). *Global entrepreneurship monitor: Women's entrepreneurship 2016/2017 report*. London: GERA.

Gupta, V. K., Turban, D. B., Wasti, S. A., & Sikdar, A. (2009). The role of gender stereotypes in perceptions of entrepreneurs and intentions to become an entrepreneur. *Entrepreneurship Theory and Practice, 33*(2), 397–417.

Hakim, C. (1998). *Social change and innovation in the labour market: Evidence from the census SARs on occupational segregation and labour mobility, part-time work and student jobs, homework and self-employment*. New York: Oxford University Press.

Halkias, D., Thurman, P. W., Harkiolakis, N., & Caracatsanis, S. M. (Eds.). (2011). *Female immigrant entrepreneurs: The economic and social impact of a global phenomenon*. Farnham: Gower.

Hatfield, I. (2015). *Self-employment in Europe*. London: Institute for Public Policy Research.

Hausmann, A.-C., & Kleinert, C. (2014). *Berufliche Segregation auf dem Arbeitsmarkt. Männer- und Frauendomänen kaum verändert*. Nuremberg: IAB-Kurzbericht.

Henkel, M., Steidle, H., & Braukmann, J. (2015). *Familien mit Migrationshintergrund: Analysen zur Lebenssituation, Erwerbsbeteiligung und Vereinbarkeit von Familie und Beruf*. Berlin: Bundesministerium für Familie, Senioren, Frauen und Jugend.

Henry, C., Foss, L., & Ahl, H. (2016). Gender and entrepreneurship research: A review of methodological approaches. *International Small Business Journal, 34*(3), 217–241.

Hillmann, F. (1999). A look at the "hidden side": Turkish women in Berlin's ethnic labour market. *International Journal of Urban and Regional Research, 23*(2), 267–282.

Hillmann, F. (Ed.). (2011). *Marginale Urbanität: Migrantisches Unternehmertum und Stadtentwicklung*. Bielefeld: Transcript.

Hughes, K. D. (2003). Pushed or pulled? Women's entry into self-employment and small business ownership. *Gender, Work & Organization, 10*(4), 433–454.

Kay, R., Schneck, S., & Suprinoviĉ, O. (2014). *Erwerbsbiografische Einflüsse auf das Gründungsverhalten von Frauen* (IfM-Materialien Nr. 230). Bonn: Institut für Mittelstandsforschung.

Kermond, C. L., Luscombe, K. E., Strahan, K. W., & Williams, A. J. (1991). *Immigrant women entrepreneurs in Australia*. Wollongong: Centre for Multicultural Studies, University of Wollongong.

Kloosterman, R., Van der Leun, J., & Rath, J. (1999). Mixed embeddedness: (In)formal economic activities and immigrant businesses in the Netherlands. *International Journal of Urban and Regional Research, 23*(2), 253–267.

Knight, M. (2016). Race-ing, classing and gendering racialized women's participation in entrepreneurship: Racialized women's participation in entrepreneurship. *Gender, Work & Organization, 23*(3), 310–327.

Kristen, C., Edele, A., Kalter, F., Kogan, I., Schulz, B., Stanat, P., & Will, G. (2011). The education of migrants and their children across the life course. *Zeitschrift für Erziehungswissenschaft, 14*, 121–137.

Lauxen-Ulbrich, M., & Leicht, R. (2003). *Unternehmerin und daneben auch noch Kinder? Lebensformen und Arbeitsgestaltung selbständiger Frauen in Deutschland. Eine empirische Untersuchung anhand von Mikrozensusdaten*. Institut für Mittelstandsforschung, Universität Mannheim.

Leicht, R. (2016). In einem gänzlich anderen Licht: Unternehmertum von Migrantinnen und Migranten. *Aus Politik und Zeitgeschichte, 66*, 32–38.

Leicht, R., Berwing, S., & Langhauser, M. (2015). Heterogenität und soziale Position migrantischer Selbständigkeit in Deutschland. *Sozialer Fortschritt, 64*(9–10), 233–241.

Leicht, R., Berwing, S., Philipp, R., Block, N., Rüffer, N., Ahrens, J.-P., Förster, N., Sänger, R., & Siebert, J. (2017). *Gründungspotenziale von Menschen mit ausländischen Wurzeln: Entwicklungen, Erfolgsfaktoren, Hemmnisse (Studie im Auftrag des Bundesministeriums für Wirtschaft und Energie)*. Institut für Mittelstandsforschung, Universität Mannheim.

Leicht, R., & Lauxen-Ulbrich, M. (2005). Entwicklung und Determinanten von Frauenselbständigkeit in Deutschland. Zum Einfluss von Beruf und Familie. *Zeitschrift für KMU und Entrepreneurship, 2*, 1–15.

Leicht, R., Strohmeyer, R., Leiß, M., Philipp, R., Welter, F., & Kolb, S. (2009). *Selbständig integriert? Studie zum Gründungsverhalten von Frauen mit Zuwanderungsgeschichte in Nordrhein-Westfalen*. Düsseldorf.

Leoni, T., & Falk, M. (2010). Gender and field of study as determinants of self-employment. *Small Business Economics, 34*(2), 167–185.

Marlow, S. (2015). Women, gender and entrepreneurship: Why can't a woman be more like a man? In R. A. Blackburn, U. Hytti, & F. Welter (Eds.), *Context, process and gender in entrepreneurship* (pp. 23–33). Cheltenham: Edward Elgar.

McManus, P. A. (2001). Women's participation in self-employment in western industrialized nations. *International Journal of Sociology, 31*(2), 70–97.

Morokvasic, M. (1991). Roads to independence. Self-employed immigrants and minority women in five European states. *International Migration, 29*(3), 407–419.

Munkejord, M. C. (2017). Immigrant entrepreneurship contextualised: Becoming a female migrant entrepreneur in rural Norway. *Journal of Enterprising Communities: People and Places in the Global Economy, 11*(2), 258–276.

Neuffer, S. (2015). Unternehmerische Selbstständigkeit als Karriereoption für frauen. *Statistisches Monatsheft Baden-Württemberg, 3,* 23–28.

Niefert, M., & Gottschalk, S. (2015). *Gründerinnen auf dem Vormarsch? Die Entwicklung der Beteiligung von Freuen am Gründungsgeschehen.* Discussion Paper No. 13-085. Zentrum für Europäische Wirtschaftsforschung, Mannheim.

Organisation for Economic Co-operation and Development (OECD). (2017). *The missing entrepreneurs 2017.* Paris: OECD.

Pio, E. (2007). Ethnic minority migrant women entrepreneurs and the imperial imprimatur. *Women in Management Review, 22*(8), 631–649.

Ram, M., Jones, T., & Villares-Varela, M. (2017). Migrant entrepreneurship: Reflections on research and practice. *International Small Business Journal, 35*(1), 3–18.

Sachs, A., Hoch, M., Münch, C., & Steidle, H. (2016). *Migrantenunternehmen in Deutschland zwischen 2005 und 2014. Ausmaß, ökonomische Bedeutung, Einflussfaktoren und Förderung auf Ebene der Bundesländer.* Gütersloh: Verlag Bertelsmann Stiftung.

Schaland, A.-J. (2010). Selbstständige Migrantinnen und Migranten in wissensintensiven Dienstleistungsbranchen: Marktzutrittschancen durch "kulturelle Kompetenzen"? In S. S. Eckart Koch (Ed.), *Internationale Migration: Chancen und interkulturelle Herausforderungen* (pp. 115–128). Augsburg: Rainer Hampp Verlag.

Schneider, J., Yemane, R., & Weinmann, M. (2014). *Diskriminierung am Ausbildungsmarkt. Ausmaß, Ursachen und Handlungsperspektiven.* Berlin: Sachverständigenrat deutscher Stiftungen für Integration und Migration (SVR).

Statistisches Bundesamt. (2018a). *Migration & integration.* Retrieved May 01, 2018, from https://www.destatis.de/EN/FactsFigures/SocietyState/Population/MigrationIntegration/Methods/MigrationBackground.html

Statistisches Bundesamt. (2018b). *Erläuterungen zur arbeitsmarktstatistik.* Retrieved May 01, 2018, from https://www.destatis.de/DE/ZahlenFakten/GesamtwirtschaftUmwelt/Arbeitsmarkt/Methoden/Begriffe/Selbststaendige.html

Strohmeyer, R., Tonoyan, V., & Jennings, J. E. (2017). Jacks-(and Jills)-of-all-trades: On whether, how and why gender influences firm innovativeness. *Journal of Business Venturing, 32*(5), 498–518.

Verduijn, K., & Essers, C. (2013). Questioning dominant entrepreneurship assumptions: The case of female ethnic minority entrepreneurs. *Entrepreneurship & Regional Development, 25*(7–8), 612–630.

Villares-Varela, M., Ram, M., & Jones, T. (2017). Female immigrant global entrepreneurship: From invisibility to empowerment? In C. Henry, T. Nelson, & K. Lewis (Eds.), *The Routledge companion to global female entrepreneurship* (pp. 342–357). London: Routledge.

Waldinger, R., Aldrich, H., & Ward, R. (1990). Opportunities, group characteristics, and strategies. In R. Waldinger, H. Aldrich, & R. Ward (Eds.), *Ethnic entrepreneurs: Immigrant business in industrial societies* (pp. 13–48). London: Sage Publications.

Weichselbaumer, D. (2016). *Discrimination against female migrants wearing headscarves.* Bonn: Forschungsinstitut zur Zukunft der Arbeit.

Welter, F. (2011). Contextualizing entrepreneurship. Conceptual challenges and ways forward. *Entrepreneurship Theory and Practice, 35*(1), 165–184.

Welter, F., & Gartner, W. B. (Eds.). (2016a). *A research agenda for entrepreneurship and context.* Cheltenham: Edward Elgar.

Welter, F., & Gartner, W. B. (2016b). Advancing our research agenda for entrepreneurship and contexts. In F. Welter & W. B. Gartner (Eds.), *A research agenda for entrepreneurship and context* (pp. 156–163). Cheltenham: Edward Elgar.

Business Transferability Chances: Does the Gender of the Owner-Manager Matter?

Rosemarie Kay, André Pahnke, and Susanne Schlepphorst

Abstract In this chapter, we examine the question of whether possible differences in the economic behavior and development of female- and male-led family enterprises prior to successions affect their transferability to the next generation. Using large-scale panel data, we find no general gender-specific differences in economic behavior in the pre-transfer phase, except the fact that women tend to invest less in capacity expansion and generate less turnover. These differences however are not the case in the profit situation of men- and women-led enterprises. Accordingly, men- and women-led enterprises do not differ in anticipating existence-threatening problems in the course of the business succession process. Differences in investment behavior therefore do not seem to harm the transfer process, although structural differences, including the company size or industry affiliation might.

1 Introduction

In Germany and other European countries, the share of women-owned and -led enterprises has increased only marginally (Haunschild and Wolter 2010; Marlow et al. 2008) despite a considerable increase in founding activities among women since 1980 (e.g. Kay et al. 2003; Niefert and Gottschalk 2014). One important reason for this is that compared with men-founded enterprises, women-founded enterprises have a lower survival rate, resulting from among other things sector choice, limited time resources, and lower start-up capital (Jungbauer-Gans 1993; Fertala 2008; Niefert and Gottschalk 2014). Another reason might be an occurrence in a later stage of the family enterprise's life cycle, i.e. the business succession. Gender-related business succession research has almost invariably focused on women as successors (Campopiano et al. 2017; Martinez Jimenez 2009). Women as managers of their own businesses and potential predecessors are rarely considered, even though for example the gender of the incumbent plays

R. Kay (✉) · A. Pahnke · S. Schlepphorst
Institut für Mittelstandsforschung (IfM) Bonn, Bonn, Germany
e-mail: kay@ifm-bonn.org; pahnke@ifm-bonn.org; schlepphorst@ifm-bonn.org

an important role regarding the successor's credibility in the eyes of employees (Koffi et al. 2014) or the sex of the successor: Male incumbents favor male successors, while female incumbents favor female successors (Schlömer-Laufen and Kay 2015). Thus, the sex "imbalance" on the part of the incumbents perpetuates the sex imbalance on the part of the successors. In other words, the selection mechanism homophily applied in the family business succession context results at best in maintaining the share of women-owned and -led businesses at the previous level. Another argument in the context of business succession refers to the chances of transferability of a family business. We assume that specific characteristics that are attributed to women-owned and -led businesses might have a direct or indirect negative impact on these chances.

We base our assumptions on various findings regarding the business succession process as well as gender differences in entrepreneurial behavior. Transferring their business is usually a once-in-a-lifetime event for entrepreneurs. This means they cannot base their decisions on experience, which intensifies their decision-making uncertainties when managing the business succession process. This is one reason why business succession is commonly considered a precarious phase in the life cycle of a family business. In extreme cases, wrong decisions might even result in its closure. With this in mind, the investment decisions prior to the business transfer are important because, among other things, the amount and type of investments affect the capitalized value of the firm and, consequently, its attractiveness to successors (Hauser et al. 2010). Following the empirical evidence that an increase in uncertainty adversely affects the investments of family enterprises (e.g. in innovations, see Caggese 2012), and considering the increasing uncertainties that accompany business transfers, it's not surprising that predecessors tend to cut back investment activities in the pre-transfer phase (e.g. Haunschild et al. 2010; Pahnke et al. 2017a). However, these studies have not addressed the question of gender differences in investment behavior during the course of business successions. Given the large body of research that implies that females are generally more risk-averse than males (e.g. Byrnes et al. 1999; Nikiforow and Siekmann 2012), we assume that women who are planning to transfer their business are more reluctant to invest than their male counterparts. If this holds true, women-led and -owned businesses consequently have fewer chances of transferability. The following therefore examines the question of whether possible differences in the economic behavior and development of female- and male-led family enterprises prior to successions also affect their transferability to the next generation.

In addressing our research question, we also draw on liberal feminist theory (Fischer et al. 1993) and literature on gender differences in entrepreneurial behavior. We contribute to the existing literature by providing new insights into gender differences in investment behavior and performance in the context of business succession. Finally, this chapter helps improve the understanding of why the share of women-owned and -led businesses has largely remained constant over time.

2 Literature Review and Hypothesis Development

Research on gender differences in entrepreneurial behavior has to date proceeded along different lines (for an overview see e.g. Jennings and Brush 2013; Minitti 2009). Three strands are of particular interest for this study: business performance, risk attitude, and business investment. Among these topics, the investment behavior of female and male family business owners prior to a business transfer has to date been scarcely researched (see also Hira and Loibl 2008). Haunschild et al. (2010) and Pahnke et al. (2017a) show that predecessors tend to cut back investments at this stage. The importance of the gender of the incumbent in this context has only been addressed by Pelger (2012) who provides evidence that compared with male firm owners, female owners are less likely to invest. And if they do invest, their average investment rate is lower. Using experimental data on German and Kazakh farmers, Holst et al. (2016) contribute the finding that female farmers often do not choose the most optimal timing for investments. And because females are inclined to invest too early compared to their male counterparts, the quality of their investments might suffer.

The gender differences observed in the business investment behavior of male and female entrepreneurs are in line with the general findings regarding gender differences in risk preferences. Studies in this strand of research mostly find that women are more risk-averse than men (e.g. Badunenko et al. 2009; Byrnes et al. 1999; Nikiforow and Siekmann 2012), which is presumably a primary result of socialization norms (Marlow and Swail 2014). However, the gender gap in risk-taking has obviously declined over time (Byrnes et al. 1999). Barasinska and Schäfer (2013) also find that after controlling for risk tolerance, the actual risk-taking of males and females no longer differs.

Most studies on gender differences in risk-taking are furthermore not conducted in a business environment. So it's unclear whether the lower risk propensity of females holds true for female entrepreneurs. As Pelger (2012) suggests, female entrepreneurs—as a subsample of women—may be as risk-taking as their male counterparts. The findings by Johnson and Powell (1994) support this notion insofar as males and females with managerial education display a similar risk propensity. However, in their comparison of growth-oriented female and male business owners, Sexton and Bowman-Upton (1990) show that females achieve lower scores when it comes to characteristics attributed to risk-taking.

Female entrepreneurs are therefore likely to harbor certain reservations with regard to business investments if they have a lower average risk-taking propensity than male entrepreneurs. Given the importance of investments for business success, this general difference in risk-taking propensities between male and female entrepreneurs could then be one explanation for why many studies observe lower outcomes in terms of sales, employment, income, profit, or growth of women-owned enterprises (e.g. Fairlie and Robb 2009; Gottschalk and Niefert 2013; Klapper and Parker 2011; see Watson and Robinson 2003 for a brief review).

With the third research strand, many scholars conclude that gender itself does not affect entrepreneurial performance. This is in line with liberal feminist theory that principally considers both men and women as "essentially rational, self-interest-seeking agents" (Fischer et al. 1993, p. 154). Disparity in achievements is here caused by other underlying mechanisms, e.g. differing access to education or variations in socialization processes (Fischer et al. 1993). In their exploration of Korean new ventures, Lee and Marvel (2014) for example show that differing firm asset endowments and industry affiliations mediate performance differences and gender. In a similar vein, Johnsen and McMahon (2005) find no performance differences between female- and male-controlled SMEs in Australia when demographic factors are also taken into account. In recapitulating the literature on the relationship between gender and performance in entrepreneurship, Klapper and Parker (2011) attribute the lower performance to the concentration of female entrepreneurs in lower capital-intensive sectors with lower average returns on capital, to smaller business size, and to the utilization of less capital and funding. Fairlie and Robb (2009) add that less work experience gives rise to the average lower performance of female businesses. It therefore comes as little surprise that women-owned businesses face higher closure rates than men-owned businesses (Fairlie and Robb 2009) and are less likely to survive (e.g. Robb 2002; Bosma et al. 2004).

Taken together, a review of the literature on the three research strands—business performance, risk attitude, and business investment—reveals a certain level of ambiguity regarding the existence of gender-specific differences. Nonetheless, it does in fact note dissimilarities in entrepreneurial behaviors and attitudes. Most importantly, female and male business owners possibly differ in their risk-taking propensity and obviously differ in their investment behavior. To our knowledge, these findings have not been taken into account in the specific context of business succession, which leads us to hypothesize the following:

H1: Directors of female-led and -owned businesses are more reluctant to invest in the pre-transfer phase than directors of male-led and -owned businesses.

While the risk propensity of male and female business owners may converge due to learning effects, this may be countered by the uniqueness of the situation in which the investment decision occurs. Especially in the pre-transfer phase, "wrong" decisions will likely yield a failure of the business succession and company closure as a result. The incumbent's uncertainty regarding whether the successor will value the expected returns on investment in a similar way can lead to (unexpected) decreases in the successor's willingness to pay to the point that an agreement about a successful business transition is no longer possible. A risk-averse decision-maker may then tend to refrain from certain investments (Pahnke et al. 2017a).

If female business owners are continually more reserved when investing than their male counterparts, this is likely to result in a comparatively more pronounced deterioration of their market position. This deterioration can express itself in various ways, e.g. loss of market share, decline in sales, profit loss, or employee layoffs. Moreover, it is likely that possible differences between female and male entrepreneurs that affect investment decisions also spill over into decisions in other areas. We pose the following hypothesis based on these arguments:

H2: Women-led and -owned businesses have lower performance outcomes in the pre-transfer phase than men-led and -owned businesses.

The rational decision of whether potential successors take over firms largely depends on the firm's prevailing and expected economic situation. Here, lower outcomes decrease the chances of finding a successor and increase the risk of failure in the course of business successions. Women-led and -owned businesses are more often faced with existential problems in pursuing a business succession. Moreover, according to liberal feminist theory, men and women are essentially both rational agents (Fischer et al. 1993). This means that female and male entrepreneurs are aware of their respective behavior and the consequences thereof. We hypothesize the following based on this argument:

H3: Compared with directors of male-led businesses, directors of female-led businesses more frequently anticipate problems in the course of the business succession process that might jeopardize the existence of their firms.

3 Sample and Key Variables

We use the Establishment Panel provided by the German Institute for Employment Research (IAB) as the database to test our propositions. Data access was provided remotely at the Research Data Centre of the German Federal Employment Agency at the IAB in Nuremberg. This panel is a large-scale, general-purpose survey, and is based on a stratified random sample of establishments from the population of all German establishments that have at least one employee covered by German social insurance. The sampling basis is the Federal Employment Agency's establishment file, which contains approximately 2 million establishments. From its outset, the IAB Establishment Panel was intended to be a longitudinal survey in which a large majority of the plants are annually interviewed. The data are augmented regularly to correct for panel closures, and newly founded firms. The panel has grown over time and currently surveys around 16,000 plants. It is generally carried out in the form of face-to-face interviews (Ellguth et al. 2014; Fischer et al. 2009).

In 2012, the survey contained a set of questions on business succession that captured information on whether a business succession would occur in the foreseeable future; on the planned mode of business transfer; on the current state of planning; and on the existence of problems regarding the business succession. Using this, we were able to identify those businesses that were planning a business succession and, by applying the longitudinal structure of the data, observe them in the pre-transfer phase over several years.

In line with existing research (e.g. Ballarini and Keese 2002; Müller et al. 2011; Zellweger et al. 2011), we limited our analyses to business successions that were reported to occur within a defined period of 5 years in the period between 2012–2016. In other words, we only investigated management decisions of enterprises with a certain "awareness" of the upcoming business succession. To observe their development and the entrepreneurs' strategic behavior, we traced them back to the 2007–2012 time period.

In principle, the IAB Establishment Panel surveys establishments only. However, with the questions on business successions, all information is related to the (superordinated) firm level. So to avoid measurement errors and ensure that the responses on business transfers were not biased by data on subsidiaries or institutions from the public sector (which are generally not affected by successions and mostly act differently from economically-minded businesses), we limited our sample to establishments that did not have subsidiaries and to private-sector establishments on which we had information on annual sales. Our analyses were therefore based on up to 574 enterprises *with*, and 6736 enterprises *without* an upcoming business succession in the near future.

We use different indicators as dependent variables in our regression analyses to obtain robust results. To measure the investment behavior of female and male business owners, we specifically estimate models on the amount of investment per capita (PC), the amount of investment in capital expansion PC, and the percentage of investment in capital expansion. Regression analyses on total sales, the profit situation, and total employment, complemented by a model for the anticipation of firms' jeopardizing problems, provide information on the business situation and the transferability chances of these companies. These indicators are important to consider because they can affect the incumbent's and potential successor's rational decision on whether it is worth transferring or taking over the company.

It should be noted that we increased the validity of our sample by exploiting the longitudinal structure of the data in two ways. First, as the information on sales and investments always references the preceding year of data collection, we generated variables with a correct time reference from two consecutive waves. Second, we occasionally used information from waves prior to 2012, for example when information on past performance was needed.

The data provide detailed annual information on executive boards, i.e. their total size, the total number of women on the boards and whether the executive boards consist of owners, external managers, or a combination of both. However, the data are less informative regarding the exact ownership structure and distribution of shares. Because intergenerational transfer specifically affects family businesses, we restricted our analyses to family businesses by considering only enterprises that are solely managed by their owners. So for the purpose of this study we defined those businesses as women-led businesses—our key variable—whose executive board consists of more than 50% females who also own/have shares in the enterprise. This threshold ensured that females exert a dominating influence within the decision-making body of the family business, which allowed us to argue that our key variable captured female business behavior. Finally, we included a number of control variables in our regressions, which may affect females' and males' investment behaviors in the pre-transfer phase. We aimed to account for the effect of industry, firm size, level of technology, place of business, legal form, payroll, and industrial relations on the dependent variables. Since we were trying to examine possible changes in the companies' development and/or entrepreneurial behavior via their nuances, we controlled for the number of years remaining until the planned business succession would occur. We also added dummy variables that in total cover the study period of up to 5 years prior to the planned business succession.

The estimation model on anticipated problems that may put the existence of firms at risk contains additional control variables on the type of planned transfer mode and the current level of planning.

4 Economic Characteristics and Behavior of Women-Led Enterprises Prior to a Planned Business Succession

4.1 Key Characteristics of Women-Led Enterprises

The outcome of this study demonstrates well-established facts on women-led enterprises. First, women-led enterprises are not very common in Germany (e.g. Haunschild and Wolter 2010; Pahnke et al. 2017b). The large majority of companies are generally men-led: In nearly three out of four enterprises, the executive boards consist of less than 50% women. 21% of all enterprises are mainly or exclusively led by women, and 6% are equally led by both men and women. A similar picture emerges from an examination of companies facing a business transfer within the next 5 years, with a slightly smaller share of women-led companies (see Fig. 1).

Further, women-led enterprises facing a business succession employ nine individuals on average and are thus smaller than their men-led counterparts, which employ an average of 14 people. This result coincides with prior studies that demonstrate the general differences between them (e.g. Kay et al. 2003; Pahnke et al. 2017b). As shown in Table 1, a larger fraction of women-led businesses with an upcoming business succession are active in trade and commerce, catering, and other services, which is consistent with the general sectoral distribution of women-led enterprises in Germany (see also Pahnke et al. 2017b). In addition, women-led enterprises are younger than male-led enterprises (see also Kay et al. 2003). This also holds true for the group of enterprises with business succession plans: Women lead about every fifth enterprise founded before 1990, and they lead nearly every fourth enterprise founded in 1990 or later. Finally, women-led enterprises are more often located in West Germany than in East Germany. This also applies to women-led businesses with succession plans.

These descriptive results suggest a few structural differences between women- and men-led enterprises with business succession plans in terms of company size, age and industry affiliation. In principle, the results are in line with other related studies on female entrepreneurship, indicating that the specific characteristics of our data do not bias the results. Taking these structural differences into account in the following multivariate analyses allows us to determine whether these structural differences and/or gender drive potential investment behavior differences in the pre-transfer phase.

Fig. 1 Distribution of companies by company type in 2012, weighted results. Source: IAB Establishment Panel, wave 2012, own calculation

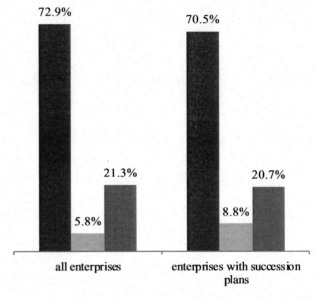

■ executive board with less than 50% women
■ executive board with exactly 50% women
■ executive board with more than 50% women

Table 1 Distribution of enterprises by company type and structural characteristics in 2012, weighted results in %

		Enterprises with business succession plans		All enterprises	
		Women-led	Men-led	Women-led	Men-led
Industry	Manufacturing	13.4	86.6	7.6	92.4
	Trade and commerce, catering	23.4	76.6	22.0	78.0
	Business services, finance, insurance	9.8	90.3	17.8	82.2
	Other services	33.0	67.0	37.3	62.7
Firm age	Founded before 1990	18.2	81.8	18.0	82.0
	Founded 1990 or later	24.8	75.2	22.8	77.2
Location	West Germany	21.5	78.5	20.0	80.0
	East Germany	17.6	82.4	26.1	73.9
Total		20.7	79.3	21.3	78.7

Source: IAB Establishment Panel, wave 2012, own calculation

4.2 Investments

4.2.1 Total Investments Per Capita

We begin our analyses of the investment behavior by examining the average total investments PC in the 2008–2012 period. Figure 2 illustrates that the average investments of men-led enterprises with business succession plans are somewhat closer to the average PC investments of all enterprises. However, the total PC investments of women-led enterprises with business succession plans are lower at the beginning and the end of the observation period, but higher in the middle of the time frame. At first glance, this development suggests differing investment behavior between men-led and women-led enterprises.

To investigate these patterns in more detail, we use ordinary least-square (OLS) estimations, with total PC investments inserted as log values (see Table 2). As shown by the estimated coefficients of our first model based on all enterprises, regardless of actual succession plans (column I), owners of women-led enterprises generally tend to invest less per capita than owners of men-led enterprises. This also applies if control variables are included.

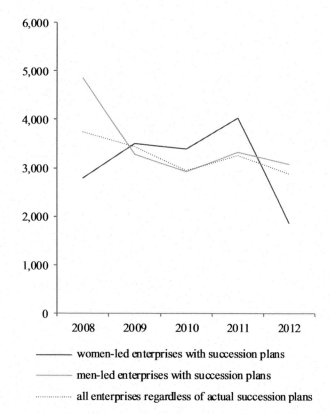

Fig. 2 Development of investments PC (in euros), 2008–2012. Source: IAB Establishment Panel, own calculation

Table 2 Results of pooled OLS estimations on (log.) total investments PC

	I	II	III	IV
		Enterprises with succession plans		
	Complete sample	All	Men-led	Women-led
Women-led enterprise	−0.576***	0.107	–	–
	(0.589)	(0.269)		
Number of years until planned business succession	–	−0.264***	−0.232**	−0.486*
		(0.090)	(0.097)	(0.265)
Firm size (reference: at least 50 employees):				
Up to 9 employees	−1.869***	−2.734***	−2.610***	−2.743***
	(0.072)	(0.273)	(0.300)	(0.824)
10–49 employees	−0.758***	−1.569***	−1.639***	−0.690
	(0.065)	(0.231)	(0.245)	(0.821)
State of technology	0.575***	0.724***	0.865***	0.126
	(0.029)	(0.118)	(0.127)	(0.317)
Uncertain future business development	−0.752***	−1.369***	−1.410***	−1.507
	(0.075)	(0.355)	(0.377)	(1.097)
Export share of at least 10%	0.634***	0.576**	0.571**	1.248
	(0.068)	(0.258)	(0.272)	(0.964)
Existence of a collective agreement	−0.175***	0.208	0.473**	−0.843
	(0.045)	(0.201)	(0.218)	(0.522)
Founded before 1990	−0.159***	−0.002	−0.015	0.164
	(0.046)	(0.215)	(0.232)	(0.675)
Sole trader (legal form)	−0.331***	−0.489**	−0.601**	−0.116
	(0.052)	(0.231)	(0.252)	(0.611)
Location West Germany	0.193***	0.251	0.198	−0.090
	(0.047)	(0.224)	(0.241)	(0.650)
Constant	3.857***	3.243***	2.677***	4.867***
	(0.143)	(0.581)	(0.620)	(1.812)
R-squared	0.089	0.1445	0.1605	0.2194
Number of observations	33,547	1678	1420	258

All estimations include seven industry and five time dummies. Coefficients are significant at the ***1%, **5% and *10% levels. Robust standard errors are in parentheses
Source: IAB Establishment Panel, own calculation

Column II reveals that women-led enterprises are obviously less different from men-led enterprises in the run-up to a (planned) business succession. Applying the described model only to enterprises with succession plans, we no longer observe a statistically significant (negative) effect of female leadership on total PC investments, while the results of all other variables more or less stay the same. Interestingly, we identify a decline in investments with respect to the remaining time interval until the planned business succession. This effect can also be observed when we run separate models only for men-led and women-led enterprises with business succession plans (columns III and IV). While only significant at the 10% level, the corresponding coefficient is larger for women-led than men-led enterprises with business succession plans.

4.2.2 Total Investments in Capital Expansion Per Capita

Because total investments in capital expansion reflect the extension of capacities instead of the replacement and preservation of existing production capabilities, they are of particular interest in the context of business successions. These kinds of activities are very informative for potential successors in determining the value of the company to be transferred.

And we do in fact observe bold differences between men- and women-led enterprises in the pre-transfer phase (see Fig. 3). Again, the average investment of men-led enterprises with business succession plans largely parallels the general development of investments in PC capital expansion. In contrast, women-led enterprises with business succession plans tend to invest less in capital expansion. We also observe an increase during the last 2 years of the time frame—the point in time where the business succession plans are likely to become more specific.

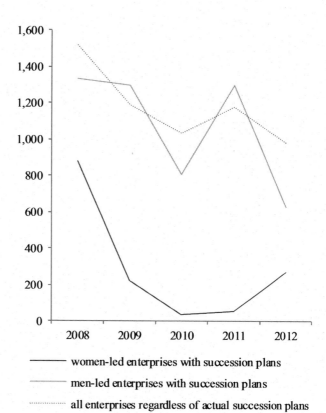

Fig. 3 Development of investments PC (in euros) in capital expansion, 2008–2012. Source: IAB Establishment Panel, own calculation

Our estimations of the general investment behavior in PC capital expansion again confirm that, all things being equal, women-led enterprises act more conservatively than men-led enterprises (see column I, Table 3). In contrast to the results on total PC investments, this outcome persists even when we take into account only enterprises with actual business succession plans (see column II, Table 3). The remaining time until the planned business succession occurs however has no further effect. We also observe no major differences when calculating separate estimations on men- and women-led enterprises (see columns III and IV, Table 3).

Table 3 Results of pooled OLS estimations on (log.) total investments in PC capital expansion

	I	II	III	IV
		Enterprises with succession plans		
	Complete sample	All	Men-led	Women-led
Women-led enterprise	−0.320***	−0.508***	–	–
	(0.044)	(0.179)		
Number of years until planned business succession	–	−0.117	0.128	−0.099
		(0.080)	(0.089)	(0.154)
Firm size (reference: at least 50 employees):				
Up to 9 employees	−1.449***	−2.167***	−2.256***	−1.967***
	(0.071)	(0.290)	(0.317)	(0.743)
10–49 employees	−0.845***	−1.989***	−2.048***	−1.648**
	(0.069)	(0.271)	(0.289)	(0.777)
State of technology	0.425***	0.462***	0.478***	0.463***
	(0.024)	(0.101)	(0.118)	(0.150)
Uncertain future business development	−0.371***	−0.841***	−1.021***	0.247
	(0.056)	(0.241)	(0.266)	(0.512)
Export share of at least 10%	0.765***	0.775***	0.699**	1.557*
	(0.067)	(0.256)	(0.271)	(0.799)
Existence of a collective agreement	−0.055	−0.071	0.011	−0.503*
	(0.037)	(0.167)	(0.192)	(0.291)
Founded before 1990	−0.336***	−0.057	−0.033	−0.457
	(0.038)	(0.178)	(0.201)	(0.396)
Sole trader (legal form)	−0.242***	−0.616***	−0.608***	−0.743
	(0.042)	(0.194)	(0.214)	(0.455)
Location West Germany	−0.168***	−0.589***	−0.573***	−0.708*
	(0.039)	(0.185)	(0.206)	(0.405)
Constant	2.045***	2.729***	2.687***	2.061***
	(0.124)	(0.521)	(0.588)	(1.186)
R-squared	0.078	0.161	0.148	0.226
Number of observations	32,839	1639	1385	254

All estimations include seven industry and five time dummies. Coefficients are significant at the ***1%, **5% and *10% levels. Robust standard errors are in parentheses
Source: IAB Establishment Panel, own calculation

4.2.3 Share of Investments in Capital Expansion

Finally, we investigate the share of investments in capital expansion in terms of total investments. Again, a comparison of finances during the 2008–2012 period indicates structural differences between men- and women-led enterprises with business succession plans. In general, the share of investments in capital expansion seems somewhat volatile, while its level is lower in women-led enterprises with business succession plans (see Fig. 4).

In line with the estimation results of the general investment behavior of women-led businesses stated above, fractional logit estimations (Papke and Wooldridge 1996) reveal general gender differences in the share of investments in capital expansion. As indicated in Fig. 4, this also applies for enterprises with an upcoming business succession (see columns I and II, Table 4). However, there is no indication that the proportion of investments in capital expansion changes as the year of succession becomes closer.

In sum, we find evidence for a general tendency of women-led businesses to invest less than their male-led counterparts. However, when restricting the sample to businesses that are approaching a succession within 5 years, the findings are more ambiguous. With total PC investments, women- and male-led businesses show no

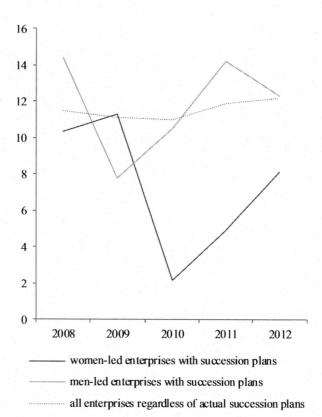

Fig. 4 Development of the share of investments in capital expansion in total investments, 2008–2012. Source: IAB Establishment Panel, own calculation

Table 4 Results of fractional logit estimations of the share of investments in capital expansion

	I	II	III	IV
		Enterprises with succession plans		
	Complete sample	All	Men-led	Women-led
Women-led enterprise	−0.196***	−0.508**	–	–
	(0.044)	(0.222)		
Number of years until planned business succession	–	−0.102	−0.100	0.232
		(0.064)	(0.066)	(0.426)
Firm size (reference: at least 50 employees):				
Up to 9 employees	−0.696***	−0.977***	−1.035***	−1.458*
	(0.044)	(0.195)	(0.208)	(0.792)
10–49 employees	−0.286***	−0.772***	−0.786***	−1.141
	(0.038)	(0.151)	(0.157)	(0.808)
State of technology	0.271***	0.340***	0.313***	0.759***
	(0.057)	(0.085)	(0.091)	(0.238)
Uncertain future business development	0.271***	−1.029***	−1.233***	2.392**
	(0.057)	(0.384)	(0.388)	(1.093)
Export share of at least 10%	0.288***	0.438***	0.390**	1.610**
	(0.038)	(0.157)	(0.156)	(0.726)
Existence of a collective agreement	−0.011	0.039	0.066	−0.351
	(0.029)	(0.130)	(0.136)	(0.545)
Founded before 1990	−0.266***	−0.001	0.013	0.923
	(0.031)	(0.151)	(0.158)	(0.711)
Sole trader (legal form)	−0.109***	−0.468***	−0.442**	−0.849
	(0.034)	(0.168)	(0.178)	(0.538)
Location West Germany	0.243***	0.565***	−0.532***	−0.837
	(0.030)	(0.161)	(0.166)	(0.705)
Constant	1.850***	−1.865***	−1.782***	3.383**
	(0.093)	(0.384)	(0.408)	(1.426)
Pseudo-log-likelihood	−12,308.180	−5833.950	−526.744	−45.248
Number of observations	33,108	1645	1389	254

All estimations include seven industry and five time dummies. Coefficients are significant at the *** 1%, **5% and *10% levels. Robust standard errors are in parentheses
Source: IAB Establishment Panel, own calculation

differences in their investment behaviors; both tend to invest less as the succession date approaches. However, differences emerge with the (total investments and share of) investments in capital expansion. Regarding the expansion of the enterprises' capacities pre-transfer, women-led businesses are more reserved. So Hypothesis 1 which postulates that directors of female-led businesses are more reluctant to invest in the pre-transfer phase than directors of male-led businesses cannot be fully confirmed. We now turn to the question of whether the observed differences in the investment behavior between women-led and men-led enterprises have an impact on their performance and employment situation.

4.3 Performance and Employment

4.3.1 Total Sales Per Capita

At first glance, women-led enterprises appear to record higher PC sales on average prior to business successions than their male-led counterparts. These sales however tend to decrease at the end of the observation period. At the same time, we observe an opposing general development in men-led enterprises with business succession plans (see Fig. 5).

Our multivariate estimations reveal that women-led enterprises tend to generate smaller PC turnover than men-led companies, both in general as well as when they face an upcoming succession (see columns I and II, Table 5). However, no statistically significant sales differences are seen: neither men- nor women-led enterprises change as the year of succession draws closer.

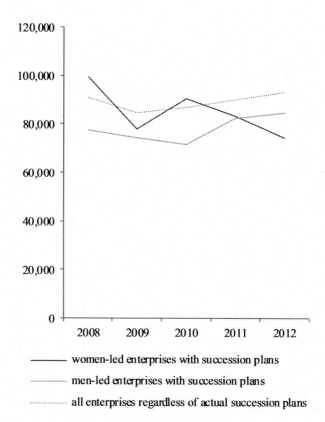

Fig. 5 Development of sales per capita (in euros), 2008–2012. Source: IAB Establishment Panel, own calculation

Table 5 Results of pooled OLS estimations on (log.) total sales per capita

	I	II	III	IV
		Enterprises with succession plans		
	Complete sample	All	Men-led	Women-led
Women-led enterprise	−0.177***	−0.127**	–	–
	(0.012)	(0.050)		
Number of years until planned business succession	–	−0.013	−0.010	−0.019
		(0.016)	(0.017)	(0.051)
Firm size (reference: at least 50 employees):				
Up to 9 employees	−0.079***	−0.011	−0.017	−0.018
	(0.015)	(0.056)	(0.060)	(0.195)
10–49 employees	0.015	0.104**	0.127***	0.052
	(0.014)	(0.050)	(0.053)	(0.187)
State of technology	0.113***	0.118***	0.132***	0.061
	(0.006)	(0.022)	(0.024)	(0.057)
Uncertain future business development	−0.100***	−0.157**	−0.143*	−0.230
	(0.016)	(0.075)	(0.083)	(0.145)
Export share of at least 10%	0.369***	0.421***	0.399***	0.530**
	(0.013)	(0.050)	(0.052)	(0.259)
Existence of a collective agreement	0.012	−0.014	−0.004	−0.044
	(0.009)	(0.035)	(0.038)	(0.099)
Founded before 1990	0.085***	−0.015	−0.077*	0.286**
	(0.009)	(0.041)	(0.045)	(0.126)
Sole trader (legal form)	−0.312***	−0.293***	−0.331***	−0.019
	(0.010)	(0.042)	(0.045)	(0.112)
Location West Germany	0.124***	0.217***	0.210***	0.161
	(0.009)	(0.040)	(0.042)	(0.131)
Constant	10.762***	10.604***	10.594***	10.494***
	(0.028)	(0.117)	(0.127)	(0.279)
R-squared	0.329	0.412	0.394	0.560
Number of observations	28,536	1525	1299	226

All estimations include seven industry and five time dummies. Coefficients are significant at the ***1%, **5% and *10% levels. Robust standard errors are in parentheses
Source: IAB Establishment Panel, own calculation

4.3.2 Profit Situation

Since relatively low PC sales do not automatically equal bad profit situations, we also take a closer look at the profits of women-led enterprises with business succession plans. The descriptive analyses reveal that a smaller proportion of women-led enterprises with business succession plans are—according to subjective perceptions—in a (very) good profit situation compared to men-led enterprises. However, there is a positive development over time (albeit a decline in 2012) which stands in contrast to men-led enterprises with business succession plans (see Fig. 6).

Fig. 6 Proportion of enterprises with a (very) good profit situation, 2008–2012. Source: IAB Establishment Panel, own calculation

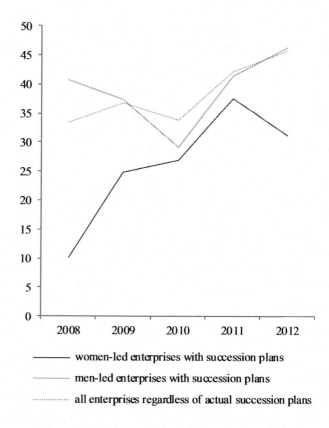

——— women-led enterprises with succession plans
·········· men-led enterprises with succession plans
············ all enterprises regardless of actual succession plans

Corresponding logit estimations on the determinants of a (very) good profit situation show that the directors of women-led enterprises are generally less likely to report a (very) good profit situation (see column I, Table 6). However, despite the visual impression given by Fig. 6, this does not hold true for enterprises with business succession plans. Beyond this, there are no indications of significant changes preceding the business succession.

4.3.3 Employment

A closer look at the employment development in men- and women-led enterprises that are planning a business transfer in the near future reveals stable levels in employment in the pre-transfer phase. However, men-led enterprises with business succession plans are noticeably larger than the general average enterprise in the sample and their women-led counterparts (see Fig. 7).

Our estimation results confirm this difference in firm size (see column I, Table 7). However, OLS regressions only on enterprises with actual business succession plans do not show statistically significant differences between the two groups. Beyond this, the results provide no evidence for a continuous change in employment when the planned date of the business succession approaches. Thus, there are no highly

Table 6 Results of pooled logit estimations of a (very) good profit situation

	I	II	III	IV
		Enterprises with succession plans		
	Complete sample	All	Men-led	Women-led
Women-led enterprise	−0.061**	0.141	–	–
	(0.029)	(0.154)		
Number of years until planned business succession	–	−0.043	−0.019	−0.167
		(0.051)	(0.055)	(0.164)
Firm size (reference: at least 50 employees):				
Up to 9 employees	−0.503***	−0.084	−0.069	−0.369
	(0.039)	(0.177)	(0.190)	(0.555)
10–49 employees	−0.145***	0.134	0.170	−0.413
	(0.036)	(0.159)	(0.166)	(0.567)
State of technology	0.473***	0.545***	0.560***	0.423**
	(0.015)	(0.069)	(0.076)	(0.180)
Uncertain future business development	−0.814***	−0.642***	−0.652**	−0.595
	(0.040)	(0.247)	(0.261)	(0.764)
Export share of at least 10%	0.162***	0.250*	0.266*	0.479
	(0.034)	(0.150)	(0.156)	(0.601)
Existence of a collective agreement	0.058***	0.238**	0.213*	0.425
	(0.022)	(0.112)	(0.122)	(0.300)
Founded before 1990	−0.270***	−0.185	−0.209	0.656
	(0.023)	(0.120)	(0.131)	(0.327)
Sole trader (legal form)	0.128***	0.182	0.271*	−0.292
	(0.025)	(0.131)	(0.141)	(0.400)
Location West Germany	−0.091***	−0.081	−0.045	0.266
	(0.023)	(0.123)	(0.134)	(0.328)
Constant	−1.435***	−2.269***	−2.316***	−1.624
	(0.073)	(0.358)	(0.385)	(1.042)
Pseudo-log-likelihood	−26,724.401	−1129.796	−961.764	−156.796
Number of observations	41,833	1784	1507	271

All estimations include seven industry and five time dummies. Coefficients are significant at the *** 1%, **5% and *10% levels. Robust standard errors are in parentheses
Source: IAB Establishment Panel, own calculation

noticeable differences between men- and women-led enterprises with business succession plans in terms of total employment (see columns III and IV, Table 7).

In summarizing the results of the outcomes of the business activities of women-led and men-led enterprises, there is certain evidence that women-led enterprises are generally "smaller" than men-led enterprises regarding sales and the number of employees, while the remaining time until the planned business successions does not further affect the development of these indicators for either women- or men-led enterprises. There is only one noticeable difference regarding business succession: Women-led enterprises which are pending a transfer generate lower sales.

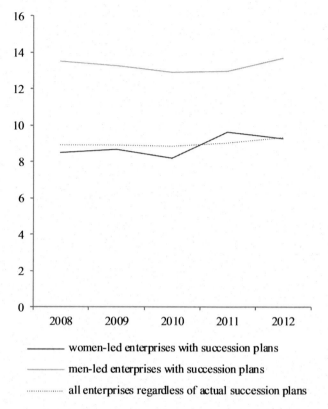

Fig. 7 Average total employment, 2008–2012. Source: IAB Establishment Panel, own calculation

Interestingly, this difference between women-led and men-led enterprises in sales is not mirrored by the results of the profit situation. Because profit is more important than total annual sales in the context of business successions, and given the fact that the identified differences in sales do not further increase in the pre-transfer phase, we reject Hypothesis 2, which postulates that women-led and -owned businesses have lower performance outcomes in the pre-transfer phase than men-led and -owned businesses.

We finally turn to the question whether women- and men-led enterprises—in awareness of their respective entrepreneurial behavior and the consequences thereof—more often anticipate problems occurring in the course of the business succession process.

4.4 Problems in the Course of the Business Transfer Process

A quarter of all enterprises with business succession plans anticipate problems in the business transfer process (26.1%), which might jeopardize the existence of the business. Among these enterprises, 24.5% are led by women. This proportion

Table 7 Results of pooled OLS estimations on (log.) total number of employees

	I	II	III	IV
		Enterprises with succession plans		
	Complete sample	All	Men-led	Women-led
Women-led enterprise	−0.093***	−0.010	–	–
	(0.012)	(0.062)		
Number of years until planned business succession	–	0.018	0.259	−0.065
		(0.023)	(0.024)	(0.091)
(log) Wages PC	0.242***	0.345***	0.343***	0.389***
	(0.004)	(0.035)	(0.040)	(0.091)
State of technology	0.114***	0.203***	0.216***	0.119*
	(0.006)	(0.029)	(0.032)	(0.061)
Uncertain future business development	−0.073***	0.155	0.193*	−0.089
	(0.016)	(0.097)	(0.109)	(0.175)
Export share of at least 10%	0.365***	0.552***	0.579***	0.180
	(0.017)	(0.074)	(0.076)	(0.292)
Existence of a collective agreement	0.202***	0.200***	0.237***	0.001
	(0.010)	(0.051)	(0.056)	(0.127)
Founded before 1990	0.230***	0.133**	0.180***	−0.129
	(0.010)	(0.052)	(0.057)	(0.128)
Sole trader (legal form)	−0.946***	−0.883***	−0.891***	−0.734***
	(0.010)	(0.054)	(0.058)	(0.165)
Location West Germany	0.044***	0.122**	0.079	0.429***
	(0.010)	(0.053)	(0.058)	(0.118)
Constant	0.773***	−0.397	−0.471	−0.335
	(0.037)	(0.278)	(0.315)	(0.702)
R-squared	0.440	0.449	0.442	0.444
Number of observations	36,881	1625	1379	246

All estimations include seven industry and five time dummies. Coefficients are significant at the *** 1%, **5% and *10% levels. Robust standard errors are in parentheses
Source: IAB Establishment Panel, own calculation

exceeds the overall proportion of women-led enterprises among all enterprises planning a business succession between 2012 and 2016 (15.5%), which indicates that women-led enterprises are more prone to existence-threatening problems in the business succession process.

However, estimating the effects on the probability of expecting any kind of problems (see column I, Table 8) or even existence-threatening problems (see column II, Table 8), we do not observe any gender effects stemming from women-led enterprises. Hence, the higher percentage of women-led businesses anticipating problems results from structural and other differences between male- and female-led businesses. We therefore reject Hypothesis 3, which postulates that compared to directors of male-led businesses, directors of female-led businesses more often anticipate problems occurring in the course of the business succession process that might jeopardize the existence of their firms.

Table 8 Results of logit estimations on anticipating problems in the business transfer process

	I	II
Women-led enterprise	0.226	0.832
	(0.470)	(0.675)
Number of years until planned business succession	0.118	0.114
	(0.140)	(0.208)
(log) Wages PC	0.378	0.449
	(0.342)	(0.467)
No changes in the executive board	0.966	1.751*
	(0.680)	(0.975)
Firm size (reference: at least 50 employees):		
Up to 9 employees	−0.210	0.587
	(0.644)	(0.986)
10–49 employees	−0.515	−0.079
	(0.619)	(0.964)
Competition	0.756*	1.386**
	(0.405)	(0.579)
Internal succession	−1.093***	−2.004***
	(0.358)	(0.683)
Sale of the firm	0.149	0.61
	(0.410)	(0.480)
Business succession not planned	3.398***	15.853***
	(1.078)	(0.813)
Business succession partly planned	2.611**	14.819***
	(1.049)	(0.894)
State of technology	−0.699***	−0.675***
	(0.174)	(0.245)
Uncertain future business development	−0.504	−0.039
	(0.689)	(0.824)
Export share of at least 10%	−0.067	−0.139
	(0.561)	(0.855)
Existence of a collective agreement	0.647*	−0.087
	(0.362)	(0.672)
Founded before 1990	0.181	0.712
	(0.386)	(0.574)
Sole trader (legal form)	0.083	0.386
	(0.413)	(0.596)
Location West Germany	−0.464	−0.762
	(0.413)	(0.667)
Constant	−5.063*	−21.058***
	(2.836)	(4.075)
Pseudo-log-likelihood	−143.119	−67.275
Pseudo R-squared	0.259	0.387
Number of observations	355	

All estimations include seven industry and five time dummies. Coefficients are significant at the ***1%, **5% and *10% level. Robust standard errors are in parentheses

Source: IAB Establishment Panel, own calculation

5 Discussions and Implications

This study aimed to elucidate whether female business leaders are more reluctant to invest in their enterprises before business successions occur and whether they consequently have lower chances of transferring their businesses. Our deliberations are based on findings on business successions and gender-related literature that highlight gender differences in general investment behavior, risk preferences, and business performance. To answer these questions, we used large-scale panel data provided by the IAB Establishment panel on German establishments.

First, our empirical results corroborate prior general findings on women-led enterprises: Compared with men-led enterprises, they are smaller in terms of total sales and the number of employees, and they more frequently perceive that their business is in a less well-positioned profit situation. As expected, women-led enterprises tend to invest more conservatively than their male counterparts, even if contextual factors such as industry or firm size are taken into account.

However, the differences between male- and female-led enterprises are considerably smaller if we focus on enterprises that face a business transfer in the near future. All things being equal, female-led enterprises invest as much in their business as their male counterparts. It is however remarkable that both male- and female-led enterprises reduce their investments prior to upcoming business successions. Strictly speaking, cut-back tendencies increase as the year of succession draws closer.

Notwithstanding, female-led enterprises pursue different investment purposes: They invest less in expanding the capacities of their businesses than their male counterparts. They instead invest more in the replacement of equipment and/or in improvements in productivity.

Overall, our findings on the investment behavior of female business owners suggest that they are generally more risk-averse than male business owners. However, contrary to our expectations, this obviously does not affect the decisions of business owners anticipating a business succession. If business owners are essentially rational agents (as liberal feminist theory supposes) they are despite the uniqueness of the business transfer process at least roughly aware of the prerequisites of a successful business succession. These prerequisites include the maintenance of an appropriate level of technology gained by industry-specific investments. Business owners who do not reach this level of technology might anticipate the lower chances of finding a successor and consequently might from the outset intentionally disregard a business succession. If this holds true, female business owners more frequently refrain from pursuing a business succession than their male counterparts because of their generally lower investments. As a result of this mechanism, the gender effect on business investments disappears.

The observed gender differences in investment behavior have relatively little impact on the performance of enterprises with business succession plans. While women-led enterprises generate lower sales, they enjoy a (very) good profit situation as often as male-led enterprises prior to business succession. Against our expectations, the gender differences in the investment behavior thus do not result in a specific deterioration of the market position of women-led businesses. From this perspective, there is no indication that female investment behavior leads to a reduction in the attractiveness of female-led and -owned businesses planning a succession.

So all things being otherwise equal, compared with men-led enterprises, women-led enterprises do not more often anticipate problems, let alone existence-threatening problems, in the business transfer process. In fact, as liberal feminist theory proposes, female and male entrepreneurs seem to be similarly aware of their respective behavior and are able to assess its outcomes. This finding indirectly contributes to the inconsistent research on gender differences in overconfidence. While some studies show that males are overconfident in comparison to females (e.g. Barber and Odean 2001), others do not (e.g. Johansson Stenman and Nordblom 2010; Deaves et al. 2009; Cesarini et al. 2006). Our finding indicates that male and female business owners planning a business succession do not differ in the assessment of their own abilities. This supports the notion that gender differences in confidence depend among other things on the respective context(s) (e.g. Muthukrishna et al. 2017).

Taking our findings as a whole, we conclude that women-led businesses have the same chance of being transferred to the next generation as men-led businesses. Both objective as well as subjective measures support this conclusion. This also means that the hurdles towards business succession success are as high for women-led businesses as they are for men-led businesses. From this point of view, women-led businesses are not more frequently prone to failure in the business succession process than their male-led counterparts. We do however have to keep in mind the structural differences between women- and men-led businesses we controlled for in our analyses. The nature of these structural differences leads us to assume that women-led businesses close more frequently in the course of business successions than men-led businesses. A lower transfer rate of women-led businesses would indeed contribute to the constant share of women-owned and -led businesses.

The study at hand contributes to the current research on business succession processes and gender in several ways. Our primary contribution is that we shed better light on the still under-researched role of gender in business succession (Haberman and Danes 2007; Martinez Jimenez 2009). The study thus promotes knowledge on female incumbents in the succession process, whereas attention has commonly been paid to male incumbents or female successors. In particular, it shifts the focus to an under-researched area: female incumbents' entrepreneurial behavior.

One of the study's strengths lies in the application of a large-scale data set. As a result, it overcomes the shortcomings of quite a few case studies that only considered women in business succession, without having a control group of male-led enterprises. The study results allow for generalization beyond the sample. The weaknesses of this study should however not be disregarded. The unavailability of information on the ownership structure and distribution of shares in the data set forced us to restrict the sample in two ways. First, we confined the sample to those businesses that are solely managed by their owners. Second, among these businesses, we defined those to be led by women in the case where the executive boards had female majorities. This ensured we would only capture the influence of female executives on the decision-making process in family enterprises. This procedure is however not without limitations if the board is in fact comprised of both men and women. Regardless of the number of male and female executives, the voting rights of male executives might exceed those of females. Furthermore, the influence of female executives might be restricted depending on their specific areas of responsibilities.

We also recognize that although all long-lasting family businesses in Europe face the challenge of succession, it is unclear whether our findings are transferable to other European countries. Carney et al. (2014) suggest that external institutional factors such as inheritance law and inheritance taxes as well as deeply embedded political and social values have an impact on among other things the probability of successful intra-family succession. It is up to future research to conduct an international comparison and answer the questions of whether and how such institutional differences influence the respective entrepreneurial behavior in the context of business succession.

References

Badunenko, O., Brasinska, N., & Schäfer, D. (2009). *Risk attitudes and investment decisions across European countries – Are women more conservative investors than men?* (Discussion Papers 928). Berlin: DIW.

Ballarini, K., & Keese, D. (2002). *Generationswechsel in Baden-Württemberg. Zum richtigen Zeitpunkt den richtigen Nachfolger ins Spiel bringen.* Stuttgart: Studie im Auftrag der Landeskreditbank Baden-Württemberg.

Barasinska, N., & Schäfer, D. (2013). *Is the willingness to take financial risk a sex-linked trait? Evidence from National Surveys of household finance* (Discussion Papers 1278). Berlin: DIW.

Barber, B. M., & Odean, T. (2001). Boys will be boys: Gender, overconfidence, and common stock investment. *The Quarterly Journal of Economics, 116*(1), 261–292.

Bosma, N., van Praag, M., Thurik, R., & de Wit, G. (2004). The value of human and social capital investments for the business performance of startups. *Small Business Economics, 23*(3), 227–236.

Byrnes, J. P., Miller, D. C., & Schafer, W. D. (1999). Gender differences in risk taking: A meta-analysis. *Psychological Bulletin, 125*(3), 367–383.

Caggese, A. (2012). Entrepreneurial risk, investment and innovation. *Journal of Financial Economics, 106*(2), 287–307.

Carney, M., Gedajlovic, E., & Strike, V. M. (2014). Dead money: Inheritance law and the longevity of family firms. *Entrepreneurship Theory and Practice, 38*(6), 1261–1283.

Campopiano, G., de Massis, A., Rinaldi, F. R., & Sciascia, S. (2017). Women's involvement in family firms: Progress and challenges for future research. *Journal of Family Business Strategy, 8*(4), 200–212.

Cesarini, D., Sandewall, O., & Johannesson, M. (2006). Confidence interval estimation tasks and the economics of overconfidence. *Journal of Economic Behavior and Organization, 61*, 453–470.

Deaves, R., Lüders, E., & Luo, G. Y. (2009). An experimental test of the impact of overconfidence and gender on trading activity. *Review of Finance, 13*, 555–575.

Ellguth, P., Kohaut, S., & Möller, I. (2014). The IAB establishment panel – methodological essentials and data quality. *Journal for Labour Market Research, 47*(1–2), 27–41.

Fairlie, R. W., & Robb, A. M. (2009). Gender differences in business performance: Evidence from the characteristics of business owners survey. *Small Business Economics, 33*(4), 375–395.

Fertala, N. (2008). The shadow of death: Do regional differences matter for firm survival across native and immigrant entrepreneurs? *Empirica, 35*(1), 59–80.

Fischer, E. M., Reuber, A. R., & Dyke, L. S. (1993). A theoretical overview and extension of research on sex, gender, and entrepreneurship. *Journal of Business Venturing, 8*(1), 151–168.

Fischer, G., Janik, F., Müller, D., & Schmucker, A. (2009). The IAB establishment panel – things users should know. *Schmollers Jahrbuch, Zeitschrift für Wirtschafts- und Sozialwissenschaften, 129*(1), 133–148.

Gottschalk, S., & Niefert, M. (2013). Gender differences in business success of German start-up firms. *International Journal of Entrepreneurship and Small Business, 18*(1), 15–46.

Haberman, H., & Danes, S. M. (2007). Father-daughter and father-son family business management transfer comparison: Family FIRO model application. *Family Business Review, 20*(2), 163–184.

Haunschild, L., & Wolter, H.-J. (2010). *Volkswirtschaftliche Bedeutung von Familien- und Frauenunternehmen*. Bonn: IfM-Materialien Nr. 199.

Haunschild, L., Tchouvakhina, M., & Werner, A. (2010). *Unternehmensnachfolge im Mittelstand: Investitionsverhalten, Finanzierung und Unternehmensentwicklung*. Frankfurt/Main: KfW-Standpunkt Nr. 5.

Hauser, H.-E., Kay, R., & Boerger, S. (2010). *Unternehmensnachfolgen in Deutschland 2010 bis 2014, Schätzung mit weiterentwickeltem Verfahren*. Bonn: IfM-Materialien Nr. 198.

Hira, T. K., & Loibl, C. (2008). Gender differences in investment behavior. In J. J. Xiao (Ed.), *Handbook of consumer finance research* (pp. 253–270). New York: Springer.

Holst, G. S., März, A., & Mußhoff, O. (2016). Experimentelle Untersuchung der Optimalität von Investitionsentscheidungen. *Schmalenbachs Zeitschrift für betriebswirtschaftliche Forschung, 68*(2), 167–192.

Jennings, J. E., & Brush, C. G. (2013). Research on women entrepreneurs: Challenges to (and from) the broader entrepreneurship literature? *The Academy of Management Annals, 7*(1), 663–715.

Johansson Stenman, O., & Nordblom, K. (2010). *Are men really more overconfident than women? A natural field experiment on exam behavior* (Working Papers in Economics No. 461). School of Business, Economics and Law, University of Gothenburg.

Johnsen, G. J., & Mcmahon, R. G. P. (2005). Owner-manager gender, financial performance and business growth amongst SMEs from Australia's business longitudinal survey. *International Small Business Journal, 23*(2), 115–142.

Johnson, J., & Powell, P. (1994). Decision making, risk and gender: Are managers different? *British Journal of Management, 5*, 123–138.

Jungbauer-Gans, M. (1993). *Frauen als Unternehmerinnen. Eine Untersuchung der Erfolgs- und Überlebenschancen neugegründeter Frauen- und Männerbetriebe*. Frankfurt/Main: Peter Lang.

Kay, R., Günterberg, B., Holz, M., & Wolter, H.-J. (2003). *Unternehmerinnen in Deutschland* (Gutachten im Auftrag des Bundesministeriums für Wirtschaft und Arbeit - Langfassung – BMWA-Dokumentation Nr. 522). Berlin.

Klapper, L. F., & Parker, S. C. (2011). Gender and the business environment for new firm creation. *World Bank Research Observer, 26*(2), 237–257.

Koffi, V., Guihur, I., Morris, T., & Fillion, G. (2014). Family business succession: How men and women predecessors can bring credibility to their successors? *Entrepreneurial Executive, 9*, 67–85.

Lee, I. H., & Marvel, M. R. (2014). Revisiting the entrepreneur gender-performance relationship: A firm perspective. *Small Business Economics, 42*(4), 769–786.

Marlow, S., & Swail, J. (2014). Gender, risk and finance: Why can't a woman be more like a man? *Entrepreneurship & Regional Development, 26*(1–2), 80–96.

Marlow, S., Carter, S., & Shaw, E. (2008). Constructing female entrepreneurship policy in the UK: Is the US a relevant benchmark? *Environment and Planning C: Government and Policy, 26*(1), 335–351.

Martinez Jimenez, R. (2009). Research on women in family firms: Current status and future directions. *Family Business Review, 22*(1), 53–64.

Minitti, M. (2009). Gender issues in entrepreneurship. *Foundations and Trends, 5*(7–8), 497–621.

Müller, K., Kay, R., Felden, B., Moog, P., Lehmann, S., Suprinovič, O., Meyer, S., Mirabella, D., Boerger, S., Welge, B., & Coritnaia, I. (2011). *Der Generationswechsel im Mittelstand im demografischen Wandel*. Duderstadt: Mecke Druck.

Muthukrishna, M., Henrich, J., Toyakawa, W., Hamamura, T., Kameda, T., & Heine, S. J. (2017). Overconfidence is universal? Elicitation of genuine overconfidence (EGO) method reveals systematic differences across domain, task knowledge, and incentives in four populations. *SSRN Working Paper*. https://doi.org/10.2139/ssrn.3064202

Niefert, M., & Gottschalk, S. (2014). Gründerinnen auf dem Vormarsch? Die Entwicklung der Beteiligung von Frauen am Gründungsgeschehen. *AStA Wirtschafts- und Sozialstatistisches Archiv, 8*(3), 115–145.

Nikiforow, M., & Siekmann, J. (2012). Risikoverhalten nach Geschlechtern: ein Überblick. *Wirtschaftswissenschaftliches Studium, 41*(5), 254–260.

Pahnke, A., Kay, R., & Schlepphorst, S. (2017a). *Unternehmerisches Verhalten im Zuge der Unternehmensnachfolge*. Bonn: IfM-Materialien Nr. 254.

Pahnke, A., Ettl, K., & Welter, F. (2017b). Women-led enterprises in Germany: The more social, ecological, and corporate responsible businesses? In V. Ratten, L.-P. Dana, & V. Ramadani (Eds.), *Women entrepreneurship in family business* (pp. 46–62). New York: Routledge.

Papke, L. E., & Wooldridge, J. M. (1996). Econometric methods for fractional response variables with an application to 401(k) plan participation rates. *Journal of Applied Econometrics, 11*, 619–632.

Pelger, I. (2012). *Of firms and (wo)men: Explorative essays on the economics of firm, gender and welfare*. Dissertation. Volkswirtschaftliche Fakultät, LMU München.

Robb, A. M. (2002). Entrepreneurial performance by women and minorities: The case of new firms. *Journal of Developmental Entrepreneurship, 7*(4), 383–397.

Schlömer-Laufen, N., & Kay, R. (2015). Zum Einfluss des Geschlechts des Übergebenden auf die Wahl des familieninternen Nachfolgenden. *Zeitschrift für KMU und Entrepreneurship, 63*(1), 1–23.

Sexton, D. L., & Bowman-Upton, N. (1990). Female and male entrepreneurs: Psychological characteristics and their role in gender-related discrimination. *Journal of Business Venturing, 5*(1), 29–36.

Watson, J., & Robinson, S. (2003). Adjusting for risk in comparing the performances of male- and female-controlled SMEs. *Journal of Business Venturing, 18*(6), 773–788.

Zellweger, T., Sieger, P., & Halter, D. (2011). Should I stay or should I go? Career choice intentions of students with family business background. *Journal of Business Venturing, 26*(5), 521–536.

Does Gender Make a Difference? Gender Differences in the Motivations and Strategies of Female and Male Academic Entrepreneurs

Vivien Iffländer, Anna Sinell, and Martina Schraudner

Abstract Academic entrepreneurship is increasingly seen as significantly advancing national efforts to innovate and compete globally. Despite long-term attempts to promote academic spin-off formation however, its numbers across Europe remain relatively low. At the same time, the scarce available data on women in entrepreneurship suggests that while their numbers may be lower, they also appear to choose different business models and focus on different markets than men. The goal of this study therefore was to examine potential differences in motivations and strategies between female and male academic entrepreneurs and, based on this, to project how greater participation by women may benefit the German transfer landscape. We interviewed 40 academic entrepreneurs for this exploratory case study. Their motivations (including gender differences) were identified using open-ended, qualitative content analysis. Our findings suggest that female academic entrepreneurs are often driven by the ideals of creating something for the common good and making a social difference. Male academic entrepreneurs on the other hand appear to pursue more personal goals.

1 Objective and Research Questions

Independent of one another, academic entrepreneurship (European Commission 2016c; Grimaldi et al. 2011; Siegel and Wright 2015; Etzkowitz et al. 2008) and gender (European Commission 2016b; Etzkowitz et al. 2008; Expertenkommission Forschung und Innovation [EFI] 2014, 2017) are receiving increasing political attention within the European Union as well as national innovation economies. Academic entrepreneurship is understood as the commercialization of scientific

---

V. Iffländer (✉) · A. Sinell · M. Schraudner
Fraunhofer Center for Responsible Research and Innovation (CeRRI), Berlin, Germany
e-mail: vivien.ifflaender@iao.fraunhofer.de; anna.sinell@iao.fraunhofer.de; martina.schraudner@iao.fraunhofer.de

© Springer International Publishing AG, part of Springer Nature 2018
S. Birkner et al. (eds.), *Women's Entrepreneurship in Europe*, FGF Studies in Small Business and Entrepreneurship, https://doi.org/10.1007/978-3-319-96373-0_4

findings (Grimaldi et al. 2011) and constitutes one form of knowledge and technology transfer (KTT). KTT is playing an increasingly greater role in advancing national capacities to innovate and compete globally (Wissenschaftsrat 2016). In this context however, the European transfer landscape has been referred to as an "emerging industry" because of its relatively humble achievements, particularly compared to the US (European Commission 2016a). Europe does however continue to promote women's participation in research and science, which is considered very important for the viability of national innovation systems (Etzkowitz et al. 2008).

While academic entrepreneurship and gender each enjoy their own vast scholarly interest and study, they are rarely considered in combination with one another. Link and Strong (2016) found that this was the focus of only six out of over 500 scholarly contributions that examine the relationships between gender and entrepreneurship as such (published between 1979 and 2016 and each cited at least 25 times). To fill this research gap, our exploratory case study builds on existing literature and addresses the following research question: *What might the differences in motivations and strategies between female and male academic entrepreneurs be?* Our findings include a number of propositions and suggest that scientific organizations can increase the variety of spin-offs by specifically sensitizing their transfer strategies to gender.

2 Current State of Research

Academic entrepreneurship constitutes one major form of knowledge and technology transfer. It occurs through patenting, licensing, contract research, and spin-off formation (Grimaldi et al. 2011; Siegel and Wright 2015). The last type is considered essential because of its broad range of long-term advantages: it helps make scientific development publicly available, creates jobs, and promotes economic and technological advancement (Bijedić et al. 2014; Walter and Auer 2009; Lautenschläger et al. 2014). Because of spin-offs' vast capacity for radical, technological innovation, they can achieve profound economic impacts spanning multiple markets (Dickel 2009). At the same time, the numbers of academic spin-offs in Europe remains comparatively low despite long-term efforts to promote their formation (European Commission 2016c).

Gender refers to a range of individual characteristics resulting from socially and culturally constructed ideas about the behavior men and women are expected to assume (Gildemeister 2010). These ideas can change dynamically and be influenced by other socio-cultural conditions (Walgenbach 2012). While gender can affect entrepreneurial conduct, the ways in which it plays out can manifest themselves through different entrepreneurial identities (Bruni et al. 2004; Stead 2015) and vary with economic context (Lewellyn and Muller-Kahle 2016).

Studies examining women's contribution to academic entrepreneurship are few (Best et al. 2016), and often limit their focus to quantitative statistics in which gender serves as a control variable (Perkmann et al. 2013). Even though this data is scarce, it indicates that substantially fewer women than men participate in academic entrepreneurship in Europe. Women's tendencies to choose comparatively transfer-unrelated occupations (Abreu and Grinevich 2017) and avoid risks (Caliendo et al. 2015) have been proposed as possible explanations for this.

The more general subject of *gender in entrepreneurship* has received much greater attention through a broad range of surveys and qualitative studies (Link and Strong 2016), indicating that women start their own businesses less often and dedicate less time to them than men (European Commission and Organisation for Economic Co-operation and Development 2017; Organisation for Economic Co-operation and Development 2016). In Europe in the second quarter of 2017, 32.3% of self-employed individuals were women; women also comprised 27.0% of those employing one or more people (Eurostat 2018). At 33.3% and 26.1% respectively, the proportions were nearly identical in Germany (Eurostat 2018), suggesting that these numbers can serve as a good representative of the general European trend.

On average, women-owned businesses appear to be smaller, employ less staff, and generate less revenue than male-owned companies (Dautzenberg et al. 2013; Hisrich and Brush 1984). Female-owned businesses have also been shown to often provide services (Ettl 2010; Barret 2006; Neergard et al. 2006; Coleman 2000), as was found to be the case with small and mid-size women-led businesses in both Europe in general (European Commission and Organisation for Economic Co-operation and Development 2017) and Germany in particular (Schwartz 2015). Finally, there appear to be more women in social than in business entrepreneurship (Pines et al. 2012), one theory for this being that women often seek to resolve social issues (Lauxen-Ulbricht and Leicht 2005; Lortie et al. 2017).

A number of causes have been posited to explain these tendencies. And the low share of women in entrepreneurial networks has been found to have a negative impact on the likelihood of women starting businesses (Markussen and Røed 2017). In academia in particular, women often appear to choose fields that provide less opportunity for entrepreneurship (Leoni and Falk 2010). Women also typically bear a greater share of family obligations such as caring for children, the elderly, and those who are sick. Possibly for this reason, women have been found to engage in entrepreneurship in pursuit of a greater work-life balance in both Europe (Organisation for Economic Co-operation and Development 2012) and Germany in particular (Abel-Koch 2014; KfW Research 2011).

Personal traits and preferences exert their influences as well. Women have been observed as being motivated intrinsically and by their long-term pursuits such as personal development, social recognition, and work-life balance rather than by financial considerations (Dalborg et al. 2012; Dautzenberg and Müller-Seitz 2011; Lauxen-Ulbricht and Leicht 2005). With regard to entrepreneurship, they also have been found to be more risk-averse (Carter 2002; Dawson and Henley 2015; Caliendo et al. 2015; Dalborg et al. 2015; Dautzenberg et al. 2013; Koellinger et al. 2008). Women also appear to find entrepreneurship less compelling, perceive the environment as less encouraging, and show less commitment to their businesses (Furdas et al. 2009). While women's less optimistic attitudes may account for their lower propensity to start a business (Koellinger et al. 2008; Dalborg et al. 2015), these attitudes may also lead to more stable business behavior and greater long-term success (Furdas and Kohn 2010).

These findings are reflected in studies on business strategies. Women appear to prefer "staying small" strategies that focus on job security, and slower but steady development (Reichborn-Kjennerud and Svare 2014; Dalborg et al. 2012). In times of crisis, women's businesses in Germany have been shown to remain more stable and have fewer declines in revenue (KfW et al. 2010). While Davis and Shaver (2012) found young men to be especially likely to express high/aggressive growth intention, women with children in their study did so more frequently than other women. Dalborg (2015) also observed female-owned businesses as following specific life cycles in which the achievement of stability typically preceded the pursuit of business growth, and therefore proposed that support programs should be sensitized to these kinds of cycles.

Women also appear to invest less start-up capital than men (Abel-Koch 2014; Marom et al. 2015), choose less capital-intensive industries (KfW Research 2011; Dautzenberg and Müller-Seitz 2011; Loscocco et al. 1991), and employ fewer staff (KfW Research 2011; Loscocco et al. 1991). Accounting for differences in size and industry, Pelger and Tchouvakhina (2013) statistically analyzed large-scale survey data on start-ups in Germany and found equity capital rates in female-owned businesses to be higher than in their male-owned counterparts. While these scholars determined only minor differences in access to loans between women and men, they also found women to be more inclined to apply for credit when they expected their businesses to succeed. The scholars therefore considered the possibility that the former finding may be largely explained by choice and thus does not necessarily indicate the absence of gender biases (Pelger and Tchouvakhina 2013). Brush et al. (2014) on the other hand expressly posited both gender biases and lower proportions of women in the venture capital industry as causes of the lower venture capital rates observed in highly growth-oriented businesses in the USA that were run by women.

As part of a German representative sample, the percentages of start-ups introducing either regional or supra-regional market innovations were determined to be nearly identical among female-owned and male-owned businesses at approximately 14% each (KfW Research 2011). The data gathered by the Global Entrepreneurship Monitor suggests that throughout Europe as well, women introduce innovative products about as frequently as men (European Commission 2014). At the same time, proportions of women have been found to be particularly low in highly growth-oriented, highly innovative technological businesses (Dautzenberg and Müller-Seitz 2011; Lee and Marvel 2014; Lauxen-Ulbrich and Leicht 2005). The European Start-up Monitor surveyed start-ups that introduced highly innovative technologies, employed highly innovative business models, and/or pursued rapid growth. The percentages of women within the sample ranged from 7.1% in Austria to 33.3% in the UK with an overall average of 14.8%. The fact that the percentage in Germany was 13.9% once again suggests that this country is in fact representative of the general European trend (Kollmann et al. 2016).

At first glance, female-owned businesses may appear to be less successful than male-owned businesses, possibly because women typically choose less profitable industries (Loscocco et al. 1991). Within individual industries however, no significant relationships between the owner's gender and success have been established (KfW Research 2011; Abel-Koch 2014; Brush et al. 2014; Robb and Watson 2012; Lee and Marvel 2014). Furthermore, bankruptcy rates among women-owned technological businesses have been found to be lower than among male-owned companies (Dautzenberg 2010), and success rates in capital-intensive businesses have been found to be equal or even higher (Brush et al. 2014). While women have been shown as more likely to leave the businesses they start, the probability of them doing so because of failure was found to be lower than for men (Justo et al. 2015). These findings suggest that women and men may be similarly successful in their ventures even if they do in fact often pursue different goals.

Building on the literature discussed above, the goal of this case study was to examine the motivations and strategies of academic entrepreneurs from a gender perspective. Germany was chosen because, as stated, it is a solid representative of the general European trend when it comes to female entrepreneurship. At the same time, it provides a particularly interesting example because while it boasts globally recognized achievement in innovation, its years of effort to promote both transfer and gender equality appear to have been considerably less successful (Wissenschaftsrat 2016; EFI 2014). Our findings provide a basis of evidence for the development of strategies to encourage women researchers.

Similar to the "typical" spin-off, it's also difficult to formulate a description of the "typical" female entrepreneur because the backgrounds and goals of women vary greatly. Women who were "pulled" into entrepreneurship by an opportunity for example were shown to be significantly more growth-oriented than those who were "pushed" by circumstances such as economic necessity (Morris et al. 2006). Different terms have been used to describe these phenomena. While Gilad and Levine (1986) and Amit and Muller (1995) also distinguish between "push" and "pull," the Global Entrepreneurship Monitor program differentiates between "necessity" and "opportunity-based" entrepreneurship (Reynolds et al. 2001). Hessels et al. (2008) recognize "necessity" entrepreneurship as well, and Thurik et al. (2008) speak of "refugee" entrepreneurship. Other scholars identify a third type of "lifestyle/family" entrepreneurship in which individuals aim to fulfill lifestyle objectives such as achieving a greater work-life balance. These motivations appear to predominate among female entrepreneurs (Stevenson 1986; Brush 1992; Hughes 2006; Kirkwood 2009).

"If motivations are largely external opportunity related then self-employment can be viewed positively. However, if entrepreneurship is a reluctant activity associated with absence of other opportunity or, particularly for women, family pressures, then self-employment may [be] viewed far less positively" (Dawson et al. 2012, p. 699). While most empirical studies focus on the differences between entrepreneurs and employees, less research has been done on individual entrepreneurial motivations. Existing literature suggests that pull or opportunity-based motivations predominate among both men and women founders (Gilad and Levine 1986; Segal et al. 2005). At the same time, other considerations can also play an important part.

Table 1 Sample demographics[a]

		Female	Male	∑
Number		19	21	40
Age in years, n = 37	20–29	5	3	8
	30–39	8	13	21
	40–49	2	3	5
	50–59	2	1	3
Most recent employer, n = 40	University	10	2	12
	Research institute	8	17	25
	Business firm	1	2	3
Field of work, n = 36	Physics or mathematics	3	2	5
	Chemistry, biology, or medicine	7	3	10
	Humanities	1	2	3
	Engineering	5	12	17
	Media technology	1	0	1

Source: Own table
[a]Gathered with the help of a short second questionnaire; some participants provided only incomplete information

3 Methodology

This study was conducted within the research project *Gender in Knowledge and Technology Transfer*,[1] funded by the German Ministry of Education and Research, and pursued the development of strategies that can help encourage researchers, particularly women, to engage in entrepreneurship. The focus was placed on STEM fields in which the proportion of female founders remains extremely low. For the project, we interviewed 40 individuals from throughout Germany who had either recently initiated an academic spin-off or planned to do so in the near future. We identified these individuals by contacting transfer offices as well as through online research. To ensure that the data was gender-balanced, men and women were included in approximately equal proportions. The sample demographics are shown in Table 1.

The interviews were guided by a questionnaire to achieve consistency and comparability. This was developed by building upon the literature described above, and focused on current work conditions, the employer's practices with regard to entrepreneurship, motivations to engage in entrepreneurship, the specifics of decision-making and business-starting processes, perceived sources of support and barriers, personal traits, and gender-related experiences. Interviewees were encouraged to speak freely in response to these questions, with each interview lasting approximately 90 minutes.

The interviews were transcribed, and also included non-verbal communication and strong expressions of emotion. They were also slightly edited for readability.

---

[1]Project ID 03IO1505, ends in August 2018.

Protocols were broken down into units of meaning and analyzed within a particular theoretical framework. Relevant information was extracted and categorized by using Mayring's method of open-ended, qualitative content analysis which allows systematic "conclusions about communication's specifics" (Mayring 2010, p. 12). The categories were derived based on the extracted information. This information was then distilled and the categories revised and refined in an iterative process using an extension of Gläser and Laudel's method (Gläser and Laudel 2009), the purpose of which is to determine core content and patterns.

The results of this analysis, including identified entrepreneurial motivations organized by type, are described in the following sections in greater detail. These descriptions are often followed by quotations that best illustrate identified characteristics in accordance with the main principle of generalization in qualitative social research.[2] They are intended to support the argumentation (Haas and Scheibelhofer 1998) rather than provide a representative sample of opinions.

4 Findings

4.1 The Motivations of Academic Entrepreneurs

Based on the assumption that academic entrepreneurs must believe in the market value of their findings (as was the case in the sample), this particular motivation was excluded from the analysis. All other motivations that were expressed can be identified either as *pushes* to "escape the present" as experienced in academia or *pulls* toward the "hopes for the future" associated with entrepreneurship. Each type additionally manifests itself either through *ideal-driven* or more *practical* desires (see Table 2).

The first expression of practical pushes is the pursuit of improving upon unsatisfactory work conditions experienced in the current research environment such as insufficient salary, contract duration, and problems with leadership: "I'd wanted to start my own business forever, but lacked ideas. [...] Then my three-month contract with the university expired for the 15th time. That forced me to look into other options. Also, I was relatively unhappy because my professor kept assigning me these, in my opinion, not particularly meaningful tasks" (Female F1, University).

National funding policies typically result in research projects being limited to specific institutions and periods of time, with spin-off grants providing the only opportunity to continue the research and ultimately develop marketable products. This effect might explain the second manifestation of practical pushes, i.e. the desire to advance the own research and/or secure a job by acquiring start-up grants. Participants who expressed one or both of these however could not claim with absolute certainty that they intended to continue their entrepreneurial pursuits after

---

[2]Translated from the German original.

Table 2 Motivations by type

Pushes	
Ideal-driven	
Increase transfer	Make research results more useful to the public and broaden their application
	Respond to people's needs and market demands
Practical	
Improve upon your unsatisfactory work conditions	Salary
	Contract duration
	Problems with leadership
Acquire start-up grants	Secure your job
	Advance your research
Pulls	
Ideal-driven	
The common good	Benefit particular groups
	Protect the environment
	Create new jobs and strengthen the local economy
Practical	
Personal pursuits	Capitalize on your research
	Achieve professional aspirations and/or advance the own career
	Achieve recognition and/or make a mark
	Create a sense of purpose and/or see your research "in action"
	Fulfill and/or advance yourself

Source: Own table

the grant money had run out: "To maybe keep my job and continue my work, that's my motivation at the moment; also my future aspirations, maybe to do a Ph.D. someday. I see myself more in academia, maybe even being a professor someday" (Male M1, Research Institute).

Ideal-driven pushes to increase transfer on the other hand originate in the discontent with the minimal effort currently spent on making research results useful to the public and broadening their application, which was regarded as a massive systemic flaw and the result of wrong priorities in academia: "It happens all the time that research projects end and the results just 'sit there.' And that's [...] a shame because it's a lot of effort [...wasted]" (Female F2, Research Institute). This kind of regret was the most frequently expressed motivation within this subtype as well as one of the most frequent overall. In this regard, many participants found it necessary to take the matter in their own hands, for which they often even used the same analogy: "I didn't want for it to just 'be left to rot on the vine.' [...] I see it way too often how great research results never find their way into industry. And not because they're not good enough, but because apparently, there are all these obstacles to make sure they never do. [...] And so I said, 'Alright. I guess the only choice is to do it myself'" (Female F3, University). Participants also mentioned their disapproval of the fact that rather than responding to people's needs and market demands, research trajectories were largely determined by research agendas: "Being closer to the market and looking at what people need, that's what I find really, really exciting. That doesn't happen enough here at the institute, in my opinion" (Male M2, Research Institute).

Within the second type, practical pulls contain more personal pursuits such as financial or professional advancement (see Table 2 for the complete list): "I haven't even thought in these social terms. [...] What I actually find motivating is my own development, which happens over time when you apply yourself, and on which you can really build your own business and then actually benefit from it if it works" (Male M3, Research Institute).

Ideal-driven pulls on the other hand manifest themselves through the pursuit of the common good. One goal is to benefit particular groups such as medical patients through the creation of new drugs, technologies, and therapy methods. Another is to protect the environment through the development of products such as solar and energy-saving technologies: "I want to make the world a better place. [...] I want to help protect the environment and reduce the energy wasted in data transfer. And I can do that best when I get this firm up and running. The socio-economic aspect is as huge a factor as the technological" (Female F4, Research Institute). The third and final desire is to create new jobs and strengthen the local economy. The motivations of this subtype can therefore also be considered social, environmental, and economic: "It's my vision, it's my dream. When you look at all these photos from Ghana and see how they burn all that electronic waste there [...]. Our technology is capable of solving that problem right there on location. [...] That's my other, inner motivation. But I can also see myself trying to change things here in my own country, while creating jobs of course" (Male M4, Research Institute).

The major distinction between ideal-driven and practical pulls thus lies in the desire to benefit some group, not just yourself. Academic entrepreneurs in the sample always expressed having at least two of the motivations described above, i.e. always at least one push and often at least one pull, which leads to:

Proposition 1 The desire to engage in academic entrepreneurship is always motivated by dissatisfaction with particular factors within academia and generally supported by recognition of opportunity, either for yourself or a group of other people.

4.2 The Gender Differences in Entrepreneurial Motivations

The entrepreneurial motivations described above, and that are organized by gender and frequency of mention are shown in Table 3. We see that women were pulled by ideals twice as frequently as men in the not-representative sample and especially by the desire to benefit particular groups: "It is, of course, to some degree, ideal-driven: I may help others. That's a big factor" (Female F5, University) and "We may be too idealistic here, my co-founder and I. Our goal is not to make more profit. That

Table 3 Entrepreneurial motivations by gender and frequency of mention[a]

			Motivations[b]	Female	Male
Pushes	Ideals	Transfer	Broader application	8	5
			people's needs	3	1
		Σ		11	6
	Practical	Work conditions	Contract duration	3	3
			Leadership	2	0
			Salary	0	2
		Σ		5	5
		Grant	Your research	1	2
			Your job	0	2
		Σ		1	4
Pulls	Ideals	The common good	Benefits to groups	5	0
			Environmental protection	1	2
			New jobs	0	1
		Σ		6	3
	Practical	Personal pursuits	Sense of purpose/research in action	7	4
			Self-fulfillment/advancement2	5	6
			Career/professional aspirations	2	7
			Recognition/making a mark	1	4
			Capitalization on research	0 (−5)[c]	5
		Σ		15	26

Source: Own table
[a]At least two different motivations mentioned by each participant, the total number therefore exceeding the sample size
[b]See Table 2 for a precise description
[c]Of little appeal to five participants and the only mentions of non-motivating factors

couldn't be all there is to it" (Female F6, University). This pursuit was mentioned five times out of six within this subtype, as opposed to never being mentioned by the men. Women also spoke of personal pursuits such as career advancement much less frequently. Moreover, 5 out of 19 interviewed female researchers, as the only participants to express non-motivating factors, found the idea of capitalizing on their research of little appeal: "When seeking applications [for my invention], rather than money, it's ways [of helping] the patient that matter most to me. That's key" (Female F7, University). With regard to pushes, 11 of the 19 women and, with that, almost twice as many as the men mentioned the ideal of increasing transfer, particularly to compensate for the systemic flaw described above and reduce massive waste: "Research that doesn't go straight to the archive, that's the motivation. That's what's so sad about this system: 99% of our findings just disappear into thin air. This spin-off is not the 'application,' it's the way of finding and achieving this application. That's my driver" (Female F8, Research Institute).

The practical pulls expressed 15 times out of 19 were either creating a sense of purpose or self-fulfillment, which can be considered the most ideal-driven within this subtype: "The question of application is a huge factor in my research. [...] It's important to me to contribute to something that I believe in. [...] I don't do things that I don't find particularly meaningful" (Female F4, Research Institute).

These findings lead to:

Proposition 2a Female academic entrepreneurs are often driven by their ideals of finding application for research results and thereby creating the common good; their more personal pursuits are often ideal-driven as well.

As mentioned above, men expressed being pulled by their ideals half as frequently as women and pushed by them slightly over half as frequently in the not-representative sample. They were also more frequently pulled by their personal pursuits such as becoming their own boss and capitalizing on the own research: "We work very hard, under all this pressure to make money, only to get pretty much nothing for ourselves. We're wearing ourselves out in this [poorly paid] position" (Male M1, Research Institute). As opposed to women, men never mentioned the pull towards benefitting particular groups and often even appeared unconcerned about social issues: "Commercialization provides the rare opportunity to improve at least your own financial prospects. The common good, yeah, that's a good point. I'd never thought of that before" (Male M3, Research Institute) or even "I don't claim to be a 'do-gooder' who wants to save the world. [...] My goal here is to be successful of course and have lots of time and money someday, hopefully" (Male M4, Research Institute).

The men who were pulled by personal pursuits were also frequently pushed in other ways. Overall, 15 out of 21 interviewed male researchers mentioned at least one push. The pursuit of a longer-term contract and broader application of research results were the most frequently expressed practical and ideal-driven pushes respectively. The two practical pushes to acquire start-up grants were mentioned by men four times in contrast to one female mention.

These findings lead to:

Proposition 2b Male academic entrepreneurs are often driven by their personal pursuits such as professional development, financial success, and recognition.

To summarize, female researchers more often engage in entrepreneurship to achieve their ideals of compensating for systemic flaws, putting inventions to good use, and benefitting other people. Male researchers on the other hand more often seek to advance themselves socially, professionally, and/or financially.

4.3 Gender Differences in Entrepreneurial Strategies

One additional goal of this study was to examine potential relationships between entrepreneurial motivations and the choice of business model. Most spin-offs aimed to provide products, often technological, and mostly business-to-business. The only three business-to-consumer operations were initiated by women, reflecting the finding that they were also observed as focusing more on benefits to people. Because the spin-offs were in the early stages of development, so too were the business models. The plans for their expected pace of development were fairly general, and the few participants who chose to share their plans spoke about slow, steady, and natural growth.

One difference in approaches was particularly striking, and once again reflected previous findings. Women often considered their products in terms of other people's needs, while their pursuit of the best possible application appeared inseparable from that of the common good: "Yes, a military application was proposed every now and then. Possible yes, desirable no! There's a long list of potential customers, and the blind and vision-impaired are the first [on that list]. We [...] asked quite a few blind people to try the device and yes, received unanimously positive feedback" (Female F9, University) as well as: "We are not just 'customer-oriented,' we actually want to gather as much feedback as we can and use it to create new [devices]. We see on the Internet all the time how people talk about what they like and what they don't like, and then it's somehow never taken into account when new things are developed" (Female F1, University).

Men on the other hand place strong emphasis on product features and their innovative, purely technological value: "What we have is a device that takes measurements, an incredible number incredibly fast. [...] You have to understand the difference between taking single measurements and a machine working constantly within the manufacturing line. And that's how much 'ground' we cover" (Male M5, Research Institute). "We've just applied for a patent on this technology [...] which is going to be, let me put it this way, a breakthrough in this segment. It can help for the first time ever to transfer this technology to [other geographic] regions" (Male M6, Research Institute), and: "It's an aluminum nitride layer. [...] Now, you can easily name at least twenty quality features. [...] We want to be ahead of the curve there" (Male M2, Research Institute).

These findings lead to:

Proposition 3 Female academic entrepreneurs more often seek to make a social difference and create social impacts, while male academic entrepreneurs place more focus on product value and technological advantages.

5 Value and Implications

This study's goal was to examine the motivations and strategies of academic entrepreneurs, including the differences between men and women. Female academic entrepreneurs in the sample were often driven by their ideals of finding broader application for research results and thereby making a social difference. Male academic entrepreneurs on the other hand often pursued more personal, practical goals such as financial success and recognition, and placed strong focus on product value and technological advantages.

Our findings supplement those of other studies indicating that female entrepreneurs are often motivated by social considerations such as the desire to resolve social issues (Lauxen-Ulbrich and Leicht 2005; Lortie et al. 2017). Our findings also suggest that greater female participation in academic entrepreneurship can lead not only to a diversification of academic spin-offs, but also to increased numbers of those focusing on people's benefits and needs. This kind of development can in turn help promote social entrepreneurship, a topic which is growing in significance (Bielefeld 2011).

Academic career options in Germany have been identified as limited (EFI 2014; Wissenschaftsrat 2014), while it has been argued that a broader range of options may be necessary to maintain research quality (Schütz et al. 2016). In view of our findings, we propose that scientific organizations institutionalize academic entrepreneurship and thus position it as a valid option. By paying better attention to broader arrays of researchers' motivations—including but not limited to those related to gender—these organizations can encourage both male and female researchers to participate in transfer. In doing so, they can increase its amount and diversity. Policymakers and funding agencies can contribute to the achievement of these goals by similarly reconsidering their priorities, such as only promoting the most innovative and growth-oriented spin-offs, and by tailoring support initiatives to a greater variety of possibilities.

Because this study was conducted in Germany, it may well be that participants were somewhat influenced by cultural norms and values, as well as by the specifics of the national research environment. Many European countries on the other hand have similar laws and regulations, such as the rule that intellectual property rights belong to the employer but not the inventors themselves. Many research institutions also orient their strategies towards the criteria proposed by major European funding initiatives such as Horizon 2020, presumably resulting in certain similarities in mind sets. In this regard, future cross-national studies should establish the degree to which our findings apply across Europe.

The study has other limitations as well. Its qualitative and exploratory character intended to provide initial insights into the differences in motivations between female and male academic entrepreneurs. Larger-scale analyses, particularly of a statistical nature that place a greater focus on strategies could validate and expand upon our results.

References

Abel-Koch, J. (2014). *Gründerinnen holen auf – Selbstständigkeit als Weg in die Erwerbstätigkeit* (p. 71). Fokus Volkswirtschaft.

Abreu, M., & Grinevich, V. (2017). Gender patterns in academic entrepreneurship. *The Journal of Technology Transfer, 42*, 763–794. https://doi.org/10.1007/s10961-016-9543-y

Amit, R., & Muller, E. (1995). 'Push' and 'pull' entrepreneurship. *Journal of Small Business and Entrepreneurship, 12*(4), 64–80.

Barrett, M. (2006). Women's entrepreneurship in Australia: Present and their future. In C. G. Brush, N. Carter, E. Gatewood, P. Greene, & M. Hart (Eds.), *Growth oriented women entrepreneurs and their businesses: A global research perspective – New horizons in entrepreneurship* (pp. 23–52). Cheltenham: Edward Elgar.
Best, K., Sinell, A., Heidingsfelder, M. L., & Schraudner, M. (2016). The gender dimension in knowledge and technology transfer – The German case. *European Journal of Innovation Management, 19,* 2–25. https://doi.org/10.1108/EJIM-07-2015-0052
Bielefeld, W. (2011). Social entrepreneurship and business development. In K. A. Agard (Ed.), *Leadership in non-profit organizations: A reference handbook* (pp. 475–483). Thousand Oaks: Sage
Bijedić, T., Maass, F., Schröder, C., & Werner, A. (2014). *Der Einfluss institutioneller Rahmenbedingungen auf die Gründungsneigung von Wissenschaftlern an deutschen Hochschulen. Individual and Structural Influences on the Entrepreneurial Activities of Scientists in German Universities* (IfM-Materialien Nr. 223). Bonn. Retrieved September 15, 2015, from http://www.ifm-bonn.org/uploads/tx_ifmstudies/IfM-Materialien-233_2014.pdf
Bruni, A., Gherardi, S., & Poggio, B. (2004). Doing gender, doing entrepreneurship: An ethnographic account of intertwined practices. *Gender, Work and Organization, 11*(4), 406–429.
Brush, C. (1992). Research on women business owners: Past trends, a new perspective and future direction. *Entrepreneurship Theory and Practice, 16*(4), 5–30.
Brush, C., Green, P., Balachandra, L., & Davis, A. E. (2014). *Women entrepreneurs 2014: Bridging the gender gap in venture capital: Diana Report.* Retrieved June 6, 2016, from http://www.babson.edu/Academics/centers/blank-center/global-research/diana/Documents/diana-project-executive-summary-2014.pdf
Caliendo, M., Fossen, F. M., Kritikos, A. S., & Wetter, M. (2015). The gender gap in entrepreneurship: Not just a matter of personality. *CESifo Economic Studies, 61,* 202–238. https://doi.org/10.1093/cesifo/ifu023
Carter, N. M. (2002). *The role of risk orientation on financing expectations in new venture creation: Does sex matter?* (Frontiers of Entrepreneurship Research). Retrieved August 9, 2017, from http://fusionmx.babson.edu/entrep/fer/Babson2002/VI/VI_P2/VI_P2.htm
Coleman, S. (2000). Access to capital and terms of credit: A comparison of men- and women-owned small businesses. *Journal of Small Business Management, 38*(3), 37–52.
Dalborg, C. (2015). The life cycle in women-owned businesses: From a qualitative growth perspective. *International Journal of Gender and Entrepreneurship, 7,* 126–147. https://doi.org/10.1108/IJGE-06-2014-0019
Dalborg, C., von Friedrichs, Y., & Wincent, J. (2012). Beyond the numbers: Qualitative growth in women's businesses. *International Journal of Gender and Entrepreneurship, 4*(3), 289–315.
Dalborg, C., von Friedrichs, Y., & Wincent, J. (2015). Risk perception matters: Why women's passion may not lead to a business start-up. *International Journal of Gender and Entrepreneurship, 7,* 87–104. https://doi.org/10.1108/IJGE-01-2013-0001
Dautzenberg, K. (2010). Frauen gründen Technologieunternehmen – eine Untersuchung im Land Brandenburg. *Sozialwissenschaftlicher Fachinformationsdienst (soFid) Frauen- und Geschlechterforschung, 2010*(2), 1–22.
Dautzenberg, K., & Müller-Seitz, G. (2011). Technologieorientierte Unternehmensgründungen als Männerdomäne?: Eine genderspezifische Untersuchung von Unternehmenscharakteristiken. *Die Unternehmung – Swiss Journal of Business Research and Practice, 65*(3), 238–262.
Dautzenberg, K., Steinbrück, A., Brenning, L., & Zinke, G. (2013). *Wachstumspotenziale inhaberinnengeführter Unternehmen – wo steht Deutschland im EU-Vergleich?* (Studie im Auftrag des Bundesministeriums für Wirtschaft und Technologie, Endbericht). Berlin. Retrieved June 9, 2015, from http://www.bmwi.de/DE/Mediathek/publikationen,did=555294.html
Davis, A. E., & Shaver, K. G. (2012). Understanding gendered variations in business growth intentions across the life course. *Entrepreneurship Theory and Practice, 36,* 495–512. https://doi.org/10.1111/j.1540-6520.2012.00508.x

Dawson, C., & Henley, A. (2012). "Push" versus "pull" entrepreneurship: An ambiguous distinction? *International Journal of Entrepreneurial Behavior & Research, 18*(6), 697–719.

Dawson, C., & Henley, A. (2015). Gender, risk, and venture creation intentions. *Small Business Management, 53*(2), 501–515.

Dickel, P. (2009). *Marktbezogenes Lernen in Akademischen Spin-offs: Gewinnung und Integration von Marktinformationen in der frühen Phase technologiebasierter Ausgründungen (Betriebswirtschaftslehre für Technologie und Innovation)*. Wiesbaden: Gabler Verlag.

Ettl, K. (2010). *Unternehmerinnen und Erfolg aus individueller und kontextueller Perspektive, KMU-Forschung* (Vol. 4, 1st ed.). Frankfurt am Main: Peter Lang.

Etzkowitz, H., Ranga, M., Conway, C., & Dixon, L. (2008). Gender patterns in technology transfer: Social innovation in the making. *Research Global, 8*(2), 4–5.

European Commission. (2014). *Statistical data on women entrepreneurs in Europe*. Retrieved January 08, 2018, from http://ec.europa.eu/DocsRoom/documents/7481/attachments/1/translations

European Commission. (2016a). *Connecting the technology transfer offices of major European public research organisations*. Retrieved from https://ec.europa.eu/jrc/communities/community/629/about

European Commission. (2016b). *Vademecum on gender equality in horizon 2020*. Retrieved June 12, 2017, from http://ec.europa.eu/research/swafs/pdf/pub_gender_equality/2016-03-21-Vademecum_Gender%20in%20H2020-clean-rev.pdf

European Commission. (2016c). *Horizon 2020. Work programme 2016–2017. Food security, sustainable agriculture and forestry, marine and maritime and inland water research and the bioeconomy*. Retrieved June 21, 2016, from http://ec.europa.eu/research/participants/data/ref/h2020/wp/2016_2017/main/h2020-wp1617-food_en.pdf

European Commission, & Organisation for Economic Co-operation and Development. (2017). *Policy brief on women's entrepreneurship*. Retrieved January 8, 2018, from https://publications.europa.eu/de/publication-detail/-/publication/a50f1af1-e470-11e7-9749-01aa75ed71a1/language-en

Eurostat. (2018). *Selbstständigkeit nach Geschlecht, Alter und Wirtschaftszweigen (ab 2008, NACE Rev. 2). (lfsq_esgan2)*. Retrieved January 8, 2018, from http://ec.europa.eu/eurostat/web/lfs/data/database

Expertenkommission Forschung und Innovation (EFI). (2014). *EFI-Gutachten: Deutschland verliert zu viele seiner Spitzenforscher*. Retrieved from March 06, 2016, from http://www.e-fi.de/fileadmin/Pressemitteilungen/Pressemitteilungen_2014/EFI-2014-Deutschland_verliert_zu_viele_seiner_Spitzenforscher.pdf

Expertenkommission Forschung und Innovation (EFI). (2017). *Gutachten zu Forschung, Innovation und technologischer Leistungsfähigkeit Deutschlands 2017*. Berlin. Retrieved from September 10, 2017, from http://www.e-fi.de/fileadmin/Gutachten_2017/EFI_Gutachten_2017.pdf

Furdas, M., & Kohn, K. (2010). *What's the difference?! Gender, personality, and the propensity to start a business* (IZA Discussion Paper 4778). Bonn. Retrieved September 11, 2014, from http://ftp.iza.org/dp4778.pdf

Furdas, M., Kohn, K., & Ullrich, K. (2009). *Gründungsaktivität von Frauen und Männern in Deutschland: Gleiche Voraussetzungen, andere Einstellungen?!* (KfW Research Nr. 48). Frankfurt am Main.

Gilad, B., & Levine, P. (1986). A behavioral model of entrepreneurial supply. *Journal of Small Business Management, 24*(4), 45–53.

Gildemeister, R. (2010). Doing Gender: Soziale Praktiken der Geschlechterunterscheidung. In R. Becker & B. Kortendiek (Eds.), *Handbuch Frauen- und Geschlechterforschung: Theorie, Methoden, Empirie, Geschlecht und Gesellschaft* (Vol. 35, 3rd ed., pp. 137–145). Wiesbaden: VS Verlag für Sozialwissenschaften; Springer Fachmedien Wiesbaden GmbH.

Gläser, J., & Laudel, G. (2009). *Experteninterviews und qualitative Inhaltsanalyse: Als Instrumente rekonstruierender Untersuchungen* (3rd ed.). Wiesbaden: VS Verlag für Sozialwissenschaften.

Grimaldi, R., Kenney, M., Siegel, D. S., & Wright, M. (2011). 30 years after Bayh–dole: Reassessing academic entrepreneurship. *Research Policy, 40*, 1045–1057. https://doi.org/10.1016/j.respol.2011.04.005

Haas, B., & Scheibelhofer, E. (1998). *Typenbildung in der qualitativen Sozialforschung: Eine methodologische Analyse anhand ausgewählter Beispiele, Reihe Soziologie* (Vol. 34). Wien: Institut für Höhere Studien.

Hessels, J., van Gelderen, M., & Thurik, A. R. (2008). Entrepreneurial aspirations, motivations and their drivers. *Small Business Economics, 31*(3), 323–393.

Hisrich, R., & Brush, C. (1984). The woman entrepreneur: Management skills and business problems. *Journal of Small Business Management, 22*(1), 30–37.

Hughes, K. (2006). Exploring motivation and success among Canadian women entrepreneurs. *Journal of Small Business and Entrepreneurship, 19*(2), 107–120.

Justo, R., Detienne, D. R., & Sieger, P. (2015). Failure or voluntary exit? Reassessing the female underperformance hypothesis. *Journal of Business Venturing, 30*(6), 775–792.

KfW, Creditreform, IfM, RWI, ZEW. (2010). *Konjunkturelle Stabilisierung im Mittelstand – aber viele Belastungsfaktoren bleiben: MittelstandsMonitor 2010 –Jährlicher Bericht zu Konjunktur- und Strukturfragen kleiner und mittlerer Unternehmen*. Frankfurt am Main. Retrieved from http://ftp.zew.de/pub/zew-docs/mimo/MittelstandsMonitor_2010.pdf

KfW Research. (2011). *Gründerinnen – Frauen als eigene Chefs*. Akzente 44. Retrieved August 08, 2017, from https://www.kfw.de/Download-Center/Konzernthemen/Research/PDF-Dokumente-Akzente/Akzente-Nr.-44-Juli-2011.pdf

Kirkwood, J. (2009). Motivational factors in a push-pull theory of entrepreneurship. *Gender in Management, 24*(5), 346–364.

Koellinger, P., Minniti, M., & Schade, C. (2008). *Seeing the world with different eyes: Gender differences in perceptions and the propensity to start a business* (Discussion Paper 035/3). Tinbergen Institute. Retrieved September 8, 2017, from http://citeseerx.ist.psu.edu/viewdoc/download?doi=10.1.1.530.898&rep=rep1&type=pdf

Kollmann, T., Stöckmann, C., Hensellek, S., & Kensbock, J. (2016). *European startup monitor*. Retrieved January 4, 2018, from http://europeanstartupmonitor.com/fileadmin/esm_2016/report/ESM_2016.pdf

Lautenschläger, A., Haase, H., & Kratzer, J. (2014). Contingency factors on university spin-off formation: An empirical study in Germany. *Journal of Entrepreneurship and Public Policy, 3*, 160–176. https://doi.org/10.1108/JEPP-02-2012-0013

Lauxen-Ulbrich, M., & Leicht, R. (2005). *Wie Frauen gründen und was sie unternehmen: Nationaler Report Deutschland: Teilprojekt: Statistiken über Gründerinnen und selbstständige Frauen*. Mannheim. Retrieved June 6, 2016, from http://www.ifm.uni-mannheim.de/unter/fsb/pdf/nationaler_report_ifm2005.pdf

Lee, H., & Marvel, M. R. (2014). Revisiting the entrepreneur gender–performance relationship: A firm perspective. *Small Business Economics, 42*(4), 769–786.

Leoni, T., & Falk, M. (2010). Gender and field of study as determinants of self-employment. *Small Business Economics, 34*, 167–185. https://doi.org/10.1007/s11187-008-9114-1

Lewellyn, K. B., & Muller-Kahle, M. I. (2016). A configurational approach to understanding gender differences in entrepreneurial activity: A fuzzy set analysis of 40 countries. *International Entrepreneurship and Management Journal, 2016*, 765–790. https://doi.org/10.1007/s11365-015-0366-3

Link, A. N., & Strong, D. R. (2016). Gender and entrepreneurship: An annotated bibliography. *Foundations and Trends in Entrepreneurship, 12*, 287–441. https://doi.org/10.1561/0300000068

Lortie, J., Castrogiovanni, G. J., & Cox, K. C. (2017). Gender, social salience, and social performance: How women pursue and perform in social ventures. *Entrepreneurship & Regional Development, 29*, 155–173. https://doi.org/10.1080/08985626.2016.1255433

Loscocco, K. A., Robinson, J., Hall, R. H., & Allen, J. K. (1991). Gender and small business success: An inquiry into women's relative disadvantage. *Social Forces, 70*(1), 65–85.

Markussen, S., & Røed, K. (2017). The gender gap in entrepreneurship – The role of peer effects. *Journal of Economic Behavior& Organization, 134*, 356–373. https://doi.org/10.1016/j.jebo.2016.12.013

Marom, D., Robb, A., & Sade, O. (2015). Gender dynamics in crowdfunding (Kickstarter): Evidence on entrepreneurs, investors, deals and taste based discrimination. *SSRN Electronic Journal.* https://doi.org/10.2139/ssrn.2442954

Mayring, P. (2010). *Qualitative Inhaltsanalyse: Grundlagen und Techniken (Beltz Pädagogik).* Weinheim: Beltz.

Morris, M. H., Miyasaki, N. N., Watters, C. E., & Coombes, S. M. (2006). The dilemma of growth: Understanding venture size choices of women entrepreneurs. *Journal of Small Business Management, 44*, 221–244. https://doi.org/10.1111/j.1540-627X.2006.00165.x

Neergaard, H., Nielsen, K., & Kjeldsen, J. (2006). State of the art of women's entrepreneurship, access to financing and financing strategies in Denmark. In C. G. Brush, N. Carter, E. Gatewood, P. Greene, & M. Hart (Eds.), *Growth oriented women entrepreneurs and their businesses: A global research perspective* (New horizons in entrepreneurship, pp. 88–111). Cheltenham: Edward Elgar.

Organisation for Economic Co-operation and Development. (2012). Key motives for starting an enterprise by gender of founder and type of motivation. In *Closing the gender gap: Act now*.

Organisation for Economic Co-operation and Development. (2016). Entrepreneurship at a glance 2016. *Organisation for Economic Co-operation and Development.* https://doi.org/10.1787/22266941

Pelger, I., & Tchouvakhina, M. (2013). *Low Debt Entrepreneurs: Unternehmerinnen gehen bei Finanzierung auf Nummer sicher* (Fokus Volkswirtschaft Nr. 26). Retrieved August 8, 2017, from https://www.kfw.de/PDF/Download-Center/Konzernthemen/Research/PDF-Dokumente-Fokus-Volkswirtschaft/Fokus-Nr.-26-Juli-2013-Frauen-Finanzierung.pdf

Perkmann, M., Tartari, V., McKelvey, M., Autio, E., Broström, A., D'Este, P., et al. (2013). Academic engagement and commercialisation: A review of the literature on university–industry relations. *Research Policy, 42*, 423–442. https://doi.org/10.1016/j.respol.2012.09.007

Pines, A. M., Lerner, M., & Schwartz, D. (2012). Gender differences among social vs. business entrepreneurs. In T. Burger-Helmchen (Ed.), *Entrepreneurship: Gender, geographies and social context* (pp. 3–14). Rijeka: InTech.

Reichborn-Kjennerud, K., & Svare, H. (2014). Entrepreneurial growth strategies: The female touch. *International Journal of Gender and Entrepreneurship, 6*(2), 181–199.

Reynolds, P. D., Camp, S. M., Bygrave, W. D., Autio, E., & Hay, M. (2001). *Global entrepreneurship monitor: 2001* (Executive Report). Retrieved January 11, 2018, from http://unpan1.un.org/intradoc/groups/public/documents/un/unpan002481.pdf

Robb, A. M., & Watson, J. (2012). Gender differences in firm performance: Evidence from new ventures in the United States. *Journal of Business Venturing, 27*, 544–558. https://doi.org/10.1016/j.jbusvent.2011.10.002

Schütz, F., Sinell, A., Trübswetter, A., Kaiser, S., & Schraudner, M. (2016). Der Science-Case attraktiver Karrierewege – Eine gegenstandsbezogene Perspektive auf Karrierebedingungen und -modelle im deutschen Wissenschaftssystem. *Beiträge zur Hochschulforschung, 38*(1–2), 64–84.

Schwartz, M. (2015). *Wie weiblich ist der Mittelstand? Frauen als Unternehmenslenker* (Fokus Volkswirtschaft Nr. 101). Retrieved August 8, 2017, from https://www.kfw.de/PDF/Download-Center/Konzernthemen/Research/PDF-Dokumente-Fokus-Volkswirtschaft/Fokus-Nr.-101-Juli-2015-Frauen-als-Unternehmenslenker.pdf

Segal, G., Borgia, D., & Schoenfeld, J. (2005). The motivation to become and entrepreneur. *International Journal of Entrepreneurial Behaviour and Research, 11*(1), 42–57.

Siegel, D. S., & Wright, M. (2015). Academic entrepreneurship: Time for a rethink? *British Journal of Management, 26*, 582–595. https://doi.org/10.1111/1467-8551.12116

Stead, V. (2015). Belonging and women entrepreneurs: Women's navigation of gendered assumptions in entrepreneurial practice. *International Small Business Journal*. https://doi.org/10.1177/0266242615594413

Stevenson, L. A. (1986). Against all odds: The entrepreneurship of women. *Journal of Small Business Management, 24*(4), 30–44.

Thurik, A. R., Carree, M. A., van Stel, A., & Audretsch, D. B. (2008). Does self-employment reduce unemployment? *Journal of Business Venturing, 23*(6), 673–686.

Walgenbach, K. (2012). *Intersektionalität – eine Einführung*. Retrieved November 20, 2017, from http://portal-intersektionalitaet.de/uploads/media/Walgenbach-Einfuehrung.pdf

Walter, A., & Auer, M. (Eds.). (2009). *Academic entrepreneurship: Unternehmertum in der Forschung*. Wiesbaden: Gabler Verlag.

Wissenschaftsrat. (2014). *Empfehlungen zu Karrierezielen und -wegen an Universitäten*. Dresden. Retrieved February 16, 2016, from http://www.wissenschaftsrat.de/download/archiv/4009-14.pdf

Wissenschaftsrat. (2016). *Wissens- und Technologietransfer als Gegenstand institutioneller Strategien: Positionspapier*. Retrieved February 14, 2017, from http://www.wissenschaftsrat.de/download/archiv/5665-16.pdf

Towards Emancipatory Aspects of Women's Entrepreneurship: An Alternative Model of Women's Entrepreneurial Self-Efficacy in Patriarchal Societies

Kirsten Mikkelsen

Abstract This chapter considers societal gender mechanisms in an effort to shed light on the antecedents of women's entrepreneurial self-efficacy (ESE). While numerous studies have repeatedly assessed the relevance of ESE for developing entrepreneurial intentions, making clear that women tend to express significantly lower levels of ESE, there are hardly any contributions dealing with the antecedents of ESE. Social mechanisms resulting from national cultural attitudes appear significant when it comes to this topic. By integrating gender as a category into this investigation, a major focus lies upon the analysis of societal processes of doing gender and its effect on the construction of women's ESE. A better understanding of this construction process is an important step towards a more gender-sensitive entrepreneurial ecosystem that supports women. The following investigation of German and Danish women entrepreneurs showed that despite a higher rate of gender egalitarianism in their country, Danish women face obstacles similar to those found in Germany on their path towards becoming self-employed. In addition, founding their own business appears to be the result of an overall emancipatory process. The relation between societal processes and the construction of ESE is presented in the model of entrepreneurial self-efficacy in patriarchal structures.

1 Introduction

The vast majority of research on women's entrepreneurship has had a predominantly androcentric perspective. It is anything but gender-blind (Stevenson 1990; Ahl 2002, 2006; Achtenhagen 2014; Welter 2004). This means that women entrepreneurs as subjects of economic study have either long been neglected (Jennings 1993) or have been the subject of comparative studies against the background of a male-dominated

---

K. Mikkelsen (✉)
Europa-Universität Flensburg, Flensburg, Germany
e-mail: kirsten.mikkelsen@uni-flensburg.de

image of the entrepreneur, with masculinity and maleness being the widely accepted norm for entrepreneurial activity. This so-called *male bias* (Stevenson 1990) repeatedly puts women entrepreneurs into the position of the "others" or "not normal" ones (Bruni et al. 2004a, b). From a feminist perspective, this androcentric lens women entrepreneurs are seen through can be defined as male dominance. Put simply, it has to date placed masculine realities above those of feminine ones (Nelson 1993). This male dominance or, according to Bourdieu (2013), these patriarchal structures perpetuate our daily habits and are difficult to break. To make matters worse, more recent studies merely compare women to men when investigating "gender" in entrepreneurship. This chapter will advocate a shift towards more feminist critiques of entrepreneurship (Henry et al. 2015), contributing to a more comprehensive approach to women's entrepreneurship from a social-constructivist perspective. The starting point for understanding entrepreneurial activity by women is breaking with the hegemonies in entrepreneurship research to give women entrepreneurs' perspectives a voice.

There's a clear need for new ways of understanding entrepreneurial activity by women better and to greater extent. This is not only because of the current state of academic research and the consistently low participation rates of women in entrepreneurial activity. Numerous efforts by policymakers and scholars also appear to not fully meet their goals of a more gender-equal access to entrepreneurial activity. For example, Germany and Denmark show similarly low start-up activity by women, with only slightly less than 5% of the female population entering this field, and with Germany actually outranking Denmark (Kelley et al. 2013). This is problematic because Denmark, as a Scandinavian country otherwise assumed as providing more equal opportunities for men and women on their labor markets, should in fact be further along with entrepreneurship than Germany (Emrich et al. 2004). This is even more surprising if we consider how, according to research on one of the main factors leading to entrepreneurial activity, Danish women express lower levels of entrepreneurial self-efficacy (ESE) (Chen et al. 1998; Krueger and Dickson 1993; Krueger and Brazeal 1994). ESE, which is based on Bandura's (Bandura 1997) work on self-efficacy, is a concept within social psychology that allows social mechanisms to be taken into account. This aspect is important because although gender has been identified as impacting ESE (Kourilsky and Walstad 1998; Wilson et al. 2007, 2009), previous research has to date not offered satisfying answers and/or models that could explain this phenomenon. Actual gender effects as a result of societal gender mechanisms remain unidentified, so this chapter seeks to understand the connection between the culturally influenced social mechanisms of gender and the ESE construction. Exploring the effects of social mechanisms from a social-constructivist perspective and thus including contextual aspects into the research on women's ESE requires a qualitative approach. It's important to obtain insights on ESE from women's own perspectives to overcome the male bias in investigating women entrepreneurs. This research is therefore based on women entrepreneurs' narratives, and will present an alternative ESE model. In this context, it will highlight the emancipatory aspects of entrepreneurship which have recently gained more attention in entrepreneurship research (Rindova et al. 2009). The overall research question is:

"How do women overcome patriarchal dominance as a result of cultural norms, and how does this affect women's ESE in patriarchal structures?"

The following elaborates on these issues by providing a deeper theoretical understanding of the key concepts for this research, gender and ESE. It will present arguments for why it is necessary to switch perspectives away from prioritizing masculinity in entrepreneurship research. Gaps in contemporary conceptualizations of ESE will be outlined, opening the path for the analysis undertaken within this context.

2 Current State of Research and Theoretical Framing

Although Verheul and Thurik (2001) state in their article on gender and raising start-up funding that no group of entrepreneurs should experience any barrier for starting or developing a business, reality paints a different picture. Extant research has shown that gender indeed has an impact on entrepreneurial activity, which can be interpreted as an impediment for women. To get a better view of how these effects occur, an overall understanding of gender as a category within entrepreneurship research will be provided, and then related to the contemporary concept of ESE.

2.1 Understanding Gender as a Category Within Entrepreneurship Research

Feminist economists criticize the alleged "gender blindness" or "neutrality" in economics and entrepreneurship research. One of the main criticisms is the total exclusion of supposedly "feminine" characteristics or realities (Haidinger and Knittler 2014; Nelson 1993; Stevenson 1990). Jennings states that, through adapting cultural gender roles, research commonly excludes women, women's questions, and feminine values. Along with this, women's issues are diminished by prioritizing rational objectivity (as a masculine value) over emotional subjectivity (as a feminine value) (Jennings 1993). As a consequence, by neglecting women-related issues and questions, the majority of present research on women entrepreneurs (Henry et al. 2015) to a certain extent fails to fully capture the realities of women entrepreneurs because it ignores their social embeddedness. Employing instead the hegemonic or androcentric approach to investigating women entrepreneurs, they mainly contrast them to their male counterparts (Henry et al. 2015). In doing this, they fail to incorporate a true gender perspective, casting women in a very negative light. And in fact, the traits and characteristics that are seen as positively related to entrepreneurial activity are mostly associated with masculinity (Ahl 2006). Here, women are assumed as less qualified to be entrepreneurs, and are attributed gender-stereotypical roles and characteristics (Sexton and Bowman-Upton 1990; Baron et al. 2001).

Gender in the context of this research is not a pre-defined biological condition. It's instead the result of associated gender roles (Butler 2008; Bourdieu 2013). The unquestioned reproduction of these gender roles, even within entrepreneurship literature, facilitates the perpetuation of this hegemonic perspective and habits in the research context on women entrepreneurs, and contradicts the neutrality of science. Gender evolves as a category within entrepreneurship research at exactly this point. This is why we need to take into account the influence of gender-stereotypical habits on our way towards perceiving and re-thinking our realities which are manifested in socio-cultural mechanisms (Bourdieu 2013; Hoppe 2002). Gender as a category is defined according to Bourdieu's (2013) understanding of a person's position in the social space, which can be interpreted as a form of symbolic power. It is the result of an individual's access to and accumulation of economic, social and cultural capital (Bourdieu 1983). There is a persistent imbalance between men and women in Western capitalist societies, which keeps women in a less privileged position than men. This is the result of often subconsciously ongoing social mechanisms, which permanently reproduce the same patterns of perception, thinking and action (habits). Due to their subliminal character, these patterns of perception, thinking and behavior are hard to break (Bourdieu 2013). In other words, women are categorized according to an apparently naturalized societal position, and equipped with a different set of the three forms of capital mentioned above. Gender in this research context is therefore a label that can be explained by socio-cultural mechanisms.

Emrich et al. (2004) present *gender egalitarianism* (GE) as a cultural dimension to make these hidden (im)balances between women and men visible. GE reflects a society's beliefs about whether members' biological sex should determine the roles that they play in their homes, business organizations, and communities. GE also makes it possible to compare national cultures. The higher the GE score, the less a society believes in the allocation of roles according to biological sex (Emrich et al. 2004). Germany ranks lower than its direct Scandinavian neighbor Denmark, suggesting more gender stereotypical roles (Emrich et al. 2004). Consequently, Denmark should under these circumstances strive to offer more equal opportunities to men and women.

More recent research on women entrepreneurs emphasize the importance of the socio-cultural context women entrepreneurs are embedded in when investigating women's entrepreneurial activity (Gather et al. 2014; Bird and Brush 2002; Brush et al. 2009; Max and Ballereau 2013; Ahl 2006; Achtenhagen 2014; Ahl and Marlow 2012; Marlow 2014). But even results of contributions setting a more contextual focus and concentrating on performance factors appear to indicate gender-stereotypical results, such as women tending to adapt their entrepreneurial activity to their family situation, and how women have smaller companies, are less growth-oriented, and seem to enter markets that tend to be dominated by women (Achtenhagen 2014; De Martino and Barbato 2003; Marlow 2014). These findings are far from unimportant. The critical aspect lies in the fact that they merely focus on performance aspects. Hence, despite recent research efforts to explore gender and entrepreneurship in a more contextual fashion, there are no satisfying research results focusing on the pre-entrepreneurial phase and explaining why women show lower rates of entrepreneurial activity than men, as well as *how* this might be affected by gender. Marlow goes so far as to state that the question of how gender affects entrepreneurial ambition and behavior is critical to gaining new insights (Marlow 2014).

2.2 Entrepreneurial Self-Efficacy from a Gender–Theoretical Perspective

According to Krueger and Dickson (1993) and Krueger and Brazeal (1994), ESE has to date been assessed as one of the main factors for enhancing the probability of entrepreneurial activity. It is an incorporated part of the entrepreneurial intentions model (EIM) by Krueger and Brazeal (1994) and Krueger et al. (2000) and can be briefly defined as the belief in the own entrepreneurial competencies to successfully undertake an entrepreneurial endeavor (Mauer et al. 2009). Self-efficacy in general is a person's "belief about what one can do under different sets of conditions with whatever skills one possesses" (Bandura 1997, p. 37). This is closely related to people's self-perceptions of their skills and capabilities. We know that ESE raises the chances for the development of entrepreneurial intent (Krueger et al. 2000; Zhao et al. 2010), although in turn, the lack of ESE simply leads to no behavior at all (Krueger and Brazeal 1994). Other than the approaches to explain entrepreneurial activity purely based on personal traits, ESE as a socio-cognitive concept allows the (woman) entrepreneur to be placed into a context with her micro- and macro-social environment (Carsrud and Johnson 1989). Against the background of gender as culturally-induced social mechanisms, this concept consequently provides the opportunity for a deeper investigation of women's *pre-entrepreneurial* phase. It gives space to investigate "how gender shapes entrepreneurial ambitions and behavior" as postulated by Marlow (2014, p. 103).

Previous research on women's self-efficacy in general shows that women tend to narrow their own career paths within rather male-dominated areas (this is typical for entrepreneurship) due to a lack of confidence in their own skills and competencies (Bandura 1997). They also have a similarly low propensity to act entrepreneurially when they *think* they lack the necessary entrepreneurial competencies (Chen et al. 1998). Kourilsky and Walstad (1998) also found that although young women are in fact equally equipped with entrepreneurial competencies, they still display lower levels of ESE. In addition to this, the results of a study by Wilson et al. (2007, 2009) show a more direct influence of ESE on the development of entrepreneurial intentions for women than for men. Brännback et al. (2007) found that women in general tend to focus more on their deficits than on their actual competencies (Brännback et al. 2007). The unanswered question here involves why women express these lower levels of ESE when they objectively are at least equally well equipped in terms of entrepreneurial competencies.

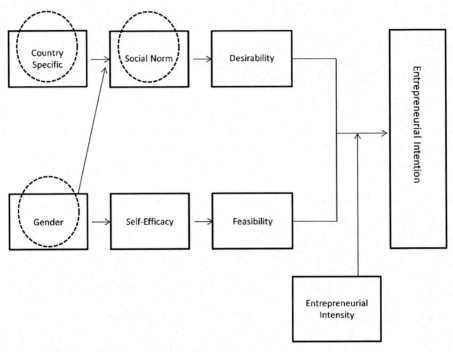

Source: Krueger and Kickul (2006)

Fig. 1 Extended Entrepreneurial Intentions Model

In their extended entrepreneurial intentions model (EEIM), Krueger and Kickul (2006) attempt to bring together gender, country-specific cultural influences, and ESE. They argue that, as suggested by research, gender influences self-efficacy and nationality influences social norms (Krueger and Kickul 2006). Their results discovered that country-specific factors influence social norms and that gender does *not* have a significant impact on them. With this discussion on gender in mind, this model identifies a flaw in its argumentation. It was stated that gender is incorporated into our daily habits, and thus is expressed through social mechanisms. But consistent with this logic, gender actually *is* a social norm and cannot be separated from the social norm aspect or treated as an external factor (Fig. 1).

In contrast to this, *country specifics* such as national cultural factors may have an impact on the intensity of these gender mechanisms in terms of how strongly gender-stereotypical behavior is manifested in a nation's habits.[1] Consequently, if ESE is influenced by gender as contemporary research suggests, then we need to focus on *how* gender in terms of social mechanisms affects the development of ESE or, as Ahl (2006, p. 612) expresses, "how gender is done" on a country-specific basis.

---

[1] As stated, GE is an index that attempts to measure this.

Germany and Denmark are two Western capitalist neighboring countries. Yet according to the cultural dimension of GE, they strongly differ in their extent of gender-stereotypical role perception. In both countries, levels of women's ESE (and entrepreneurial activity) lie far below those of men's. At the same time, Danish women are surprisingly less entrepreneurially efficacious (Kelley et al. 2013), with their actual entrepreneurial activity lagging behind that of German women. Hence, there appear to be gender-related peculiarities in developing ESE that actually lead to or impede entrepreneurial intention and activity, and that to date have not been disclosed and cannot be captured or expressed by cultural dimensions or indices. This furthermore indicates that contemporary ESE concepts are not sufficiently reliable in anticipating women's propensities to act entrepreneurially because they ignore the effects of "doing gender." Despite the undoubted relevance of ESE for entrepreneurial intention, little is known about the actual antecedents of ESE (Mauer et al. 2009), let alone its relation to gender mechanisms.

It is well known that aspects like mastery experience, also possible in the form of entrepreneurship education (Wilson et al. 2009), or role models offering vicarious learning, have a positive impact on ESE for women (BarNir et al. 2011) and that women differ from men in their level of ESE. Mauer et al. (2009) suggest that girls or women are conditioned differently. Following this and the above-mentioned logic of gender as a category, the self-efficacy model according to Bandura, which is the basis for almost all investigations on ESE, also reveals an explanatory weakness. Social influence is part of only one of the factors influencing self-efficacy. Assuming gender as a social mechanism influencing social habits, it's furthermore assumed as having a broader influence on the antecedents of (entrepreneurial) self-efficacy for women in general. That is why this study questions the status quo of the ESE concept, focusing instead on communalities between women entrepreneurs who have actually engaged in entrepreneurial activity and thus have already shown a certain level of ESE. Instead of reproducing knowledge by investigating existing models and concepts, this study explores ESE by integrating the experts' knowledge and experience, re-constructing their concepts regarding women's ESE. Furthermore, the gender theoretical perspective in accordance with Bourdieu (1983, 2013) is included, taking the relevance of (subconscious) gender mechanisms into account.

An investigation of German and Danish women entrepreneurs was conducted to answer this research question and explain the contextual phenomenon mentioned above. The following outlines the method and the methodological approach applied.

3 Methodological Approach

Starting from a feminist perspective with the aim of understanding *how* still-hidden gender mechanisms affect the construction of women entrepreneurs' ESE, this research contribution holds a social constructivist perspective, and calls for a qualitative study. As the theoretical framing has highlighted so far, this study is characterized by a highly subjective perspective. It's important to capture women's realities within their entrepreneurial contexts to overcome the male bias in entrepreneurship research regarding women entrepreneurs (Henry et al. 2015). To achieve this, and with the explorative character of this study in mind, a qualitative approach was used to conduct the study and analyze its data. Qualitative research methods appear to integrate women's realities better because they are opposed to the positivist male-associated objectivity of quantitative analysis (Flick 2009; Haidinger and Knittler 2014). The challenge of this study is to reveal the deeper structures of the culturally influenced habits regarding gender mechanisms in an entrepreneurial context. The most suitable way to do this is to obtain insights into the subjects' (here: women entrepreneurs') realities, i.e. the individuals experiencing the social mechanisms in question.

The research question is explored by applying the inductive interpretative method according to Gioia et al. (2013). This method helps create new knowledge and a theoretical concept grounded in data that is not too closely related to already-existing knowledge (in this case, the EEIM and ESE described above). Henry et al. (2015) very openly and directly encourage scholars to "be bolder" and look beyond quantitative methods (Henry et al. 2015, p. 20). This is why the Gioia method (2013) is used in the following to walk a new path in contextual and theory-building research. This method is currently gaining ground in entrepreneurship research (Wigren 2007). Methods following the idea of grounded theory are especially well-suited for the investigation of gender mechanisms as "they provide tools for analyzing processes, which hold much potential for studying social justice issues" (Charmaz 2005, p. 507). Male bias and male dominance in women's entrepreneurship can also be viewed as a form of social injustice or inequality.

Gioia's aspiration is to create new knowledge, build a theory and, as he states, new concepts (Gioia et al. 2013). Instead of modifying existing constructs, he claims to use his analysis to provide new concepts that are grounded in the collected data. This study contributes to understanding how women entrepreneurs construct their ESE, which is seen in a gender theoretical context where gender is treated as sociocultural mechanisms that guide society's habits. Hence, it is a construction *process* that is being investigated. Gioia et al. follow a few fundamental assumptions to create qualitative rigor in their method. The basic assumption is that the world is socially constructed and that people (women entrepreneurs) who construct their realities are "knowledgeable agents." They are the expert source of what they think, intend or act upon (Gioia et al. 2013). When seeking to find communalities or patterns for constructing ESE among women, women entrepreneurs themselves are the suitable research object. This assumption goes along with Stevenson's (1990) opinion that the best way to discover the world of women entrepreneurs is to ask them directly and let them explain (Stevenson 1990). Another basic assumption is about the role of the researcher who is also knowledgeable. Based on existing knowledge, the researcher is able to disclose patterns and concepts that might escape the informants' perception and eventually result in new theories (Gioia et al. 2013). A structured analyzing process was developed to incorporate this aspect, which is summarized in Fig. 2.

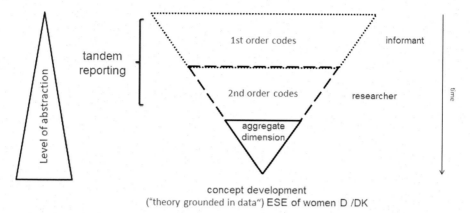

Source: Own illustration following Gioia et al. (2013)

Fig. 2 Analysis process according to Gioia et al. (2013)

The coding steps are at the core of the process. Verbal data in a first step is coded with first-order codes. The researcher's major role in this phase is to "give an adequate account that captures the meaning" of the informants' experience in their own words (Gioia 2014, p. 6). During this phase, first-order codes are formulated very closely to the original data. In a further step the next major role comes into play of identifying patterns in the data, thus allowing the surfacing of "concepts and relationships that might escape the awareness of the informants" (Gioia 2014). A crucial step is the formulation of these concepts into theoretically relevant terms, here second-order codes. The first two coding steps are described as tandem reporting where the researcher switches between the roles of an informing position during first-order coding and a more interpretative position using existing knowledge to unveil patterns during the second-order coding phase. In a third step, second-order codes which emerge from a certain amount of first-order codes disembogue into aggregate dimensions (Gioia et al. 2013). As Fig. 2 demonstrates, the more aggregate the new knowledge is, and the higher the level of abstraction, the more the researcher can interpret and build theories. Although this process is presented as strictly sequential, it is clear that the tandem reporting in particular is a rather iterative process. first-order codes, second-order codes, and aggregate dimensions build the basis for the so-called data structure, which allows a visualization of the analysis process, placing the emergent concepts (from the data structure) into a dynamic relation, which now can help to understand the phenomenon of interest (Gioia et al. 2013).

Since the aim of this study is to obtain deeper insight into the effects of gender mechanisms on women entrepreneurs' construction of ESE, asking women entrepreneurs the questions directly is obvious. The sampling strategy was initially guided by the content of the research question. Gathering the initial data set the sampling "snowball" into motion, which could be applied because the informants were able to point out other possible subjects of interest (Neergaard 2007). Altogether, 16 biographic narrative interviews were conducted (8GER+8DK) with women entrepreneurs from different industries in Germany and Denmark that were considered "not typical" for women. These women entrepreneurs' narratives aim to deliver explanatory information about facilitating and constraining factors for women's ESE and entrepreneurial activity.[2] The interviews were analyzed according Gioia et al. (2013) and Gioia (2014). via the iterative process of first- and second-order coding resulting in aggregate dimensions. These codings and dimensions form the data structure (Table 1)[3] which is the basis for the alternative model of women's ESE in patriarchal structures.

4 Empirical Findings and Discussion

Obtaining and analyzing nearly 14 hours of verbal data from 16 women entrepreneurs in Germany and Denmark aimed at the re-construction of their ESE. Table 1 summarizes the 60 first-order and 11 second-order codes that finally resulted in three aggregate dimensions. The data structure with its new concepts regarding ESE in a gender theoretical context represents the basis grounded in data for the alternative model of ESE in patriarchal structures (ESEPS) (Fig. 3). The ESEPS model sets women entrepreneurs and their individual realities (micro-level) into a context with gender mechanisms in their socio-cultural environment (macro-level). In contrast to contemporary models of ESE or EIM—in which ESE has been identified as a decisive factor—the ESEPS model does not treat gender as an external variable, but instead integrates the effects that societal gender mechanisms have on the individual woman entrepreneur. By doing so, it responds to scholars' demands of investigating women entrepreneurs and ESE in a more contextual manner (Henry et al. 2015; Ahl and Marlow 2012; Marlow 2014). The data findings further reveal that as a part of forming ESE in the context of gender theoretical assumptions, women while forming their ESE undergo an overall emancipatory self-reflective process to overcome male or patriarchal dominance. According to the interviews, time plays an important role here.

The analysis of the narratives was guided by Bourdieu's theoretical assumptions regarding patriarchal dominance as the result of the accumulation of forms of economic, social and cultural capital. This made it suitable for disclosing power relations within women entrepreneurs' realities. Following the logic patterns that

---

[2]The initial question/request was: "Please outline your pathway to your current professional situation. Start as early as you can recall." The intention was to let the interviewees themselves decide where to start and what to focus on. For additional clarity, the researcher taped the interviews, and took additional notes for further questions. Supportive questions were prepared to help the interviewees settle into a flow when needed, although the actual course of the interviews was in fact set by the interviewees themselves.

[3]The numbers in the brackets indicate how often this code was used.

Table 1 Data structure for the re-construction of women entrepreneurs' ESE in patriarchal societies

1st-Order Codes	2nd-Order Codes	Aggregate Dimensions
Being a women as a barrier in work life (31)		
Unequal chances in work life (23)		
Male dominance behavior (22)		
Masculine vs. feminine (20)		
Traditional gender roles in the (parental) home (19)	Perceived gender inequality	
Women stand out in male domains (15)		
Men in leadership positions (10)		Inequality of chances for women entrepreneurs
Male networks (9)		
Men- and women domains (8)		
Interplay between family and work life important (7)		
Typical male characteristics (6)		
Children as a career "knock-out" (5)		
No network (4)		
Role as an entrepreneur, not as a woman (2)		
Annoying (-invivo, related to male dominance)		
Country-specific influence D	Country-specific influence	
Country-specific influence DK		
Traditional schemes of thinking and perception (25)		
Women-typical characteristics (22)	Traditional patriarchal patterns of thinking and perception as a barrier	
Women as boss is extraordinary (5)		
Symbols of status as a sign of affiliation (5)		
Perception of women and money in society (2)		
Importance of upbringing (26)		
Changes in society (19)		
Breaking up of and rebelling against traditional roles (16)	Breaking up prevalent societal structures	
Breaking out of traditional role images (15)		Strategies for dealing with inequality of chances
Breaking up of traditional patterns of perception (11)		
Breaking up of traditional occupational profiles (11)		
Role conflicts with parents (2)		
Importance of being self-employed for women (57)		
Coping behavior under perceived inequality (7)	Coping behavior in masculine	
Exploiting being a woman (5)		

(continued)

Table 1 (continued)

1st-Order Codes	2nd-Order Codes	Aggregate Dimensions
Challenges accepted (20)	Coping with challenges	(Self-) Assurance with challenges
Not afraid of challenges (11)		
Bumblebee (Humleb) flies (-invivo, related to "not afraid of challenges")		
Network member (36)	Appreciation by others for self-esteem	
Women networks advantages (26)		
Encouragement by others as a positive reinforcement (25)		
Support by network of like-minded (8)		
Support by partner in career planning (8)		
Inspiration (-invivo, related to women network)		
Sparring partner (-invivo, related to women network)		
Success makes self-confident	Achievement experience	
Job experience as a positive reinforcement		
Personal success factors (50)	Person-related characteristics	
Willingness to learn as prerequisite for professional success (28)		
Urge for freedom (15)		
Orientation towards problem-solving (3)		
Mother as positive role model (9)	Family as an influence	
Mother as negative role model (2)		
Father as direct supporter (7)		
Father as indirect supporter (3)		
Family role models for being self-employed (8)		
Having an impact as a motivation for self-employment (30)	Awareness of competencies	
Unused competencies (17)		
Role models are contextual (15)		
Education as positive influence on competency awareness (17)		
Motivation through work that makes sense (7)		
Comparison with others (5)		
Cinderella work (-invivo)		

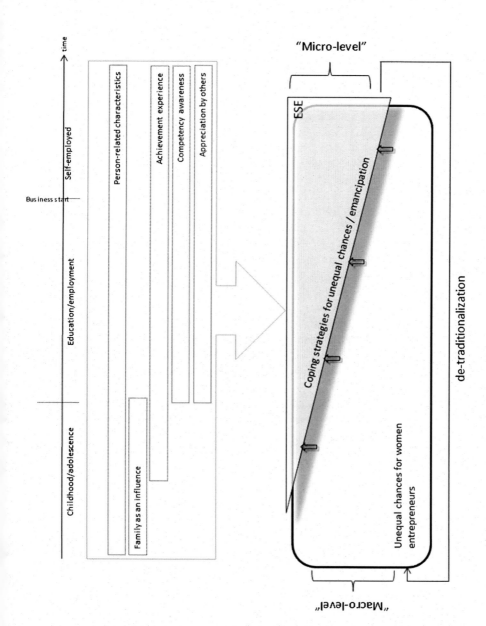

Fig. 3 Model for ESE in patriarchal structures (ESEPS)

were explored during the early coding phase facilitated the formulation of search heuristics: (1a) description of women's realities in terms of how women perceive gender equality, (2a) strategies to deal with perceived gender equality in terms of what strategies they develop to cope with their experience, and (3a) sources of ESE in terms of how they form their self-confidence in the entrepreneurial context. Accordingly, these heuristics led to the three aggregate dimensions: (1b) inequality of chances for women entrepreneurs, (2b) strategies for coping with inequality, and (3b) sources of entrepreneurial self-efficacy.

In connection with (1b) it could be assessed that despite recorded levels of gender egalitarianism within cultural science, women still face a high degree of unequal chances in their professional lives. Figure 3 shows these inequalities as a macro-level social condition women entrepreneurs are confronted with. Vertical and horizontal segregation as the result of patriarchal structures and power exclude women from socially recognized positions. Table 1 gives insight into related first- and second-order codes. Here it becomes obvious that women still perceive a certain amount of inequalities. These can range from being subtle [which is why these patterns are so hard to break (Bourdieu 2013)] to more obvious. As one of the strongest issues, women reported the intermingling of their professional roles with assumptions about their private roles as wives and mothers. One German interviewee for example reported that "In fact a consultant once asked me in the very beginning [...] what my family plans were. I found that question impudent. [...] That was cheeky. You don't do that when this might be a knock-out argument"[4] (P11, l. 203–209, D). Another Danish woman entrepreneur said that "as a mother we often need to do both...we have to do everything at the same time. You could easily suffocate from that" (P2, Z. 223–224, DK).

Interviewees either reported a high level of double stress in fulfilling both roles, or were involuntarily confronted with expectations about their presumed household roles, albeit in a professional context. In addition, women's professional success often comes at the expense of their private life and vice versa. A condition which Bourdieu identifies involves hidden gender-stereotypical assumptions that clearly discriminate against women (Bourdieu 2013). Although both German and Danish women gave examples of this, one striking quotation comes from the German owner of an IT company: "It's still difficult in Germany to combine business and family. It's not without reason that there is a business owner sitting here without children" (P8, Z. 591–593, D). Along with this, the interviewees identified having children as a career "knock-out" not least of all due to the circumstances described above (see Table 1). Another important aspect characterizing women's unequal chances is male dominance. This is expressed in various ways such as body language or verbal expressions. In both forms of communication, women reported men demonstrating and abusing their hierarchical positions and using these communication instruments disrespectfully. Also, being acknowledged as a professional in both employed and self-employed situations means women repeatedly have to prove their competencies.

---

[4]All German and Danish quotes have been translated into English.

A Danish entrepreneur operating in Germany put it in a nutshell, "Actually it's funny. Other than men women always have to be able to do at least 22 out of 20 possible things" (P2, Z. 175–176, DK). Women are thus often per se separated from competencies that are outside their "natural role" as care-takers (Bourdieu 2013, p. 168). Another example was the self-employed German woman who was addressed as a colleague's wife by potential business partners although they shared no family relation.[5] Even though she was equally in charge, her male colleague was assumed to be the boss. This incident confirms the habits observation that women in business are often portrayed as "business wives"—closer to their "naturalized role"—while men occupy the popular public sphere. In another example, a Danish business owner entered a customer's office, who then wanted to wait to talk about business until her boss was there. These two examples indicate how strongly the image of a male entrepreneur is incorporated into daily habits. In yet another example, a Danish woman entrepreneur went to get a loan from bank for her business idea and was kindly asked to bring her husband, although he had nothing to do with her business. They insisted on her bringing him along to the next meeting. It is worth mentioning that this woman was among the best global salespersons in the company she worked for before starting her own business.

Following these examples of perceived gender inequality, the verbal data also exposed some hints at the next aggregate dimension. (2b) Living and working in the described patriarchic environment, women over time develop a desire to break free from these unspoken yet strongly and regularly reproduced societal rules. The arrows in Fig. 3 indicate the relation between perceived gender inequality and coping strategies. Two main strategic behaviors of women in this context were discovered. One is breaking with societal structures. The other is associated with starting their own business. Breaking with societal rules refers to a more conscious debate regarding gender stereotypes. Women want to disrupt the status quo and question gender roles. "It's this good girl role we're breaking out of" (P2, line 366, DK) said one Danish woman entrepreneur. Also, taking on entrepreneurial action means intruding into the male-dominated sphere, representing an active interference with male dominance. The interviewees had often experienced and noticed some sort of gender inequality during their childhood. In these cases, it was a dominant father and a mother with less acknowledged social status—even if she did in fact do a great deal of work in both the household and at work. Growing up they turned these experiences or memories into their own ambitions not to give in to this imbalance. This internal will to break with traditional rules is important because it challenges the often latent structural discrimination against women (Kahlert 2012). Returning to the example of women's professional success being (so far) only possible at the expense

---

[5]"And so we quite often were in a situation that when we showed up together, also due to him being an extrovert, people—especially males—were fixated on him. And he also held a PhD, and that was one of the worst situations. We were at a trade fair and had a conversation with a client, a potential customer who addressed me as 'Mrs. Dr. [...] Oh, I'm sorry, I have to apologize. I don't know why I just said that.' Yeah, exactly. Bad enough you simply assumed that I can only be the wife and at the same time...you didn't even grant me my own name, but called me 'Mrs. Dr.'"

of their private lives, it becomes obvious how important it is to get both men and women involved in this disruptive behavior. Although men are the profiteers of existing structures (Jäger et al. 2012), they are also trapped in the binary order of gender roles, and true change can only happen if both genders work together (Bourdieu 2013). An example of this cooperation was given by a Danish woman entrepreneur who stated that it was obvious for her husband to take over the household. "It was total logic. I earned more than he did as a teacher and then it was clear that it wouldn't be me who'd stay at home" (P1, lines 299–302, DK). At the same time this points to the fact that as long as starting a business is only possible if men are willing to give up parts of their "natural roles" as breadwinners, unequal chances for women will persist. Breaking out of "being the good girl" and entering the public sphere [as opposed to staying in the private sphere, the core of patriarchal dominance (Bourdieu 2013)], is an important step towards changing the traditional rules of gender order (Jäger et al. 2012). Rindova et al. (2009) say that viewing entrepreneurial projects as emancipatory efforts helps understand the factors that motivate people to disrupt the status quo and change their position in the social order they are embedded in. From the gender-theoretical standpoint established above, becoming self-employed and starting a business is according to the available data the strongest strategy in breaking free from gender norms and coping with gender inequality in the labor market. Self-employment can be viewed as a reaction to perceived social injustice, and women re-arrange the social order they are a part of. Since entrepreneurship has been identified as a male concept, according to Bourdieu, women who start entrepreneurial activities enter male-dominated "terrain." So from a feminist perspective, self-employment serves as an act of emancipation; an emancipation not only from authorities in an employment situation, but also and especially from male dominance in employment relationships. From this perspective, each woman entrepreneur who starts her own business contributes to de-traditionalizing male-dominated or patriarchal structures (see Fig. 3).

Wanting to become self-employed is hardly a spontaneous decision. (3b) The data analysis of the biographic narrative interviews led to the conclusion that for women, becoming self-employed is the result of a longer self-reflective process during which their urge for emancipation appears to increase. Figure 3 symbolizes this with the triangular form of coping strategies related to the level of emancipation. The social circumstances, identified above as perceived gender inequality, serve as a form of motivation. As mentioned above, ESE is in this context developed over time, and the self-reflective process with an emancipatory character can be divided into three major phases: childhood/adolescence, qualification/employment, and self-employment. In all three phases, women form their ESE by learning about and experiencing episodes of breaking with habits. Figure 3 shows that there are various factors during these phases that over time have an influence on the formation of ESE. It becomes clear that these factors differ in their relevance within each phase. The analysis was able to explore how person-related characteristics such as a drive for freedom, problem-solving orientation, and willingness to learn appear to be important along the entire pathway. Although they appear to be independent from other factors, they are actually intertwined to some extent. Family influence for example could be related to being a problem solver later on. During their childhood and adolescence, family appeared to have an influence on the women's drive for freedom. For example, "in this context my mother was very untraditional for that time" (P5, lines 520–522, DK). The narratives revealed a concentration of factors influencing women entrepreneurs' ESE during the phase of education and employment. In particular, this here included competency awareness, experiencing achievement, and appreciation by others. Interestingly, the group of women almost univocally reported key episodes of comparing themselves with superior male colleagues that led to an attitude of "if he can do it, then I definitely can do it, too, if not even better." This kind of comparison with others helps people become convinced of their own competencies. The interviewees also expressed situations of being unchallenged, feeling they had the resources to accomplish more. They were also striving for work that actually made sense. Other examples show the impact that acknowledgement by others has on ESE. Interestingly, these factors influencing ESE have also been found to be important after having started a business. During this phase, and following the decisive act of emancipation, women still perceive gender inequalities. Having entered a male-dominated sphere, they reported difficulties in being acknowledged and obtaining access to important—mostly male-dominated—networks. Consequently, with limited access to important economic, social and cultural capital, women took the initiative and created their own spheres, which in turn helped become acknowledged. Women in male-dominated industries nevertheless are still rare, and have to put a great deal of effort in accumulating the required capital to position themselves as women entrepreneurs. Women networks can here serve as a source for expanding upon and improving ESE.

Remarkably, and despite the fact that Denmark ranks higher in gender egalitarianism than Germany, no considerable advantage for Danish women regarding the perception of gender mechanisms could be observed. On the contrary, gender mechanisms as a part of national culture seem to persevere in both stronger and more subtle ways than measurable gender equality indicators can show. So while the results do not seem to be surprising regarding Germany, there does in fact appear to be structural discrimination in Denmark which escapes gender equality measurements. The major difference identified was the seemingly greater willingness of Danish men to take over household roles.

5 Conclusions and Implications

The data analysis of the 16 interviews with Danish and German women entrepreneurs aimed at understanding how women construct their ESE by taking theoretical gender assumptions into account and how they overcome patriarchal dominance. In contrast to other contemporary studies on ESE which preferably employed quantitative analysis and treat gender as an external variable, this research project worked with an inductive interpretative method to find new concepts for understanding the antecedents of women entrepreneurs' ESE in the patriarchal structures of Western capitalist societies. In this context it was of special interest how gender as a social norm, influenced by national culture, affects the antecedents of ESE. A new approach was identified as necessary due to the fact that contemporary research is often guided by male-mainstream models and rationalities, and subsequently often fails to incorporate women's realities. Also, the comparison between Danish and German women entrepreneurs' ESE showed an inconsistent relation between the level of ESE and actual entrepreneurial behavior. Supposing that gender mechanisms (which have not yet been captured in ESE models) play a role, the exploratory study led to an alternative model of entrepreneurial self-efficacy in patriarchal structures (ESEPS).

This new model integrates the perceived mechanisms of gender that take place on a macro-social level into the relevance of women entrepreneurs becoming self-employed on the micro-social level. Taking the initial unequal chances for women entrepreneurs into account, ESE antecedents are extensively involved with breaking with traditional gender roles and habits. For women entrepreneurs this seems not only to include being convinced of their entrepreneurial capabilities; even more so, it involves becoming aware of actually being trapped in male-dominated structures and breaking free from them. This process of becoming aware was identified as an overall emancipatory self-reflective process which could be divided into three main phases. A phase which in the entrepreneurial context seemed to be especially poignant was the education and employment phase. The most convincing strategy for the women interviewed appeared to be starting their own business. As a limitation of this research, it is important to note that the results are based on a rather small amount of data, rendering the common rules of validity and reliability inapplicable. It nevertheless serves as a new starting point for further investigations.

Future research on women entrepreneurs' startup activity that employs a more gender-sensitive approach could elaborate more on the emancipatory effects of entrepreneurial activity. The majority of research has to date been carried out through an androcentric lens and is based on male categories. So far, it has not been possible to fully capture the emancipatory importance of self-employment for women. Entrepreneurial emancipation not only means high levels of autonomy or getting out of an authoritative relationship or employment situation in general. Male entrepreneurs may have the exact same motivation. But for women, the emancipatory process takes place on another level, one which men as the overall profiteers of patriarchy do not experience. This is why it is so important to treat gender as a category in the sense of social mechanisms influencing women entrepreneurs' realities.

Because they occupy other positions in the social space, women do not have the same opportunities as men when starting a business. Although entrepreneurial activity has an emancipatory effect on men as well, women here not only break free from authorities in business, but from patriarchal dominance as well. This indicates a greater emancipatory effect of entrepreneurial activity on women than on men in patriarchal structures.

The focus on entrepreneurial activity as an act of emancipation can additionally help to understand not only the economic but also the societal effects of women's entrepreneurship, particularly in societies with patriarchal structures. In this context, promoting women's entrepreneurship advances it towards becoming an important instrument of women empowerment.

References

Achtenhagen, L. (2014). Selbständigkeit von Frauen – Forschungsperspektiven und –resultate aus dem skandinavischen Raum. In C. Gather, I. Biermann, L. Schürmann, S. Ulbricht, & H. Zipprian (Eds.), *Die Vielfalt der Selbständigkeit – Sozialwissenschaftliche Beiträge zu einer Erwerbsform im Wandel* (pp. 49–62). Berlin: HWR Berlin Forschung: Edition Sigma. 58/59.
Ahl, H. (2002). *The making of the female entrepreneur – A discourse analysis of research texts on Women's entrepreneurship, JIBS Dissertation Series*. Jönköping: Jönköping Business School.
Ahl, H. (2006). Why research on women entrepreneurs needs new directions. *Entrepreneurship in Theory and Practice, 30*(5), 1042–2587.
Ahl, H., & Marlow, S. (2012). Exploring the dynamics of gender, feminism and entrepreneurship: Advancing debate to escape a dead end? *Organization, 19*(5), 543–562.
Bandura, A. (1997). *Self-efficacy – The exercise of control* (12th ed.). New York: W.H. Freeman and Company.
Barnir, A., Watson, W. E., & Hutchins, H. M. (2011). Mediation and moderated mediation in the relationship among role models, self-efficacy, entrepreneurial career intention, and gender. *Journal of Applied Social Psychology, 41*(2), 270–297.
Baron, R. A., Markman, G. D., & Hirsa, A. (2001). Perceptions of women and men as entrepreneurs: Evidence for differential effects of Attributional augmenting. *Journal of Applied Psychology, 86*(5), 923–929.
Bird, B., & Brush, C. (2002). A gendered perspective on organizational creation. *Entrepreneurship in Theory and Practice, 26*, 41–56.
Bourdieu, P. (1983). Ökonomisches Kapital, kulturelles Kapital, soziales Kapital. In R. Kreckel (Ed.), *Soziale Ungleichheiten, Soziale Welt Sonderband* (Vol. 2, pp. 183–198). Göttingen.
Bourdieu, P. (2013). *Die Männliche Herrschaft* (2nd ed.). Frankfurt am Main: Suhrkamp Verlag.
Brännback, M., Carsrud, A., Kickul, J., & Krueger, N. (2007). *"Watch out Isaac!!" – Re-Constructing Entrepreneurial Intentions*. Conference Paper 4th AGSE Conference, 6–9 February, Brisbane, Australia.
Bruni, A., Gherardi, S., & Poggio, B. (2004a). Entrepreneur-mentality, gender and the study of women entrepreneurs. *Journal of Organizational Change, 17*(3), 256–268.
Bruni, A., Gherardi, S., & Poggio, B. (2004b). Doing gender, doing entrepreneurship: An ethnographic account of intertwined practices. *Gender Work and Organization, 11*(4), 406–429.
Brush, C. G., de Bruin, A., & Welter, F. (2009). A gender-aware framework for women's entrepreneurship. *International Journal of Gender and Entrepreneurship, 1*(1), 8–24.
Butler, J. (2008). *Gender trouble*. New York: Routledge.
Carsrud, A. L., & Johnson, R. W. (1989). Entrepreneurship – A social psychological perspective. *Entrepreneurship & Regional Development: An International Journal, 1*(1), 21–31.
Charmaz, K. (2005). Grounded theory in the 21st century: Applications for advancing social justice studies. In N. K. Denzin & Y. S. Lincoln (Eds.), *The sage handbook of qualitative research* (3rd ed., pp. 507–535). Thousand Oaks, CA: Sage.
Chen, C. C., Greene, P. G., & Crick, A. (1998). Does entrepreneurial self-efficacy distinguish entrepreneurs from managers? *Journal of Business Venturing, 13*, 295–316.
De Martino, R., & Barbato, R. (2003). Differences between women and men MBA entrepreneurs: Exploring family flexibility and wealth creation as career motivators. *Journal of Business Venturing, 18*, 815–832.

Emrich, C. G., Denmark, F. L., & Den Hartog, D. (2004). Cross-cultural differences in gender egalitarianism. In R. J. House, P. J. Hanges, M. Javidan, P. W. Dorfman, & V. Gupta (Eds.), *Culture, leadership, and organizations: The GLOBE study of 62 societies* (3rd ed., pp. 343–394). Thousand Oaks, CA: Sage Publications.

Flick, U. (2009). *Qualitative Sozialforschung – Eine Einführung* (2nd ed.). Hamburg: Rowohlts Enzyklopädie, Rowohlt Taschenbuchverlag.

Gather, C., Biermann, I., Schürmann, L., Ulbricht, S., & Zipprian, H. (Eds.). (2014). *Die Vielfalt der Selbständigkeit – Sozialwissenschaftliche Beiträge zu einer Erwerbsform im Wandel. In HWR Berlin Forschung, 58/59.* Berlin: Edition Sigma.

Gioia, D. A. (2014). A 1st-order/2nd-order qualitative approach to understanding strategic management.

Gioia, D. A., Corley, K. G., & Hamilton, A. (2013). Seeking qualitative rigor in inductive research: Notes on the Gioia methodology. *Organizational Research Methods, 16*(1), 15–31.

Haidinger, B., & Knittler, K. (2014). *Intro – Feministische Ökonomie, mandelbaum kritik & utopie.* Wien.

Henry, C., Foss, L., & Ahl, H. (2015). Gender and entrepreneurship research: A review of methodological approaches. *International Small Business Journal, 34*(3), 1–25.

Hoppe, H. (2002). *Feministische Ökonomik – Gender in Wirtschaftstheorien und ihren Methoden.* Berlin: Edition Sigma.

Jäger, U., König, T., & Maihofer, A. (2012). Pierre Bourdieu: Die Theorie männlicher Herrschaft als Schlussstein seiner Gesellschaftstheorie. In H. Kahlert & C. Weinbach (Eds.), *Zeitgenössische Gesellschaftstheorien und Genderforschung* (pp. 15–36). Wiesbaden: Springer Verlag.

Jennings, A. L. (1993). Public or private? Institutional economics and feminism. In M. A. Ferber & J. A. Nelson (Eds.), *Beyond economic man – Feminist theory and economics* (pp. 111–129). Chicago: The University of Chicago Press.

Kahlert, H. (2012). Dis/Kontinuitäten der Geschlechterverhältnisse in der Moderne. Skizzen zu Anthony Giddens' Verbindung von Gesellschaftstheorie und Genderforschung. In H. Kahlert & C. Weinbach (Eds.), *Zeitgenössische Gesellschaftstheorien und Genderforschung* (pp. 57–79). Wiesbaden: Springer Verlag.

Kelley, D., Brush, C. G., Greene, P. G., & Litovsky, Y. (2013). *Global entrepreneurship monitor – Women's report 2012.* Global Entrepreneurship Research Association (GERA).

Kourilsky, M. L., & Walstad, W. B. (1998). Entrepreneurship and female youth: Knowledge, attitudes, gender differences, and educational practices. *Journal of Business Venturing, 13,* 77–88.

Krueger Jr., N., & Brazeal, D. V. (1994). Entrepreneurial potential and potential entrepreneurs. *Entrepreneurship Theory & Practice, 18*(3), 91–104.

Krueger Jr., N., & Dickson, P. R. (1993). How believing in ourselves increases risk-taking: Perceived self-efficacy and opportunity recognition. *Decision Sciences, 25*(3), 385–400.

Krueger, N, Jr., & Kickul, J. (2006). *So you thought the intentions model was simple?: Navigating the complexities and interactions of cognitive style, culture, gender, social norms, and intensity on the pathways to entrepreneurship.* Paper presented at USASBE conference, Tucson, AZ.

Krueger Jr., N., Reilly, M. D., & Carsrud, A. L. (2000). Competing models of entrepreneurial intentions. *Journal of Business Venturing, 15,* 411–432.

Marlow, S. (2014). Exploring future research agendas in the field of gender and entrepreneurship. *International Journal of Gender and Entrepreneurship, 6*(2), 102–120.

Mauer, R., Neergaard, H., & Linstad, A. K. (2009). Self-efficacy: Conditioning the entrepreneurial mind-set. In A. L. Carsrud & M. Brännback (Eds.), *Understanding the entrepreneurial mind* (pp. 233–257). New York: Springer.

Max, S., & Ballereau, V. (2013). Theorizing about gender and entrepreneurship: Bridging the gap with social psychology. *International Journal of Gender and Entrepreneurship, 5*(1), 97–110.

Neergard, H. (2007). Sampling in entrepreneurial settings. In H. Neergaard & J. P. Ulhøj (Eds.), *Handbook of qualitative research methods in entrepreneurship* (pp. 253–275). Cheltenham: Edward Elgar.

Nelson, J. A. (1993). The study of choice or the study of provisioning? Gender and the definition of economics. In M. A. Ferber & J. A. Nelson (Eds.), *Beyond economic man – Feminist theory and economics* (pp. 23–36). Chicago: The University of Chicago Press.

Rindova, V., Barry, D., & Ketchen Jr., D. J. (2009). Entrepreneuring as emancipation. *Academy of Management Review, 34*(3), 477–491.

Sexton, D. L., & Bowman-Upton, N. (1990). Female and male entrepreneurs: Psychological characteristics and their role in gender-related discrimination. *Journal of Business Venturing, 5*, 29–36.

Stevenson, L. (1990). Some methodological problems associated with researching women entrepreneurs. *Journal of Business Ethics, 9*, 439–446.

Verheul, I., & Thurik, R. (2001). Start-up capital: "Does gender matter"? *Small Business Economics, 16*, 329–345.

Welter, F. (2004). The environment for female entrepreneurship in Germany. *Journal of Small Business and Enterprise Development, 11*(2), 212–221.

Wigren, C. (2007). Assessing the quality of qualitative research in entrepreneurship. In H. Neergaard & J. P. Ulhøi (Eds.), *Handbook of qualitative research methods in entrepreneurship* (pp. 383–404). Cheltenham: Edward Elgar.

Wilson, F., Kickull, J., & Marlino, D. (May 2007). Gender, entrepreneurial self-efficacy and entrepreneurial career intentions: Implications for entrepreneurship education. *Entrepreneurship in Theory and Practice, 31*(3), 387–406.

Wilson, F., Kickull, J., Marlino, D., Barbosa, S. D., & Griffths, M. D. (2009). An analysis of the role of gender and self-efficacy. *Journal of Developmental Entrepreneurship, 14*(2), 105–119.

Zhao, H., Seibert, S. E., & Lumpkin, G. T. (2010). The relationship of personality to entrepreneurial intentions and performance: A meta-analytical review. *Journal of Management, 36*(2), 381–404.

Women Entrepreneurship in Estonia: Formal and Informal Institutional Context

Sanita Rugina

Abstract This paper explores the impact of gendered context on the female entrepreneurship environment in Estonia. Having introduced comprehensive structural and institutional reforms in the 1990s, Estonia is now one of the most developed and progressive post-Soviet bloc countries. Most global rankings place Estonia towards the top of their lists, presenting it as an example of long-term successful economic and fiscal policy, with effective structural reforms and state governance. Nevertheless, the women entrepreneurship rate in Estonia is surprising, with women entrepreneurs constituting only 5% of the women in the active labor force in 2012. This is significantly lower than the EU-28 average entrepreneurship rate, and one of the lowest in Europe. This paper aims to contribute to the field of entrepreneurship, illustrating how the extent of entrepreneurship is linked to its social context. A sample of 20 women entrepreneurs was taken from the main cities in Estonia (Tallinn, Tartu, Narva and Kurresaare) to explain the experience of female entrepreneurs.

1 Introduction

Estonia is a former socialist economy and Soviet republic. Introducing comprehensive structural and institutional reforms in the 1990s, Estonia's transition to the market economy was enhanced by its 2004 integration into the European Union (Lumiste et al. 2008). Estonia is now a country with an advanced, high-income economy that is among the fastest growing in the EU (Storobin 2005). Most global rankings have Estonia high on their lists, presenting it as an example of long-term successful economic and fiscal policy, with effective structural reforms and state governance. Estonia has been referred to as the "Baltic Tiger" and even an "economic miracle" (Laar 2007). In terms of business culture and ethics, Estonians like to be considered a part of Scandinavia or Northern Europe rather than one of the Baltic

---

S. Rugina (✉)
Kingston University, Kingston upon Thames, UK
e-mail: sanita.rugina@kolumbs.lv

countries or a former Soviet republic. In other words, it prefers to tend towards notions of democracy, tolerance, and equality.

The women entrepreneurship data in Estonia is quite surprising, especially when considering its successful economic and political developments, as well as its mindset of wanting to become one of the most developed nations in the world. Women entrepreneurs constituted 5% of the women in the active labor force in 2012. This was significantly lower than the EU-28 average entrepreneurship rate (10%) and one of the lowest in Europe. The situation is similar in several Eastern European countries. Women entrepreneurs in Lithuania constitute only 7% of the women in the active labor force, in Slovenia 8%, in Bulgaria 8%, in Montenegro 8%, in Hungary 8%, and in Latvia 8% (European Commission 2014a). And since 2008 the number of women entrepreneurs in Estonia has even decreased by 3% (European Commission 2014a), while the entrepreneurship rate has decreased by more than 1% in Lithuania, Romania, Poland, and Bulgaria (European Commission 2014a). Because these countries share similar pasts, it is possible that the reasons for low and decreasing female entrepreneurship rates are somehow similar. So research findings in Estonia could be related to those coming from these EU countries as well.

The goal of the European Commission's strategy for economic development in the European Union aims at smart, sustainable, inclusive growth (European Commission 2010). It goes hand in hand with the general vision of Estonia's economic policy—creation of an open, competitive, and stable economic framework supporting business activities (Lumiste et al. 2008). At the same time, the Estonian government has no track record in developing women's enterprise policy, and gender issues are not a focus of entrepreneurship and businesses development strategy at the moment. If the potential contribution of entrepreneurship to economic development and social inclusion is to be fulfilled, it is important that both women and men are fully represented as entrepreneurs (Aidis et al. 2007). Both academics and business practitioners would agree that female entrepreneurship plays a significant role within the context of socio-economic development (Sarfaraz et al. 2014).

Because the contribution of women-led businesses to the Estonian economy is largely under-researched and unmeasured, it is difficult to explain why the number of women entrepreneurs is so low and why it has even diminished over the last decade. Although no analysis has been made on this topic (Rozeik 2014), a European Commission report on encouraging female entrepreneurship in Estonia suggests that there are still relatively strong gender stereotypes supported by Estonians, which result in gender segregation both in education and on the labor market (Rozeik 2014).

Institutional and legal contexts play an important role in female entrepreneurship, influencing its nature and extent as well as its potential economic contribution (Aidis et al. 2007). Formal institutions such as laws and public policy can create opportunities for entrepreneurship. At the same time, informal institutions such as values, norms, and the general attitude of a society towards entrepreneurship can strongly influence the perception of entrepreneurial opportunities (Salimath and Cullen 2010). The existing institutional framework might limit women's entrepreneurial activities due to redefined and changed gender roles, thus restricting their access to external resources. People may generally ascribe domestic roles to women which conflict with entrepreneurial activities (Welter and Smallbone 2010).

Institutional context influences the nature, pace of development, and extent of entrepreneurship, as well as the way entrepreneurs behave (Welter and Smallbone 2011). The previous research on the influence of the institutional context on entrepreneurship mostly draws from empirical evidence about transition economies that are characterized by ambiguous, unstable, and uncertain institutional environments. This chapter aims to critically examine the institutional embeddedness of entrepreneurship in one of the most developed and stable post-Soviet bloc economies.

The purpose of this study was to explore whether there are gender stereotypes impacting female entrepreneurship in Estonia. The research also aimed to understand the individual characteristics women possessed that helped them to become entrepreneurs, as well as what motivated them. A sample of 20 women entrepreneurs from the main cities in Estonia was conducted to explain the experience of female entrepreneurs.

This chapter begins with a review of theoretical concepts from the entrepreneurship literature that focus on the interplay of formal and informal institutions with a particular emphasis on the role of informal institutions (gender stereotypes) and their influence on female entrepreneurship. The theory of human capital and entrepreneurial motivations is also studied here. The paper then proceeds with the background information on female entrepreneurship in Estonia and methodology of the study. Section 4 discusses the findings of the qualitative study of Estonian female entrepreneurs. The paper ends with conclusions and suggestions for future research.

2 Theoretical Background

2.1 Institutions and Entrepreneurship

There is currently a growing recognition in entrepreneurship research that economic behavior can only be understood within the context of its social relations (Welter and Smallbone 2011). More and more researchers are adopting institutional approaches to explain various topics of entrepreneurship and SMEs (Thornton et al. 2011). Entrepreneurs and their activities are influenced by opportunities and incentives provided by a country's context, which is made up of both formal and informal institutions (Aidis 2017). The sociocultural and the political-institutional environments influence entrepreneurial attitudes and motives, the resources that can be mobilized, as well as the constraints and opportunities on/for starting and running a business (Thornton et al. 2011). Because of this, context has an impact on the nature, pace of development, and extent of entrepreneurship as well as on entrepreneurial behavior. With regard to female entrepreneurship, the variety of institutional contexts can be either a liability or an asset.

The definitions of an institution vary among scholars. Scott (2008) proposes that institutions consist of cognitive, normative and regulative structures, and activities that provide stability and meaning in social behavior. Institutions according to North are humanly devised constraints that structure political, economic, and social interaction. They consist of both informal constraints (values, norms, sanctions, taboos, customs, traditions, and codes of conduct), and formal rules (constitutions, laws, economic rules, property rights and contracts). Together with standard constraints of economics, they define the choice of set and therefore determine transaction and production costs, and hence the profitability and feasibility of engaging in economic activity. They evolve incrementally, connecting the past with the present and the future; history in consequence is largely a story of institutional evolution in which the historical performance of economies can only be understood as a part of a sequential story. Institutions provide the incentive structure of an economy; as that structure evolves, it shapes the direction of economic change towards growth, stagnation, or decline (North 1991).

Applied to the field of entrepreneurship, institutions represent the set of rules that articulate and organize the economic, social, and political interactions between individuals and social groups, with consequences for business activity and economic development (Thornton et al. 2011). North distinguishes between formal and informal institutions, defining them as assets and constraints, and emphasizing the inertial character of informal institutions, stating that they will not change immediately in reaction to the implementation of formal rules. North opposes the mainstream approach to transition, adding that path-dependence can and will produce a wide variety of patterns of development, depending on the cultural heritage and specific historical experience of a country (North 1997). This can result in radically different economic performance, which can exist over long periods of time as a result of the embedded character of informal institutions (North 1990, 2005).

2.2 Gender Stereotypes as a Kind of Informal Institution

Formal institutions such as laws and public policy that guarantee the rule of law, protection of property rights, and gender equality will typically stimulate entrepreneurship. At the same time, informal institutions such as values, norms, and stereotypes will leave an imprint on the general attitude of a society as well as individuals when they perceive entrepreneurship and entrepreneurial opportunities (Welter and Smallbone 2003). Informal institutions represent socio-cultural factors that may shape an entrepreneur's feasibility, desirability, and legitimacy considerations in the examination of entrepreneurship as a potential career choice. For example, formal institutions such as laws may enable women to enter entrepreneurship, but social norms may still discourage them from engaging in various activities (Pathak et al. 2013). The evolving institutional framework might constrain women's formal integration into the emerging market economy due to redefined and changed gender roles, thus restricting their access to the external resources that are needed to achieve a business venture. They might even ascribe domestic roles to women, which would conflict with entrepreneurial activities (Welter et al. 2006). As informal institutions are deeply embedded within a society and its culture, they determine gender roles and prescribe typically "male" or "female" behavior (Ahl 2006), thus impacting the desirability, nature, and extent of entrepreneurship for women.

Gender stereotypes are one of the oldest informal institutions that assign certain gender roles prescribing how men and women should act and what their responsibilities in life are. Gender stereotypes are culturally defined and transmitted through interactions between people, in mass media, and by popular discourse (Ahl 2006). Social sciences distinguish between sex as ascribed to biology, anatomy, hormones, and physiology; and gender as constructed through social, cultural, and psychological factors (Ahl 2006). While sex (male and female) is something people are born with, gender is what people do, and how they act when they attribute a circumscribed meaning to males and females (Bruni et al. 2004). Gender is not simply one aspect of sex. More fundamentally, it's something people do, and repeatedly do when interacting with others (Butler 1990).

Gender stereotypes are widely held in society, and often influence attitudes and behaviors without conscious awareness (Devine 1989; Wegener et al. 2006). People tend to pursue tasks positively associated with their gender while avoiding tasks not associated with their gender (Miller and Budd 1999). Distinct gender roles lead to major inequalities in a wide range of social, economic, educational, political, social, conjugal, financial, and labor-related issues (Wirls 1886).

These stereotypes have also been found to influence assessments of male- and female-related jobs, often causing the former to be valued more highly and earn higher wages than the latter (Cohen and Huffman 2003; Karlin et al. 2002). More broadly, the stereotypical characteristics attributed to men and women in society influence the classification of various occupations as "masculine" or "feminine," which tends to affect people's aspiration and inclination toward these jobs (Cejka and Eagly 1999). Empirical evidence overall suggests that women are likely to have lower expectations than men for success in a wide range of occupations (Eccles 1994).

Not surprisingly, significantly lower levels of self-efficacy among women have been found in careers historically perceived as "non-traditional" for women (Bandura et al. 2001; Betz and Hackett 1981). Scholars argue, and evidence indicates, that gender stereotypes influence men's and women's intentions to pursue entrepreneurship, an achievement-based career domain (Gupta et al. 2005).

Even more, studies find that current views about entrepreneurs are heavily weighted toward traits traditionally viewed as masculine, and these stereotypical beliefs adversely affect the entry into and development of women in entrepreneurship (Gupta et al. 2008). Entrepreneurs are usually described using masculine words (e.g. assertive, aggressive), whereas feminine attributes either do not appear at all (e.g. affectionate, sympathetic) or are the direct opposite (e.g. gentle, shy) of entrepreneurial characteristics (Gupta et al. 2008).

More specifically, scholars have argued that socially constructed and educated ideas about gender and entrepreneurship limit women's ability to accrue social, cultural, human, and financial capital, and place limitations upon their ability to generate personal savings, have credit histories attractive to resource providers, or engage the interest of loan officers, angel investors, and venture capitalists (Gupta et al. 2009). These factors are believed to impact the kinds of ventures men and women entrepreneurs start as well as their subsequent development. For example, women entrepreneurs are more likely than men to have businesses in the service or retail sector that are smaller, slower-growing, and less profitable, which in turn reinforces the stereotypical image of men and women in self-employment (Gupta et al. 2005).

2.3 Human Capital and Entrepreneurship

From an individual's perspective, the constituting factors of entrepreneurship are demographic characteristics such as age, gender, and individual human capital. Human capital expresses itself through factors such as (professional) education, work experiences, and previous management experiences (Dombrovsky and Welter 2006). Entrepreneurship research suggests that previous education and professional experience have a positive effect on entrepreneurship and business development (Evans and Leighton 1990). Human capital theory argues that knowledge improves the cognitive abilities of individuals. As a result, their potential activities are more productive and efficient (Mincer 1974; Schultz 1959). Formal education is one component of human capital that may assist in the accumulation of explicit knowledge that may provide skills useful to entrepreneurs (Davidsson and Honig 2003).

Human capital not only consists of formal education. It includes learning and practical knowledge that is acquired during previous work experiences. Previous knowledge plays a critical role in intellectual performance because it assists in the integration and accumulation of new knowledge, and helps integrate and adapt to new situations (Weick 1996). A common influence on entrepreneurship in western countries is family background, where family origin is generally found to offer positive role models (Shapero and Sokol 1982). A stylized fact emerging from research shows individuals whose parents were either self-employed or business owners to be more likely to become entrepreneurs than those from families without this kind of entrepreneurial experience (Dunn and Holtz-Eakin 2000). An entrepreneurial family background is said to transport knowledge, skills, self-confidence, and positive attitudes into entrepreneurship, thus facilitating the entry of the family's children into it.

Most work in both the popular and academic press about the decision to start a business includes background or antecedent factors underlying the entrepreneurial decision. Included among those antecedent factors is the influence of role models on the potential entrepreneur's thought process (Dombrovsky and Welter 2006). Researchers have argued that role models provide an observational learning experience for the individual. Additionally, the role model can directly influence an individual by actively participating in the learning experience (Van Auken et al. 2006). Seeing entrepreneurial reality every day can unquestionably be an encouraging and valuable experience, and can influence the own decision to become an entrepreneur. Furthermore, many business-owning parents involve their children in minor tasks in their companies, which also shapes their experiences. Research reports that 35–65% of entrepreneurs had one or more entrepreneurial parents (Scherer et al. 1990). By including their children in their firm, business owners provide the opportunity to gain entrepreneurial knowledge that will become valuable in future business start-ups (Van Auken et al. 2006).

2.4 Motivational Factors to Become Entrepreneurs

Being an entrepreneur, managing a business, and taking risks are difficult challenges. What is it about certain people that drives them to take on the risks, uncertainty, and instability of being an entrepreneur? Most entrepreneurial research has found very similar entrepreneurial motivations, with independence and the need for self-achievement always ranked first (Hisrich 1984). Other motivational factors are often less important. However, when flexibility in the workplace is included in the survey, it is also identified as another important factor motivating female entrepreneurship (DeMartino et al. 2006).

Independence entails taking the responsibility to use one's own judgment. It also involves taking responsibility for the own life rather than living off the efforts of others. In his competitive study of women entrepreneurs in the U.S. and Puerto Rico, Hisrich (1984) found that one of the primary motivations to start a business was a desire for greater independence. Some of the literature on empirical evidence has suggested that entrepreneurs are more independent than others (Shane et al. 2003).

Another motivational trait that has received attention is the locus of control—the belief in the extent to which individuals believe that their actions or personal characteristics affect outcomes. Individuals who have an external locus of control believe that outcomes are out of their control, whereas individuals with an internal locus of control believe that their personal actions directly affect the outcome of an event (Rotter 1966).

Some women choose not to enter or return to corporate life, preferring instead to establish their own business in the expectation that it will offer a better work-family balance. Other women are attracted by greater flexibility in the use of their time, and the ability to accommodate professional goals alongside personal responsibilities (Marlow and Carter 2004). Women business owners are not necessarily seeking reduced hours; instead, they aim to achieve more or better control over the hours they work (Mattis 2004).

3 The Economic Environment in Estonia and Female Entrepreneurship

Estonia was stripped of its independence and became part of the Soviet Union when it was annexed by Russia in 1941. This ended the first Estonian independence that lasted from 1918 to 1941 and was marked by relative economic, social, and political development as well as advances in cultural and national values. Women participation rates in labor were high during Soviet rule. McCauley (1981) gives figures that show women's participation rates (i.e. the proportion of women of working age in employment) for the USSR in 1975 as 83% for women aged 16–54 years, and 65% for those aged 15–70 years. The Soviet rule made work mandatory and prosecuted those without it. Gender equality was also high on the Soviet party agenda. Although there were few women among party elite members and top management positions, women occupied many middle-level management positions. They were scientists, doctors, and lawyers. The media portrayed women as front-line labor heroes in every sector, and the general perception was that women were equal to men and could succeed in any field.

In 1991, Estonia regained its independence from the Soviet Union and started to rebuild its political and economic institutions. Estonia's integration into the European Union in 2004 accelerated the further development of the market economy, enhancing its institutional framework. The EU integration process played an important role in creating and supporting the development of a liberal, private sector-based market economy. Implementation of the European Union recommendations, rules, standards, and norms helped to increase the competitiveness of Estonian companies by improving access to the EU and other markets (Lumiste et al. 2008). Since the early 1990s, Estonian women have taken an active part in the labor market; overall female employment in Estonia is high. According to Statistics Estonia, the employment rate of women in Estonia was 71% for the age group 15–69 in 2016 (Fig. 1).

Gender equality is guaranteed in Estonian female entrepreneurship, and women's rights are legally protected by the constitution. Estonia ranks number 12 among 190 countries in the World Bank's ease-of-doing business, surpassing countries such as Finland, Australia, Canada, and Switzerland, showing that regulations for creating and running a business are straightforward and transparent, with effective protection of property rights (World Bank 2016). According to GEM, 64% of Estonians agree with the statement that entrepreneurs enjoy a high status in their country (regional average 66%). 53% of Estonians consider starting a business as a desirable career choice (regional average 57%) (GEM 2016). In addition, women in Estonia are significantly more educated than men (46.4% of the female and 28% of the male labor force; aged 15–74 had third-level education in 2012) (Karu 2014).

Considering the achievements of Estonia as well as the country's aspiration to become one of the most developed nations in the world, as well as its favorable entrepreneurial framework and high education level of women, the women entrepreneurship reality in Estonia is quite surprising. Only 5% of women in the active labor force were entrepreneurs in 2012. This is one of the lowest in the EU whose

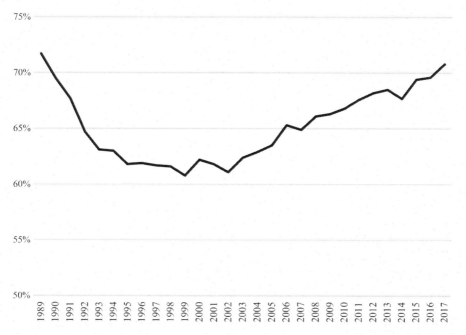

Fig. 1 Employment rate of women in Estonia for the age group 15–69. Source: Statistics Estonia

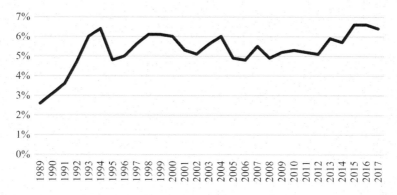

Fig. 2 Female entrepreneurship rate in the Estonian active labor force. Source: Statistics Estonia

average female entrepreneurship rate is 10%. This rate has not changed significantly since the 1990s (Fig. 2).

The education level of women entrepreneurs in Estonia is very high. It is higher than the education level of men entrepreneurs. Both figures are higher than the respective EU-28 averages. The rate of Estonian women remarkably exceeds the average of the EU-28 and is the highest in the EU (Table 1).

Moreover, women who decide to become entrepreneurs earn more and work fewer hours per week than their male counterparts in Estonia (Rozeik 2014).

Table 1 Education level in Estonia, 2012

	Women (%)	Men (%)
Tertiary educational attainment for the age group 15–64, Estonia	41	25
Tertiary educational attainment for the age group 15–64, EU-28 average	26.8	23.7

Source: Rozeik (2014)

According to EU data in 2012, women entrepreneurs in Estonia worked on average fewer hours than men entrepreneurs (35 and 40 h respectively) (European Commission 2014a, b). Despite a high education level, Estonian women are concentrated in certain sectors such as education, wholesale and retail trade, health care and social work, public administration, and accommodation and food services (Fig. 3). Moreover, the "glass ceiling" in Estonia results from the fact that women are underrepresented in managerial positions. A study on gender pay gaps indicates that men predominate among managers in general, making up two-thirds of their ranks (Anspal et al. 2010).

The *Gender equality monitor* conducted by the Ministry of Social Affairs in 2016 reports that in most Estonian families, women are responsible for household chores (laundry, cooking, washing dishes, helping children with their homework, communication with the kindergarten/school and teachers, and, in approximately half the families, house cleaning). Compared to earlier results (2009–2016) the distribution of household chores between men and women has remained widely unchanged (Vainu 2016). According to the Eurobarometer Survey on Gender Equality (European Commission 2017), 70% of Estonians think that the most important role of a woman is to take care of the home and family. This might explain the fact that women entrepreneurs work fewer hours: they have to balance their work and family responsibilities.

There is inconsistent information about the net income level of women and men entrepreneurs and their contribution to the economy. GEM Report 2012 results indicate that men earned greater profit from entrepreneurship than women, and only a fifth of those whose monthly net income was over 1500 euros were women (Rozeik 2014). At the same time, the Eurostat data for 2012 indicate that the mean net income of women entrepreneurs (8688 euros) is higher than that of men entrepreneurs (8118 euros) in Estonia (European Commission 2014b). Considering that the gender pay gap here is the largest in Europe, these figures are surprising (Karu 2014). It can be argued that women are able to make use of their skills in a more productive way as entrepreneurs compared to being employed somewhere else.

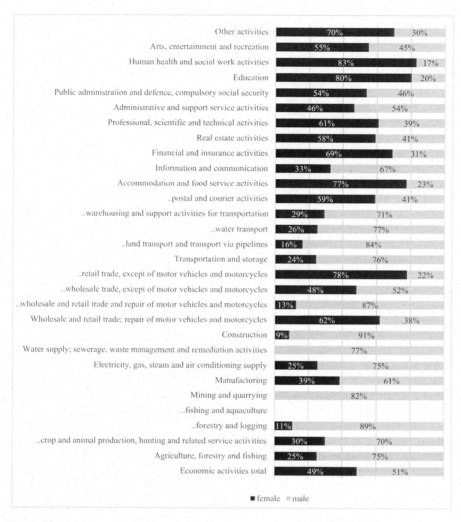

Fig. 3 Employed persons by sector of the economy, 2016. Source: Statistics Estonia

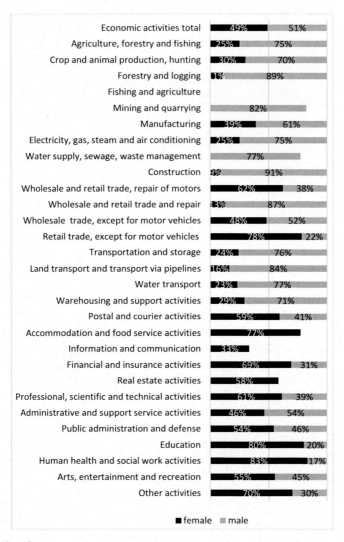

Fig. 3 (continued)

4 Methodology

4.1 Research Approach and Sample

The results of this study empirically draw on 20 in-depth interviews with female entrepreneurs, and two interviews with experts in Estonia. These were performed from October 2016 to June 2017. All female participants were entrepreneurs at the time of the interview, except one who was no longer at her company. All participants lived and operated their businesses in Estonia. The first contacts had received assistance from the Estonian Chamber of Commerce, Estonian trade associations, and personal networks, and furthermore had received recommendations from already-interviewed women entrepreneurs. It was important to have entrepreneurs from different areas, with different backgrounds and different demographics. Altogether more than 50 female entrepreneurs were contacted and asked to participate in the research. At the beginning, the willingness to participate was slow, although later more and more female entrepreneurs expressed a willingness to be part of the research. Once the responses became repetitive, the researcher felt an acceptable saturation had been achieved to perform effective data analyses.

The largest number of respondents came from the Estonian capital Tallinn (15 of 20 respondents), although an effort was made to interview female entrepreneurs from other regions of Estonia. Tallinn is economically the most active, with almost half of all Estonians living there. Several respondents that operate their businesses in Tallinn and live there were born in other parts of Estonia and moved to the capital for economic reasons.

The participants ranged from 26 to 55 years of age. During the study, eight respondents had no children, three had adult children who no longer lived at home, and eight had children who were younger than 18 and lived in the same household. All businesses were at least 2 years old, and the oldest business was 16 years old. In the latter case, the respondent had become a shareholder 8 years ago after working in the company for several years, i.e. she was not considered a company founder. The oldest business founded by a respondent was 14 years old. One of the interviewed women has meanwhile exited the business, although she has in fact been an entrepreneur for 8 years and is now actively seeking new business opportunities. Three of the respondents owned more than one company. The companies operated both locally and internationally, and many had international staff members. The companies ranged in size from 2 to 40 employees. For all respondents, their businesses were the main source of income. Three women were from very masculine sectors—one was from the construction sector, and two others were from the timber and logistics industry, although the latter two were in the field of developing software solutions (Table 2).

Two experts on gender equality and female entrepreneurship were additionally interviewed. One was the head of the board of the Estonian Women's Studies and Resource Centre. She has been working in the center since its foundation, receiving the *Woman of the Year* honor in 2016 for her efforts in promoting gender equality in Estonia. The other was the president of the Estonian Association of Professional and Business Women. These experts were interviewed only after the entrepreneurs' interviews were completed; here, the researcher did not want to be influenced by expert opinion during the interview process.

The interview process was guided by a set of open-ended questions that had been developed beforehand encompassing the following issues: gender stereotypes and their influence on women entrepreneurs in Estonia; the reasons and motivation for the respondents to become entrepreneurs; and the background and previous experiences of respondents.

Table 2 The interviewed female entrepreneurs and their businesses

		Industry	Employees	Scope	Location	Age	Education	Relationship	Children	No. of companies
1	AA	Software for learning languages	40	International	Tallinn	27	Bachelor	Partner	1	2
2	BB	Business consulting	7	Local	Tallinn	34	Bachelor	Partner	–	1
3	CC	Natural cosmetics	6	International	Kose	34	Bachelor	Partner	1	1
4	DD	Software solutions for start-ups and investors	28	International	Tallinn	42	Master	Married	2	1
5	EE	Sustainable fashion		Local	Tallinn	41	PhD	Partner	2	
6	FF	Medical software solutions	7	International	Vismaa	52	PhD	Married	2 adults	2
7	GG	NGO	2	Local	Tallinn	26	Master	Partner	–	1
8	HH	Business consulting	4	Local	Tallinn	38	Bachelor	Married	2	2
9	II	Music production	7	International	Tallinn	24	Bachelor	Partner	–	2
10	JJ	Heavy machinery rental	2	Local	Tallinn	34	–	Partner	2	1
11	KK	Digital design	7	International	Tallinn	30	Bachelor	Partner	–	
12	LL	Beauty salon		International	Tallinn	31	Bachelor	Partner	–	
13	MM	Business consulting	1	Local	Haapsalu	36	Master	Partner	–	1
14	NN	Construction		International	Saaremaa	46	Bachelor	Divorced	2 adults	1
15	OO	Logistics software development	12	International	Tallinn	30	Bachelor	Partner	–	1
16	PP	Software development for timber industry	9	International	Tallinn	35	Master	Married	2	1
17	QQ	Digital design	3	International	Tallinn	29	Bachelor	Partnership	–	1
18	RR	Sales of kids' clothes	2	International	Tallinn	40	High school	Divorced	1 (12 years)	2
19	SS	Financial consulting	11	Local	Narva	55	Bachelor	Partnership	3 adults	1
20	TT	Online shop for spices and exotic foods	10	International	Tartu	37	Master	Married	2 (12, 4)	1

Source: Empirical study

4.2 Data Analysis

The in-depth interviews were conducted in person by the author. According to Wakkee et al. (2007), face-to-face interviews are one of the most effective qualitative methods. The general level of English proficiency is quite high in Estonia, so most interviews were performed in English, as this language was spoken by both the respondents and the researcher. It also made the transcription process easier. Only one respondent was not confident enough with her English language skills, so she brought an interpreter with her.

The interview process was done in accordance with the previously developed interview guide. The interviews were recorded with the permission of the interviewees. The interviews were then manually transcribed (the automatic transcription software was not able to recognize non-native English speakers).

Analyzing interview data is a multistep "sense-making" endeavor. To make sense of interviews, researchers must engage in data coding (DeCuir-Gunby et al. 2011). Codes are defined as "tags or labels for assigning units of meaning to the descriptive or inferential information compiled during a study" (Miles and Huberman 1994, p. 56). Data-driven codes were developed though repeated examination of raw data. As a result of the inductive analysis of the interviews, data codes were developed into topics, and crucial issues were defined (Table 3).

A within-case to cross-case analysis strategy was used to examine the interviews. (Eisenhardt 1989) points out that within-case analysis helps to build familiarity with the data, while the search for cross-case patterns forces the investigators to go beyond initial impressions. The initial issues emerged during the interview process, with some issues being repeated during the interviews and discussions with the experts. By its nature, qualitative data can be chaotic and messy. The analysis of the data has to be methodical and systematic if we want to extract value out of it (Miles and Huberman 1994). The considerable amount of interview data led to the adoption of a rigorous structure of analysis facilitated by the NVivo software. Data was also fed back to respondents for comments and clarification. The strategies to ensure credibility, transferability, dependability, and confirmability of the data analyses are listed in Table 4.

5 Research Findings

Our data analyses confirmed that there are gender stereotypes in Estonia that influence the everyday experiences of women in general, and have an impact on female entrepreneurship rates in Estonia. As the owner of the beauty salon described the situation, "We have a lot of gender stereotypes in Estonia. Men are used to these stereotypes. 'We have so many beautiful girls here, let them stay at home, raise the kids while the men bring in the money'" (LL).

Table 3 Coding scheme

Codes	Examples of coding
Identifying gender stereotypes	
Manifestation of gender stereotypes	"It comes from childhood and from the very early beginnings that it's like if you are a woman you are raised a bit differently and you are expected to act differently. You don't have high expectations businesswise, the whole society is for some reason like that" (JJ). "I think these are stereotypes. Estonian men are, well, if you know our history, it's a patriarchal world. I know men and women are also different" (NN).
The origins of gender stereotypes	"In Soviet times it was more equal. Things changed during independence, and that's how my grandmother raised me. In the spirit like, if Estonia gets free then you don't have to work a day in your life because your husband will support you. She lived before the Second World War and that was the lifestyle. And she came from that era and for her it was a big insult that she was forced to work. Because she thought if a woman has children her job is to be a housewife. And that was the attitude she was raised with before the Second World War. And during the 1990s that was exactly what happened because men started businesses and it was very risky. Lots of people got killed, there was the mafia and business somehow got this connotation or bad publicity that it was very dangerous. Business as such was often illegal. Lots of women felt that they maybe didn't want these "dirty" things. That business is something dirty, something bad. That it's illegal. And if I want to have kids I want them to have a mother. So I kept away from that" (MM).
Influence of school	"I was a very good student, always studying well and everything. But the boys were making a mess, and everybody was laughing at them. They were cool guys. The teachers were not even trying that hard with them, but the girls had to be patient and everything had to be good" (TT).
Changes in the new generation	"There are some girls who want to come work with me, and they are like 'Oh, I don't care about the money! I just want to do the beauty treatments that I like. I have a husband/boyfriend at home who will pay for everything for me!'" (Interviewer): "Really?" "Yes. 'Oh, I can only work on these certain days, he doesn't like me working on the weekends, or at night', so they demand different schedules. But maybe this is the same in other countries as well" (LL).
Sectors	"When I went to this big international logistics conference there were thousands of men and only ten women—waitresses and me. But I came back with amazing deals because they all wanted to listen to me because I was a girl. Everybody wanted to speak to me, to see me, I was like a monkey in a zoo" (OO).
Mass media	"I sometimes give interviews and I also feel that it's very stereotypical of these journalists. How they picture this lady. Sometimes I find it very tiring. I think it's about the media a lot as well, how they picture women" (PP).

(continued)

Table 3 (continued)

Codes	Examples of coding
Attitude of men towards female entrepreneurs	"This is the problem with Estonian men. If entrepreneurs are women we don't feel that we can be women with the guys we are with. We have to make too many decisions. We have to carry this responsibility thing too high. And this is something that has to do with stereotypes" (HH).
Family life	"I've had quite a few discussions with my friends who are entrepreneurs or leaders in big companies. All of them are struggling with the fact they don't feel like a female in their relationship, and that is very sad" (SS).
Human capital	
Education	"I've studied all kinds of things. Like design-related things, design-related programs, because I found them interesting. I think education matters" (HH).
Previous experience	"I started the company about 6 or 7 years ago. Before that, I was a makeup artist, and I wanted to learn about beauty stuff because I liked working in that field. Over time, I figured out how the eyebrow area works. And then I figured why don't I teach other people about this stuff! Because I already knew quite a lot. I always liked to learn more, because I cannot know everything, and I am constantly learning" (LL).
Role models	"My dad owns a big transportation/logistics company and warehouses, and because of that I've been in this transportation business all my life like from when I was 3 years old. I worked for 9 years with my dad in logistics, I was the specialist in the field" (OO).
Motivations	
Independence and control	"Well, the reason why I was with Waterhouse Coopers for such a short time is that I simply felt irrelevant. And the fact that I was there felt like I was just a cog in a big wheel and that particular position, which was beginner level auditing, and me being there I didn't understand why this wasn't automated, why it had to be a person. It seemed like a complete waste of time. Plus having to log your time every 6 minutes or something like the exact point, and then having time in your day for like 20 minutes to read a newspaper. It seemed absolutely ridiculous, why does it matter" (AA).
Balance between work and family	"When you have kids, it's all about your flexibility. If you have the responsibility you'll do that, but you need the flexibility" (PP).
Financial gain	"I don't see myself working in a bank somewhere. To be honest, I can do what I like and make even more money by being an entrepreneur than sitting in a high position at a bank" (LL).
Other motivational factors	"I also feel [stereotypes]. I don't think I've come across this myself in my work since I think I feel I've managed to make my own rules" (QQ).

Source: Own table

Table 4 Strategies to ensure credibility, transferability, dependability and confirmability

Quality criterion	Provisions made by researcher
Credibility	Adoption of appropriate, well recognized research methods Development of familiarity with culture of participants' environment(s) Random sampling of individuals serving as informants Triangulation via use of different types of informants Tactics to help ensure honesty from informants Iterative questioning in data collection dialogues Peer scrutiny of project Use of "reflective commentary" Member checks of data collected, and interpretations/theories formed. "Thick" description of phenomenon under scrutiny Examination of previous research to frame findings
Transferability	Provision of background data to establish context of study and detailed description of phenomenon in question to allow comparisons to be made
Dependability	Employment of overlapping methods In-depth methodological description to allow study to be repeated
Confirmability	Triangulation to reduce effect of investigator bias Recognition of shortcomings in study's methods and their potential effects In-depth methodological description to allow integrity of research results to be scrutinized

Source: Adapted from Shenton (2004)

Although the reasons for gender stereotypes among Estonians are still not clear, several respondents suggested that these stereotypes originate from Estonia's early days of independence (1918–1940) or even earlier times when Estonian society was very patriarchal, with men and women having strict gender roles. Men were "breadwinners" while women stayed at home and cared for the family and children. Memories of a free Estonia were cherished during Soviet times, and nostalgia for previous independence was strong. The second independence brought denial of Soviet values, including gender equality. After independence was regained, Estonians had to build a new value system, and they turned to the values that were in their treasured memories without realizing that some of them had in the meantime become outdated and were no longer beneficial. "Estonia is a very masculine culture compared to the rest of Europe. Estonia was very masculine for a really long time even before the Soviet occupation. So maybe these stereotypes come from there because men were really honored and valued during the Soviet occupation, and later even more. Good men were killed or taken to Siberia so guys who stayed here were mostly drunks, but the culture of worshiping men remained. As there were very few men, the standards for good men dropped. That is one of the main reasons we have high rates of domestic violence here in Estonia" (MM).

Gender stereotypes influence the kinds of ventures men and women entrepreneurs start as well as the industries they choose. For example, as women are associated more with caregiving, women entrepreneurs are more likely to have businesses in the education, service, or retail sectors. This in turn reinforces the stereotypical image of men and women, resulting in double-entry barriers for many sectors—gender stereotypes, no networks and no knowledge transfer due to sector segregation. DD had been an entrepreneur for 4 years. She also was in managerial positions for more than 8 years. She acknowledges that many industries including financial and start-up sectors are male-dominated, and that the situation there is not changing quickly enough. "On the management level—nothing is changing. The deals you sign... I have not signed any contracts so far, the other counterpart being a lady, I don't remember. I have been in finances for many years—male, male, male. I have been in the start-up business now for 4 years—none. Male, male, male, male" (DD).

QQ is an owner of a design agency she founded together with her friends after graduation from her university. She had no entrepreneurial experience, but because of her personality and gender she believed she would not be able to succeed in an employed position in the fields she was interested in. "I felt it [stereotypes]. I guess that might be also one of the maybe subconscious reasons for becoming an entrepreneur because I feel for me it's very important that I'm not dependent on anyone else. So create my own job and I can choose how and who to work with because I feel especially in, like, traditionally men-ruled areas, for instance architecture or so that I think it is very difficult for female staff to get the same treatment" (QQ).

Estonian school curriculums in general do not have gender-specific programs. Programs are instead developed to promote gender equality. Nevertheless, the data analyses show that the school system in Estonia reflects the social constructs of society in general and encourages development of gendered roles and expectations. "It starts from school and of course there are still these gender stereotypes from school that girls have to be the ones who are polite with good grades who are quiet, not making a mess. That's a good student, and if the girl doesn't do that then you are a troublemaker and you're a bad girl. You shouldn't be loudly expressing your opinions or saying stuff against the teacher, or kind of challenging the teacher's authority. I'm not in our schools anymore, but that's how I remember things" (SS).

Media plays a significant role in the creation and development of socially accepted gendered roles and role models. The data analyses reveal that mass media in Estonia cultivates traditional gender roles prevailing in society. The owners and editors of women's magazines consider their readers as not being interested in women leaders and entrepreneurs, and as a result do not report on them in the mass media. This in turn stifles positive role models for society that would otherwise promote female entrepreneurship. "I was a journalist in a glossy magazine for women for three and a half years, and I wrote mostly about those feminine topics. I wanted to write about leadership and entrepreneurs, but the editors said we have so few female leaders in Estonia that there is no market. And it will not sell, there will be no market. The editors said there are no readers, so we cannot write about these topics. They said the Estonian reader is very conservative" (MM).

Gender expectations place a double burden on those women with professional or business aspirations. The general perception is that despite their professional responsibilities and achievements, women are still expected to take care of the family, home, and children. The data analyses show that although women are not satisfied with the situation, they do not feel able to change it. As a well-known female entrepreneur, the creator of a virtual meeting place for start-up companies and investors complained,

"It's tough! Even though when I go home, I have a wonderful husband, I still do the laundry, I take care of some of the household things. He's good with the kids, he does the homework and all this kind of stuff and takes care of them when I'm traveling a lot, but nevertheless sometimes I feel like it doesn't matter how much I contribute financially or whatever. Professionally, I'm still a mother and a wife" (DD).

According to GEM data, the status of entrepreneurship is high in Estonia, and entrepreneurship is even considered a good career choice. MM, a business consultant and coach for women entrepreneurs conducted informal research. Over the period of several years she talked to men about female entrepreneurship. When asked, many men would not object to their wives and partners becoming entrepreneurs, and even welcomed the idea of women entering entrepreneurship. "I've done some informal research. I mostly talked to men. I haven't seen a man who would say it's a bad idea, or women should stay at home in the kitchen, or they aren't able to run a company. I was surprised. I've met men who said that women are not interested in entrepreneurship. Like 'I have a wife and she is so shy she would never do that. Although I would appreciate it if she went out and got some more money. But she's not interested so I'll pay all the bills and I'll support her'" (MM).

This is contradictory. Although men say they are supportive of the idea that their partners and wives become entrepreneurs, at the same time, men still expect women to care for the family and children. Even more, the analyses of the data demonstrate that Estonian society expects women bosses to stay feminine and gentle even when they occupy top management positions. They are expected to not express their opinion, get "bossy," or be too loud. "The other thing is the stereotypes about entrepreneurs especially in this region, is that when you're a female entrepreneur or a female boss, you're a bitch. It's the way they look and the way they do photoshoots, and the way they wear their makeup, and this kind of stuff. And then we have these very humble stories all around the world where people do not even notice the lady who has a big fortune or has built a monopoly and is also a really nice person. In this region, there's this stereotype—If you're a female entrepreneur, you're a bitch" (DD).

Because entrepreneurs are perceived as having predominantly masculine characteristics, those who want to succeed had to learn to be more like their male colleagues. The analyses of the data show that female entrepreneurs deliberately learned more masculine behavior. Several respondents told us that they learned how to talk with men in a way that gets them heard and taken into account. It is still not clear if they learned to talk and behave in a more masculine way in response to society's perceptions, or simply because men do not consider women to be equally qualified.

NN: "I was the only woman in the company. Men act and talk differently. I read a lot of psychology books about how men talk and about companies. I learned how to communicate with men, I didn't expect men to learn that. I had to make sure these guys listened to me. You have to pick your sentences very correctly—I think so, I guess so. Men don't want women in their work places to act like their moms and wives at home."

Interviewer: "Did men listen to you before you read these books?"

NN: "It was like I was talking but nobody really listened. Like some birds sing very nice, but I understood that this was not the problem about my opinions or my experiences. I had a lot of experience, but you have to act like a man if you want to be in business on a high level. Men do not want women at their work places telling them what to do or nagging them."

Interviewer: "Did the situation change after you read these books?"

NN: "Yes. 100%. In a day. I could feel it. 'What did you say? Do you think so? Really?' It was quite nice."

In a gendered society, masculinity is associated with rationality and limited emotions. Because female entrepreneurs perceive entrepreneurship as masculine territory, they think there is no place for emotions and sympathy. Nor do they perceive emotions as something natural that both sexes have. Instead they disapprove of their feelings at work and consider them inappropriate.

BB: "You have the responsibility for the people that you've hired here. You're lured in here with promises of a good job and a good environment, and if you can't deliver then that is really something that keeps you up at night. I think that we have been kind of lucky too, not having really hard times businesswise. I think relationships with others are the most heartbreaking sometimes, maybe that is a female quality."

Interviewer: "Heartbreaking?"

BB: "Meaning like it's really hard when somebody leaves. Or when there are some struggles in the team or they don't get along or something like this. It really affects a lot, maybe that is where women are more empathetic or feel for people more than men do, or I don't know. I think that we have, or I have postponed some firings because of these personal feelings, not making the right decisions as a CEO. It's hard to make these kinds of decisions."

There has been only a slight increase in female entrepreneurship rates during the last 2 years (1–2%). Non-governmental organizations have also started to voice their concerns about this. It could be expected that gender stereotypes in Estonia would decrease with further development of the country and its globalization. Nevertheless, data analyses show that there is a long way to go to change the social constructs of the female entrepreneurship environment in Estonia. Several respondents expressed their concern that there is in fact little change. "I think that gender roles are deep inside us. What I see now is kind of a new generation of female entrepreneurs coming, but their businesses are more like arts and crafts. More like creative business or like fashion or cosmetics or something like that. I see another generation coming, but they are all kind of in feminine sectors. There are some examples in start-ups like technology start-ups as well, but still very few. So I think that there is still some fear of becoming an entrepreneur" (TT).

6 The Influence of Human Capital on the Decision to Enter Entrepreneurship

6.1 Education

The goal of this research was to explore individual characteristics of the interviewed Estonian female entrepreneurs. Here it was important to understand what the unique characteristics of female entrepreneurs are that make them stand out and become entrepreneurs in the highly gendered Estonian society. From an individual's perspective, constituting factors of entrepreneurship are demographic characteristics such as age, gender, and individual human capital. Human capital consists of factors such as education (professional training as well), work experiences, and previous management experiences. Educational and family background influence women's motivation and career development, and education is one of the values that has traditionally been highly valued in Estonian society. Even more, Estonian women in general have higher educational standards than men. As the owner of a cosmetics company proclaimed, "Estonian universities are full of women!" (CC)

It is interesting to note that this entrepreneur studied office management at university and never worked in the field. Another respondent, the owner of a finance consulting company commented, "I didn't even consider not having a university degree. All my family members and friends have one. It's just something you do!"

All respondents except one have at least a bachelor's degree, five have master's degrees, and two have a PhD. All of the respondents considered university education a necessary prerequisite for success in life in general. The respondent who owns a design agency (KK) admitted that even though she did not learn much at university because her field is progressing more quickly than university programs can keep up with, she still holds a university degree.

Taking into account the gendered context of female entrepreneurs in Estonia, acquiring university education provides potential and already-existing entrepreneurs with a higher sense of self-esteem which is necessary for the establishment and management of a business. Most respondents argued that entrepreneurs need education and continuous development for their businesses to be successful.

It can be argued that in a society where education is valued and where gender stereotypes are strong, acquiring education serves as a factor that increases their self-efficacy and the chance for women to enter entrepreneurship.

6.2 The Influence of Previous Work Experience on the Decision to Enter Entrepreneurship

Fourteen out of 20 respondents established their businesses in the same field they had previously worked in. It can be argued that the previous experiences, networks, and knowledge were of crucial importance for the decision to become an entrepreneur. As the creator of a meeting place for investors and new business venture explained, "No, it wasn't scary. I knew everything. I'd been working with entrepreneurs, I knew what it means" (DD).

The shareholder and founder of the company that produces software solutions for timber measurement became a shareholder in a different sector, although she did in fact use the same set of skills she had previously acquired. She is responsible for everyday management and sales in the company. "In the beginning I was really afraid. I wanted to leave every day. But then I realized that I had done this before" (PP).

Although the studies ascertain the fact the previous knowledge plays a significant role, the higher percentage of respondents who founded their businesses in the same field they worked in before implies that Estonian female entrepreneurs try to acquire higher efficacy levels prior to their entrepreneurial attempts. Only one respondent (the owner of the cosmetics company (CC)) started to operate in a completely new field. She was a single mom who wanted to come up with an idea that would support her and her child.

Three respondents established their companies directly after attending university, having acquired some necessary knowledge and experience during their university years. They participated in the foundation of student businesses or had started to offer their services to customers before graduating. For one of them (the owner of a design agency), it was difficult to find a job, so she and a friend decided to start a company of their own. "We felt we would give it to try. There was nothing to lose" (KK). For the other two, it was a deliberate decision to start their own companies.

6.3 The Influence of Role Models Inside the Family on the Decision to Enter Entrepreneurship

One or both parents of 6 out of 20 respondents were also entrepreneurs. Business owners have the opportunity to share their wisdom and practical knowledge with learners. The founder of a start-up that develops logistics software solutions said during the interview, "My dad owns a big transportation/logistics company and warehouses, and because of that I have been in this transportation business all my life since I was 3. I worked for 9 years with my dad. I am a specialist in the field" (OO).

The owner of a business consulting company concluded, "My stepdad was an entrepreneur; he has been an entrepreneur since the beginning when he was allowed to become an entrepreneur, like in the 1990s. I think it influenced me. Entrepreneurs weren't from an unknown planet any more. And my mom was a housewife and I didn't want to be that" (BB).

It can be argued that female entrepreneurs in Estonia that decide to enter entrepreneurship and establish business ventures have acquired higher human capital and thus in turn increased their self-efficacy. Gender stereotypes act as a barrier to entrepreneurship, leading to women being less likely to pursue tasks not associated with their gender.

6.4 Motivations to Become Entrepreneurs

In this section, we examine motivations that contributed to the women's decision to become self-employed in Estonia. Data analysis revealed that respondents were motivated to start their own venture by a range of positive and, for some, negative drivers. All 20 women had experienced a positive "pull" towards entrepreneurship. For some, this arose from factors which included a desire for greater independence and control over their lives, challenges in their professional lives, and the wish for greater personal fulfilment.

6.4.1 Independence and Control as Motivational Factors to Start an Own Business

The data analyses revealed that independence and control were the highest, very strong motivational factors for all respondents. All interviewed female entrepreneurs mentioned independence as their first motivator. The owner of a design company said, "I myself have not wanted to play according to the rules. For me it's very important that I'm not dependent on anyone else. So I created my own job and I can choose how and whom to work with" (QQ).

The owner of a music production company said, "Most of all, I like the freedom that I can plan my own time. And nobody can tell me when to take a vacation. When I feel that it's been enough, that I cannot work anymore, then I take a vacation" (II).

The desire to take control over decision making was important for 17 of the 20 women who exhibited the drive and ambition to be self-employed. The co-owner of a consulting company said, "The feeling like it's my choice is important I think. And in this company I think that what I have, why I've stayed so long is because I can really control my time, I can take off a month for vacation whenever basically, or just dedicating time to things and being flexible" (BB).

The owner of a business consulting company for female entrepreneurs said, "You can choose your own time. You can always set higher goals for yourself, and earn more money. You're able to create something" (MM).

6.4.2 Balance Between Work and Family

Eighteen respondents were motivated by the desire for greater flexibility over their professional and personal lives, allowing them more time with their children and the ability to manage their time and workload more effectively. The owner of a heavy machinery rental platform said, "The flexibility is very important when you have kids" (JJ).

The owner of a cosmetic products company added, "I think that it's a privilege when my child is sick at home and I can do both things at once" (CC).

The owner of a timber measurement solution said, "When you have kids, it's all about your flexibility. If you have the responsibility you'll do that. But you need the flexibility" (PP).

Also of note is that the respondents that did not currently have children stressed that a work-life balance is important to them. The respondent from the logistics solution company commented, "I am CLO of this company, but I can arrange my time for my family. I can travel. Some women entrepreneurs take their kids and go to the conferences and it's no problem" (OO).

6.4.3 Financial Gain

Most entrepreneurs enter entrepreneurship because of the potential to make a living as well as with the hope to ensure a comfortable lifestyle. All 20 respondents stated that it was important for them to earn enough money to support themselves and the family while pursuing other business and development goals. At the same time all of them asserted that this is not their main motivation, and in some cases they could in fact earn more being employed somewhere else. The owner of a kids' retail shop commented, "Of course, money is important. This is how I support my kid and myself. But money isn't everything, I could earn more if I worked in a bank" (RR).

The previous owner of a construction company told us, "Yes, with the money I earned we could travel—me and my kids. We could go to music festivals and do sports. Yes, money is important. But it's not everything" (NN). (This entrepreneur is able to enjoy a comfortable lifestyle now that she has exited her business).

6.5 Other Motivational Factors

All respondents mentioned additional motivational factors that are important for them: that they can create their own rules; they can do something they are passionate about; they can make a difference; and can grow personally and professionally.

Although there is not much research on these phenomena, it is clear that entrepreneurs are motivated by the kinds of firms they could build and that they would ideally want to work in. The popular media is full of stories of the unique organizational structures, perks, and incentives that entrepreneurs create for their new ventures to attract and keep employees. "I also feel [stereotypes]. I don't think I've come across this myself in my work since I think I've managed to make my own rules" (QQ).

The creator and owner of an online language learning platform commented on what her future aspirations were before she became an entrepreneur: "After graduating from the university, I wasn't sure what to do. But whatever I did next, I wanted to do it with interesting people, people who are smarter than me, that I had a lot to learn from. And also, I wanted to have a nice office. I don't want to work in a windowless box" (AA).

The courage to take risks usually comes from having faith in something. In turn, faith usually arises when someone has a passion for something. A company's success is directly proportional to hard work and the owner's perseverance. It is however the passion of the owner that pushes them to work hard. Passion is an important motivating factor that drives people towards entrepreneurship.

Eighteen out of 20 respondents stressed that they can do what they really love and the way they think is the right way to do it. They don't have to follow anybody's directions. The owner of a beauty treatment company revealed how "It can be very lame, but my work is almost like my hobby. I even had a beauty blog, and I tested a lot of beauty products and talked about them" (EE).

The co-owner of a heavy machinery rental company explained, "Yes, it took a lot of courage and encouragement from my partner to take this opportunity and I am very glad I did . . ... I would never want to be an employee again" (JJ).

Previous research on female entrepreneurship has argued that women are more likely to start businesses with both social and economic goals (Meyskens et al. 2011). It can be argued that women in general are more concerned about the well-being of society and the future of coming generations. Three respondents mentioned making a difference as a motivational factor for being entrepreneurs. The owner of an event planning agency explained how "I want to leave the world a better place for my children. Most women are entrepreneurs because they want to do something. They want to make some change. They are ready to take some responsibility, and entrepreneurship is all about responsibility" (HH).

The owner of a consulting company complained about her time in public administration. "I felt like I can't really make a difference, I felt like it was waste of time and resources for everybody, so I left public administration" (BB).

When entrepreneurs run their own business, they obtain a better understanding of their personalities and capabilities. The adversity they face on a daily basis helps them become more aware of themselves and also helps them grow. The motivational factor of growing and developing as a person was mentioned by two respondents. One of the developers and owners of a medical solution development platform expressed her opinion, "For ever and ever I'm gonna be an entrepreneur. The more and more I am in, the more I get excited about how I can grow as an entrepreneur. That is super important for me—to grow as a person" (FF).

It can be argued that the motivational factors for female entrepreneurs in Estonia are similar to other entrepreneurs—independence and control, financial gain, and flexibility that can provide a successful family-work balance.

7 Conclusions and Implications for Further Research

This study identified the gender stereotypes in Estonian society that influence women's intentions to pursue entrepreneurship, something generally perceived as a masculine domain. These stereotypes limit the possibility for women entrepreneurs to start businesses in certain sectors. Gender stereotypes are therefore one of the factors that can explain low female entrepreneurship rates in Estonia.

This study also found that although the motivational factors for Estonian female entrepreneurs are similar to the motivational factors of female entrepreneurs in other countries, Estonian female entrepreneurs tend to bring greater amounts of entry prerequisites such as human capital into their businesses with them. Accordingly, it can be argued that the low number of women entrepreneurs in Estonia is not due to a lack of education or skills. Female entrepreneurial progression in Estonia is generally *not* hindered by the person's limited capability, but by artificially created obstacles for women as a whole. Women here are typically required to overcome social and cultural barriers to achieve their full potential.

The general aims of the Estonian economic policy for 2014–2020 include embedding an enterprising attitude into society, increasing productivity of enterprises, and encouraging innovation. Female entrepreneurship is not on this agenda. Nevertheless, the main focus is on the areas and enterprises with high growth potential. Vast theoretical and empirical work concludes that women are of crucial importance to the process of introducing innovations into markets. They create employment (including self-employment) that contributes to overall wealth creation in all economies (Brush 2006). Women entrepreneurs create jobs and innovation, and contribute to economies just like their male counterparts. Second and more compelling are the contributions women entrepreneurs make to society. There is growing evidence that women are more likely to reinvest their profits in education, their family, and community (Brush 2017).

The results of this study point out a greater problem emerging not only in Estonia but in other Eastern European countries that regained their independence in the 1990s as well. These governments tend to overemphasize rapid economic development, often neglecting long-term sustainable development for the entire society and economy in general. This in turn can slow down the economic development and advancement of specific social groups.

Further research on gender stereotypes and women entrepreneurship in transition economies will be necessary. Its focus should be on informal rules interplaying alongside and in conjunction with formal institutions, shaping their actors and outcomes. Along with achieving a deeper understanding of other factors that cause low women entrepreneurship and low entrepreneurship rates in general, this also has the potential to promote the development of national policies that support female entrepreneurship. Analyses of already-existing practices and policies for female entrepreneurship would be beneficial as well.

This research can be used for academics, professionals, researchers, and policymakers working in the fields of small business and entrepreneurship. This data can furthermore be used to develop evidence-based policy and actions that would increase the amount of women participating in entrepreneurship in Estonia.

References

Ahl, H. (2006). Why research on women entrepreneurs needs new directions. *Entrepreneurship: Theory and Practice, 30*(5):595–621. https://doi.org/10.1111/j.1540-6520.2006.00138.x

Aidis, R. (2017). Do institutions matter for entrepreneurial development? *IZA World of Labor*.

Aidis, R., Welter, F., Smallbone, D., & Isakova, N. (2007). Female entrepreneurship in transition economies: The case of Lithuania and Ukraine. *Feminist Economics, 13*(2), 157–183. https://doi.org/10.1080/13545700601184831

Anspal, S., Krat, L., & Tairi, R. (2010). *Sooline palgalõhe Eestis. Gender pay gap analyses*. Retrieved from https://www.sm.ee/sites/default/files/content-editors/Ministeerium_kontaktid/Uuringu_ja_analuusid/Sotsiaalvaldkond/2_raport.pdf

Bandura, A., Barbaranelli, C., Caprara, G. V., & Pastorelli, C. (2001). Self-efficacy beliefs as shapers of children's aspirations and career trajectories. *Child Development, 72*(1), 187–206. Retrieved from https://pdfs.semanticscholar.org/0dc4/ffd8d9d62a08d11b4457170a087e4d6157f0.pdf

Betz, N. E., & Hackett, G. (1981). The relationship of career-related self-efficacy expectations to perceived career options in college women and men. *Journal of Counseling Psychology, 28*(5), 399–410. Retrieved from https://www.researchgate.net/profile/Gail_Hackett/publication/232490806_The_relationship_of_career-related_self-efficacy_expectation_to_perceived_career_options_in_college_women_and_men/links/558c5ac808ae591c19d9fd84/The-relationship-of-career-related-self-efficacy-expectation-to-perceived-career-options-in-college-women-and-men.pdf

Bruni, A., Gherardi, S., & Poggio, B. (2004). Doing gender, doing entrepreneurship: An ethnographic account of intertwined practices. *Gender, Work and Organization, 11*(4), 406–429. https://doi.org/10.1111/j.1468-0432.2004.00240.x

Brush, C. G. (2006). *Growth-oriented women entrepreneurs and their businesses: A global research perspective*. London: Edward Elgar.

Brush, C. G. (2017). *How women entrepreneurs are transforming economies and communities*. Retrieved March 30, 2017, from https://www.forbes.com/sites/laurelmoglen/2017/03/29/matthew-rodriguez-makes-the-tough-job-of-teaching-writing-easier/#17a050fb7ad6

Butler, J. (1990). *Gender trouble : Feminism and the subversion of identity*. New York: Routledge. Retrieved from https://books.google.lv/books/about/Gender_Trouble.html?id=2S0xAAAAQBAJ&redir_esc=y

Cejka, M. A., & Eagly, A. H. (1999). Gender-stereotypic images of occupations correspond to the sex segregation of employment. *Personality and Social Psychology Bulletin, 25*(4), 413–423. https://doi.org/10.1177/0146167299025004002

Cohen, P. N., & Huffman, M. L. (2003). Individuals, jobs, and labor markets: The devaluation of women's work. *American Sociological Review, 68*(3), 443. https://doi.org/10.2307/1519732

Davidsson, P., & Honig, B. (2003). The role of social and human capital among nascent entrepreneurs. *Journal of Business Venturing, 18*(3), 301–331. https://doi.org/10.1016/S0883-9026(02)00097-6

DeCuir-Gunby, J. T., Marshall, P. L., & McCulloch, A. W. (2011). Developing and using a codebook for the analysis of interview data: An example from a professional development research project. *Field Methods, 23*(2), 136–155. https://doi.org/10.1177/1525822X10388468

DeMartino, R., Barbato, R., & Jacques, P. H. (2006). Exploring the career/achievement and personal life orientation differences between entrepreneurs and nonentrepreneurs: The impact of sex and dependents. *Journal of Small Business Management, 44*(3), 350–368. https://doi.org/10.1111/j.1540-627X.2006.00176.x

Devine, P. G. (1989). Stereotypes and prejudice: Their automatic and controlled components. *Journal of Personality and Social Psychology, 56*(1), 5–18. https://doi.org/10.1037/0022-3514.56.1.5

Dombrovsky, V., & Welter, F. (2006). The role of personal and family background in making entrepreneurs in a post-socialist environment. *SSRN Electronic Journal*. Retrieved from https://doi.org/10.2139/ssrn.1697581

Dunn, T., & Holtz-Eakin, D. (2000). Financial capital, human capital, and the transition to self-employment: Evidence from intergenerational links. *Journal of Labor Economics, 18*(2), 282–305. https://doi.org/10.1086/209959

Eccles, J. S. (1994). Understanding women's educational and occupational choices: Applying the Eccles et al. model of achievement-related choices. *Psychology of Women Quarterly, 18*(4), 585–609. https://doi.org/10.1111/j.1471-6402.1994.tb01049.x

Eisenhardt, K. M. (1989). Building theories from case study research. *The Academy of Management Review, 14*(4), 532. https://doi.org/10.2307/258557

European Commission. (2010). *Communication from the commission Europe 2020, a strategy for smart, sustainable, inclusive growth.*

European Commission. (2014a). *Statistical data on women entrepreneurs in Europe*, 110.

European Commission. (2014b). *Statistical data on women entrepreneurs in Europe. Directorate-general for enterprise and industry.*

European Commission. (2017). *Special Eurobarometer Report on Gender Equality.*

Evans, D. S., & Leighton, L. S. (1990). Small business formation by unemployed and employed workers. *Small Business Economics, 2*, 319–330. https://doi.org/10.2307/40228659

GEM. (2016). *Global entrepreneurship monitor*. Retrieved February 17, 2018 from http://www.gemconsortium.org/country-profile/60

Gupta, V. K., Turban, D. B., Wasti, S. A., & Sikdar, A. (2005). Entrepreneurship and stereotypes: Are entrepreneurs from mars or from venus? *Academy of Management Proceedings, 2005*(1), C1–C6. https://doi.org/10.5465/AMBPP.2005.18778633

Gupta, V. K., Turban, D. B., & Bhawe, N. M. (2008). The effect of gender stereotype activation on entrepreneurial intentions. *Journal of Applied Psychology, 93*(5), 1053–1061. https://doi.org/10.1037/0021-9010.93.5.1053

Gupta, V. K., Turban, D. B., Wasti, S. A., & Sikdar, A. (2009). The role of gender stereotypes in perceptions of entrepreneurs and intentions to become an entrepreneur. *Entrepreneurship Theory and Practice, 33*(2), 397–417. https://doi.org/10.1111/j.1540-6520.2009.00296.x

Hisrich, R. D. (1984). The woman entrepreneur in the United States and Puerto Rico. *Leadership & Organization Development Journal, 5*(5), 3–8. https://doi.org/10.1108/eb053558

Karlin, C. A., England, P., & Richardson, M. (2002). Why do "women's jobs" have low pay for their educational level? *Gender Issues, 20*(4), 3–22. https://doi.org/10.1007/s12147-002-0020-6

Karu, M. (2014). *Exchange of good practices on gender equality*. Discussion paper, Equal pay days, Estonia.

Laar, M. (2007). *The estonian economic miracle. Backgrounder, the heritage foundation*. Retrieved from https://www.heritage.org/report/the-estonian-economic-miracle

Lumiste, R., Pefferly, R., & Purju, A. (2008, January 1). *Estonia's economic development: Trends, practices, and sources*. Retrieved from http://documents.worldbank.org/curated/en/280881468025510249/Estonias-economic-development-trends-practices-and-sources

Marlow, S., & Carter, S. (2004). Accounting for change: Professional status, gender disadvantage and self-employment. *Women in Management Review, 19*(1), 5–17. https://doi.org/10.1108/09649420410518395

Mattis, M. C. (2004). Women entrepreneurs: Out from under the glass ceiling. *Women in Management Review, 19*(3), 154–163. https://doi.org/10.1108/09649420410529861

McCauley, M. (1981). *The soviet union since 1917*. London: Longman. Retrieved from https://books.google.lv/books/about/The_Soviet_Union_since_1917.html?id=YJmEAAAAIAAJ&redir_esc=y

Meyskens, M., Elaine Allen, I., & Brush, C. G. (2011). *Human capital and hybrid ventures* (pp. 51–72). UK: Emerald Group Publishing. Retrieved from https://doi.org/10.1108/S1074-7540(2011)0000013007

Miles, M. B., & Huberman, A. (1994). *Qualitative data analysisitle*. New York.

Miller, L., & Budd, J. (1999). The development of occupational sex-role stereotypes, occupational preferences and academic subject preferences in children at ages 8, 12 and 16. *Educational Psychology, 19*(1), 17–35. https://doi.org/10.1080/0144341990190102

Mincer, J. (1974). *Schooling, experience, and earnings*. Human Behavior and Social Institutions no. 2, National Bureau of Economic Research, Inc., New York ($10.00). Retrieved from https://eric.ed.gov/?id=ED103621

North, D. C. (1990). *Institutions, institutional change and economic performance*. Cambridge: Cambridge University Press.

North, D. C. (1991). Institutions. *Journal of Economic Perspectives, 5*(1), 97–112. https://doi.org/10.1257/jep.5.1.97

North, D. C. (1997). Understanding economic change. In J. Nelson, C. Tilly, & L. Walker (Eds.), *Transforming post-communist political economies*. Washington, DC: National Academy.

North, D. C. (2005). *Understanding the process of economic change*. Princeton, NJ: Princeton University Press. Retrieved from https://press.princeton.edu/titles/7943.html

Pathak, S., Goltz, S., Buche, M. W. (2013). Influences of gendered institutions on women's entry into entrepreneurship. *International Journal of Entrepreneurial Behavior & Research, 19*(5), 478–502. https://doi.org/10.1108/IJEBR-09-2011-0115

Rotter, J. B. (1966). Generalized expectancies for internal versus external control of reinforcement. *Psychological Monographs: General and Applied, 80*(1), 1–28. https://doi.org/10.1037/h0092976

Rozeik, H. (2014). *Exchange of good practices on gender equality encouraging female entrepreneurship women entrepreneurship in Estonia*. Retrieved from http://ec.europa.eu/justice/gender-equality/files/exchange_of_good_practice_uk/ee_comments_paper_uk2014_en.pdf

Salimath, M. S., & Cullen, J. B. (2010). Formal and informal institutional effects on entrepreneurship: A synthesis of nation-level research. *International Journal of Organizational Analysis, 18*(3), 358–385. https://doi.org/10.1108/19348831011062175

Sarfaraz, L., Faghih, N., & Majd, A. (2014). The relationship between women entrepreneurship and gender equality. *Journal of Global Entrepreneurship Research, 2*(1), 6. https://doi.org/10.1186/2251-7316-2-6

Scherer, F., Brodzinski, D., & Wiebe, A. (1990). Entrepreneur career selection and gender: A socialization approach. *Journal of Small Business Management, 28*(2), 37. Retrieved from https://search.proquest.com/openview/373842fc404f7cb1d411c96f0b931585/1?pq-origsite=gscholar&cbl=49244

Schultz, T. W. (1959). Investment in man: An economist's view. *Social Service Review, 33*(2), 109–117. https://doi.org/10.1086/640656

Scott, W. R. (2008). Approaching adulthood: The maturing of institutional theory. *Theory and Society, 37*(5), 427–442. https://doi.org/10.1007/s11186-008-9067-z

Shane, S., Locke, E. A., & Collins, C. J. (2003). Entrepreneurial motivation. *Human Resource Management Review, 13*(2), 257–279. https://doi.org/10.1016/S1053-4822(03)00017-2

Shapero, A., & Sokol, L. (1982). *The social dimensions of entrepreneurship*. Retrieved from https://papers.ssrn.com/sol3/papers.cfm?abstract_id=1497759

Shenton, A. K. (2004). Strategies for ensuring trustworthiness in qualitative research projects. *Education for Information, 22*, 63–75. Retrieved from https://pdfs.semanticscholar.org/452e/3393e3ecc34f913e8c49d8faf19b9f89b75d.pdf

Storobin, D. (2005). Estonian economic miracle: A model for developing countries. *Global Politician*.

Thornton, P. H., Ribeiro-Soriano, D., & Urbano, D. (2011). Socio-cultural factors and entrepreneurial activity: An overview. *International Small Business Journal, 29*, 105–118. https://doi.org/10.1177/0266242610391930

Vainu, V. (2016). *Soolise võrdõiguslikkuse monitooring 2016*. Retrieved from http://enut.ee/files/soolise_vordoiguslikkuse_monitooringu_raport_2016.pdf

Van Auken, H., Stephens, P., Fry, F. L., & Silva, J. (2006). Role model influences on entrepreneurial intentions: A comparison between USA and Mexico. *The International Entrepreneurship and Management Journal, 2*(3), 325–336. https://doi.org/10.1007/s11365-006-0004-1

Wakkee, I., Englis, P. D., & During, W. (2007). Using e-mails as a source of qualitative data. In H. Neergaard & J. P. Ulhøi (Eds.), *Handbook of qualitative research methods in entrepreneurship*. Cheltenham: Edward Elgar.

Wegener, D. T., Clark, J. K., & Petty, R. E. (2006). Not all stereotyping is created equal: Differential consequences of thoughtful versus nonthoughtful stereotyping. *Journal of Personality and Social Psychology, 90*(1), 42–59. https://doi.org/10.1037/0022-3514.90.1.42

Weick, K. E. (1996). Drop your tools: An allegory for organizational studies. *Administrative Science Quarterly, 41*(2), 301. https://doi.org/10.2307/2393722

Welter, F., & Smallbone, D. (2003). Institutional development and entrepreneurship in transition economies. In *Proceedings of the World Conference of the International Council for Small Business*.

Welter, F., & Smallbone, D. (2010, March). The embeddedness of women's entrepreneurship in a transition context. In *Women entrepreneurs and the global environment for growth. A research perspective* (pp. 96–117), Northampton: Edward Elgar.

Welter, F., & Smallbone, D. (2011). Institutional perspectives on entrepreneurial behavior in challenging environments. *Journal of Small Business Management, 49*(1), 107–125.

Welter, F., Smallbone, D., Mirzakhalikova, D., & Maksudova, C. (2006). Women entrepreneurs between tradition and modernity–the case of Uzbekistan. In N. I. Friederike Welter & D. Smallbone (Eds.), *Enterprising women in transition economies* (pp. 45–66). Aldershot: Ashgate.

Wirls, D. (1886). Reinterpreting the gender gap. *The public opinion quarterly*. Oxford University Press/American Association for Public Opinion Research. Retrieved from https://doi.org/10.2307/2748721

World Bank. (2016). *Doing business 2017: Equal opportunity for all – Estonia*. Washington, DC: World Bank.

Entrepreneurship Education and Gender in Europe

A Systematic Literature Review of Studies in Higher Education

Davy Vercruysse

Abstract Entrepreneurship is considered an important factor for economic growth. And although female entrepreneurs offer outstanding socio-economic potential, there are still more men working as entrepreneurs than women. Support for female entrepreneurs is improving in Europe but compared to the United States there is still progress to be made. Major differences can also be identified between European countries. Although one way to foster entrepreneurship is via entrepreneurship education, reviews about entrepreneurship education in combination with gender studies are rare. This paper performs a systematic literature review, presenting the state of entrepreneurship education and gender within the last decade, and generating a European map of research. European samples are descriptively analyzed, and six different issues are identified. Implications for practitioners and policymakers are provided, and the article concludes with insights revealing where more research is needed and how it could be performed in Europe.

1 Introduction and Reasoning Behind the Paper

Entrepreneurs are a source of prosperity and economic growth (European Commission 2013), so Europe needs as many of them as possible. A substantial difference exists between the amount of male and female entrepreneurs. In 2013, only 37% of all worldwide firms were run by a woman (VanderBrug 2013). This rate is even lower for Europe: although 52% of the population is female, only 34.4% of European entrepreneurs are women. Moreover, the annual firm start-up rate for males is 1.35%, while only 1.01% of females start an own company (Caliendo et al. 2014).

D. Vercruysse (✉)
Faculty of Economics and Business Administration, Ghent University, Ghent, Belgium
e-mail: davy.vercruysse@ugent.be

More women entrepreneurs would have a positive impact on economic growth, and a greater amount of female entrepreneurs would achieve a larger amount of entrepreneurs in general. More specifically, women entrepreneurs are the source of relatively more job creation. Indeed, studies by the European Parliament prove that women create relatively more small- and medium-sized enterprises (SMEs) than men; 85% of net new jobs in the EU are created by these SMEs. In other words, more women entrepreneurs would generate more SMEs, which would create more new jobs as a result. Women entrepreneurs also display higher levels of innovation than their male counterparts (European Commission 2014). If as many women as men participated in the labor force, it would contribute one trillion dollars to GDP in emerging economies (VanderBrug 2013). All in all, although the vast socio-economic potential of women's entrepreneurship is known (Hughes et al. 2012), this difference in the rate between male and female entrepreneurs (i.e. this gender gap) is still very significant.

An increasing number of studies have as a result observed what the reasons could be for this gender gap and what can be done to reduce it (Ahl 2006). Although there are in fact fewer women entrepreneurs, *entrepreneurial education* might offer a possible solution to stimulate entrepreneurial aptitude for men and women alike (Cheraghi and Schøtt 2015). According to the European Commission, entrepreneurship can be taught and learned. With this in mind, one of the missions of the European Union is to support programs that increase entrepreneurial intention (EI) and foster women entrepreneurship via educational and business networking platforms (European Commission 2013).

The Female Entrepreneurship Index (FEI) is a score measured by the individual and institutional efforts in one country to promote female start-ups. Besides the fact that this rate is much higher for the United States (82.9) and Australia (74.8) in comparison to the leading European country (the United Kingdom at 70.6), the *dissimilarity within Europe* itself is even more pronounced. Several Scandinavian and central European countries have FEI scores of around 65, the eastern part (Czech Republic, Poland, Estonia) has scores of approximately 55, while the more southern countries (Croatia, Portugal, Romania) only have scores of around 50 (Terjesen and Lloyd 2015). These noticeable European differences raise questions about how the female entrepreneurial ecosystem can be fostered by entrepreneurship education and what kind of research has been performed so far. Since reviews about entrepreneurship education in combination with gender studies are rare, the purpose of this paper is to provide the state of affairs regarding EE and gender between 2006 and 2016 from a European perspective.

Two main research questions are posed. **What kind of research is done on EE and gender on the European continent, and how is it performed? What are the main general and gender-related issues and key findings here?** To answer these questions, a brief overview of global and European research will first be discussed, followed by a descriptive analysis of the European[1] samples in order to find similar and different characteristics between the papers (study design, methods, sample characteristics, kind of EE). This paper will furthermore give a thematic overview with key findings in general and gender in particular. Based on these, implications for educators and policymakers will be discussed to show how entrepreneurial programs with a focus on female entrepreneurs can be expanded upon and even improved. Finally, the article will show which research gaps need more attention.

2 Methodology

This paper is a *literature review* with a systematic approach in accordance with the work of Pickering and Byrne (2014). In comparison to the use of narrative reviews, this method follows a series of clear steps to lower the possible subjectivity or potential biases of research. Furthermore, intercoder reliability is added, in line with the work by Lombard et al. (2002). As in previous research, a combination of deductive and inductive coding approaches is used for the content analysis (Epstein and Martin 2005).

To capture as many possible articles on the research topic, a systematic literature search was performed among international peer-reviewed articles (in English) in the following databases: Web of Science, Science Direct, Business Source Premier, and ABI/Inform. The first three databases are commonly used as databases for this research. ABI/Inform is recommended by Frank and Hatak (2014) because it provides relevant articles in entrepreneurship research. Keywords used here were (1) 'entrepreneur* education' + 'gender', (2) 'entrepreneur* education' + 'women' or 'woman', (3) 'entrepreneur* education' + 'fem*', (4) 'entrepreneur* education' + 'higher education'.[2] The articles were screened for the given keywords in the title, abstract and full text (references included). After running this search in these four databases, 6171 total articles were found. Duplicates were first reduced automatically by Endnote, and by hand in a second run to exclude unseen duplicates from the first elimination. After excluding all duplicates, 2104 articles remained. An overview of the collection and exclusion rounds can be seen in Table 1.

Each article was screened in two rounds to exclude or include them from/into the final sample. A procedure with a codebook was composed, providing the strategy regarding how to include/exclude articles in the two rounds. Only the titles and abstracts were analyzed in a first round. In this phase the main question was whether the article dealt with entrepreneurship education in higher education or not.

---

[1] We consider Europe as the entire continent, including all Scandinavian countries, Russia and the UK.

[2] 'Entrepreneur* education' stands for 'entrepreneurship education' or 'entrepreneurial education', 'fem*' stands for 'female' or 'feminine'.

Table 1 Overview of the collection and exclusion rounds

Sample	Collection/exclusion method	Amount of articles
Gross sample	Collecting all articles	6171
Net sample 1	Exclusion of duplicates	2104
Net sample 2	Does the article deal with EE in HE?	532
Net sample 3	Does the article deal with gender?	87

Source: Own table

The subjectivity of coding (including or excluding an article) was tested under *intercoder reliability* (Lombard et al. 2002). The main researcher first coded all of the articles. In addition, three other researchers (coders 1, 2 and 3) each independently coded one-third of the total sample, following the instructions in the codebook. The three coders were first independently trained: 5% of the articles for each coder were analysed together with the main researcher. Discussions about including or excluding an article were done in this phase as a means to ensure that every coder knew how the expected criteria were to be measured. In a second phase, every researcher (coders 1, 2 and 3) coded the articles independently. Krippendorff's α was calculated: the observed α gave scores of 0.916, 0.918 and 0.851 respectively for every coder, each time compared to the main researcher. Comparing this outcome with the required minimum of $\alpha = 0.800$ (Krippendorff 2012) indicated that the level of acceptance had been reached; the data possessed a fair degree of reliability.

Every article where there were still doubts following the comparison was included or excluded based on the decision made between the main researcher and the respective coder. 532 peer-reviewed articles were available following the first exclusion round. In a second exclusion round, all the articles were studied in-depth by the main researcher regarding whether the article dealt with issues like gender, females or women. Only 87 papers remained in the list following this second exclusion because in all the other articles, these terms only appeared in their references.

These 87 articles were integrated into a database that collected and manually examined 54 characteristics of every paper. Since the field of entrepreneurship education under gender aspects is heterogeneous and still under-researched, a combination of *deductive and inductive coding* approaches was applied in this content analysis (Epstein and Martin 2005). After setting up the different codes, all the articles were integrated and coded into the database. After all of the articles were examined, all of the codes were revised, and the references of the selected articles were screened to investigate whether there were other articles (cross-references) which were not seen during the previous phases. With the exception of a few articles in other languages and articles which did not originate from 2006 to 2016, no others were found except non-peer-reviewed articles.

3 Findings

This section consists of two parts. The worldwide sample is briefly discussed in the first part, followed by a descriptive analysis with a focus on the papers conducting research on European students. Here, all articles are categorized according to the respective paper's method (quantitative, qualitative, mixed or conceptual). For every categorization, the study design, the characteristics of the samples, and the stimulus (what kind of EE?) are discussed. In the second part, all European-based papers are categorized according to their topics, discussing the key findings in general and the key findings regarding gender for each of them. A general overview of the articles with their key findings and descriptive analyses is clustered according to topic and can be found in the table in Appendix.

3.1 Descriptive Analysis of the Sample with a Focus on the European Articles

The first research question concerns what kind of research is involved in the study, as well as how it is performed worldwide and, in greater detail, for the European samples. This systematic literature review started with a very broad sample, with an initial selection of 2104 articles. 87 articles from around the world were categorized as performing research on gender and EE, of which 31 articles used gender only as a control variable. While the total amount here is very poor, the last 10 years have in fact seen a positive evolution, as shown in Table 2. These articles are found in 42 different journals with disciplines including education, business, entrepreneurship, gender, social sciences, management and technology. The journals having the most articles are *Education and Training* (14), *Journal of Enterprising Culture* (6), *International Entrepreneurship and Management Journal* (5) and *International Journal of Gender and Entrepreneurship* (5).

In the 87 articles about gender and EE, 31 articles are based on studies with samples of European students from one country, while 12 compare different European samples, or one sample from Europe and one sample from another continent. 40 studies deal with non-European samples, and 4 studies are meta-regressions based on worldwide samples. The two first categories with a total of 43 articles based on (at least) one European sample are of particular interest for this study. The descriptive analysis will now focus in greater detail on the methods used, the study design, the sample characteristics, and the stimulus (what kind of EE was applied?) of these 43 European articles. Appendix provides the overview of the different papers which will be discussed in further detail. Table 3 gives an overview of the categorization of the European samples according to their method.

Of these 43 European papers, four articles are *conceptual*, based on literature reviews of previous research. The study designs of these papers vary. One article evaluates entrepreneurship programs in Germany using other literature, another

Table 2 Worldwide overview of the amount of articles about EE and gender during the last 10 years (only January–June for the year 2016)

	2006	2007	2008	2009	2010	2011	2012	2013	2014	2015	2016	Total
All articles	1	1	2	6	11	7	12	13	13	14	7	87
Gender as main focus	1	1	2	3	8	6	9	6	11	6	3	56
Gender as control variable	0	0	0	3	3	1	3	7	2	8	4	31

The research sample is from January 2006–June 2016, so 2016 is only partially integrated into the sample. This explains the decline
Source: Own table

Table 3 Categorization of the European samples according to their method

Conceptual	4
Qualitative	5
Mixed method	1
Quantitative	33
Regression	12
SEM	3
ANOVA	4
Pre-/post-t-tests	4
Chi-squared	3
Descriptive analysis	3
Other methods	4
Total European articles	43

Source: Own table

investigates if and how veterinary students can benefit from EE, a third focuses on women entrepreneurship in university education, and the last one conceptualizes the idea of testing entrepreneurial self-efficacy in relation to personality, gender and propensity to risk.

In addition, five articles are purely *qualitative*. One of them is based on semi-structured interviews with 122 students to find out how entrepreneurial courses should be organized. The other four use case studies composed of documents or diaries of students and educators, or using an evaluation of a study day for educators. These four articles deal with the following topics: EE and female entrepreneurship, the impact of EE on students' competencies and propensity, and the beliefs of students about the characteristics of entrepreneurs.

Only one article of the 43 uses a *mixed method*, with a regression analysis combining in-depth interviews to focus on the organization of EE programs in universities with 95 respondents from four different countries.

The majority (33) of the European papers base their findings on a quantitative analysis. 12 of these 33 quantitative papers use different regression techniques (sometimes combined with other techniques). Eight of the regression analyses perform studies on the entrepreneurial intention (EI) of students. Several studies directly use EI as an independent variable, while others investigate the three antecedents of EI (perceived behavior control, subjective norms, and attitude towards behavior) of the theory of planned behavior. The other five regression analyses test the need for achievement, the ambition of students, their perceived learning outcome, their entrepreneurial aptitude, or their competencies. Furthermore, in eight of the regression papers, students attended (obligatory or voluntary) entrepreneurship lectures or workshops, while in three others the samples were mixed, with students both attending or not attending EE courses. Two also worked with samples where no business students were involved. Here, the articles measured the beliefs of students concerning entrepreneurship courses.

Along with the papers using regression analyses, three papers apply structural equation modeling to perform tests on EI or its antecedents. Two of these papers look at how EI changes over several years, while the other one measures EI in its interaction with culture and gender. In one of the articles, the stimulus (what kind of EE is offered?) is not specified, while in the other two papers students from different fields of study were examined.

In addition, four papers use ANOVAs to focus on the beliefs and attitudes of students about becoming an entrepreneur (1), EE courses (2), or their entrepreneurial intention (1). Here the stimulus is not available for three articles, while in one of the articles EE courses are optionally offered.

Four other papers use different t-tests in a pre- and post-test design to study the change in self-efficacy or EI, the change in entrepreneurial knowledge and skills, or the attitude towards an entrepreneurial course. The kind of EE reviewed here varies between one entrepreneurial course to different entrepreneurial programs, of which some are residential and others are not.

Three other papers use chi-squared tests to search for differences in attitudes towards entrepreneurship or entrepreneurial intentions among different student groups, with different control variables such as taking courses on entrepreneurship education and gender or not.

Three other articles work only with a descriptive analysis to see what the proportion of participants is in EE courses, or the impact EE programs have on entrepreneurial aptitude. The remaining four articles use other methods such as rank tests, trend analyses, data mining or multi-level techniques to test beliefs or attitudes of students towards EE courses or EI in general.

Although the samples in the quantitative analyses differ greatly, in most of the papers, the amount of students tested is between 100 and 500 elements. Most studies consist of an equal amount of male and female students.

3.2 Thematic Analysis of the European Samples

The second research question concerns the main issues and their general and gender-related key findings for every topic. Based on the deductive and inductive coding, six research topics were identified: EE and female entrepreneurship, the impact of EE on students' competencies and/or entrepreneurial propensity, the study of EI and/or its antecedents in relation to EE, the beliefs of students about the characteristics of entrepreneurs, the beliefs and attitudes of students about entrepreneurial courses, and the beliefs and attitudes of students about entrepreneurship (starting up). Table 4 gives an overview.

In the following sections, all articles per topic will be described with a special focus on the general conclusion, and with a specific look at gender. Implications for educators, policymakers and further research are briefly mentioned to show the direct link to this paper's study design. The main implications will be analyzed in detail during the discussion. The papers in Appendix are placed in chronological order when used for the first time in this section, making the comparative analysis easier to follow.

Table 4 Overview of the topics

Topic	#
EE and female entrepreneurship	4
Impact of EE on students' competencies and/or entrepreneurial propensity	8
EI and/or its antecedents in relation to EE	18
Beliefs of students about characteristics of entrepreneurs	3
Beliefs and attitudes of students about entrepreneurial courses	4
Beliefs and attitudes of students towards entrepreneurship (starting up)	6
Total	43

Source: Own table

The research topics of *EE and female entrepreneurship* cover four articles. Henry and Treanor (2010) performed a literature review to conclude that EE could help women in veterinary medical fields overcome gender-specific barriers. Moreover, during a discussion workshop, educators concluded that EE courses in non-business disciplines will become increasingly important in the future, especially in sectors where more males are currently self-employed (Treanor 2012). Tegtmeier and Mitra (2015) performed a literature review on women's entrepreneurship research with a focus on university education. They state that more research is needed on the topic. Rae et al. (2012) provide a descriptive overview of enterprise education in the UK, surveying 116 higher educational institutions (HEIs). They state that there is a significantly higher proportion of male students compared to females in EE programs, meaning fewer women become entrepreneurs. Although entrepreneurship might be seen as a conventionally "male" interest, policymakers and HEIs should promote entrepreneurship as a desirable cultural norm in general as well as in courses.

The *impact of EE courses on students' competencies or entrepreneurial propensity* comprises eight articles. Competencies or propensity involve intended knowledge, skills, aptitudes and abilities to start up. Petridou and Sarri (2011) found a positive impact of EE on the *knowledge, skills and entrepreneurial aptitude* of students. Here, a greater portion of men are interested in entrepreneurship than women. Since female entrepreneurs face different obstacles than males, females should be encouraged to follow an entrepreneurship program. In the study by Vilcov and Dimitrescu (2015), 171 students appeared to obtain more competencies via entrepreneurship education, while gender differences manifested themselves only later in their career choices.

Radovic-Markovic et al. (2012) studied how *entrepreneurial abilities* can be stimulated via EE; their study had a specific focus on women. Using qualitative in-depth interviews and a quantitative approach with 95 respondents, they noticed that entrepreneurial abilities can be best fostered when multi-dimensional relationships are established between the course concepts and entrepreneurship experiences. Gender-based EE should facilitate a more "women-centered" approach with an adaptation to everyone's individual needs. Here, more freedom in learning and reducing existing stereotypes is important to promote the self-confidence and individual development of the students. Jones et al. (2008) found that males initially showed more *commitment* towards a future entrepreneurial career, although both sexes displayed a very high rate of interest following the course. The authors concluded that enterprise education can have a positive impact on entrepreneurial career aspiration. More studies should be taken into account in a longitudinal setting to investigate whether these results are transferable to other countries. Kriz and Auchter (2016) found that educational simulation games increase the entrepreneurial knowledge and skills of students. Gender-based, extended debriefing appears to promote the entrepreneurial motivation of women. Because of this, the authors suggest organizing different game formats and programs for specific target groups. Following a thematic analysis of surveys on German-speaking students, Kailer (2009) furthermore infers that more variation is needed in EE when it is applied to specified target groups. Based on other studies, he states that female students express a special need for individual coaching and networking events where experienced and female entrepreneurs could serve as role models. Tiago et al. (2015) deduced that attending an EE course was the main determinant of the differences between students' propensity to start a company, while age and gender showed no significant results. Kurczewska et al. (2014) performed a content and thematic analysis comparing Finnish with Egyptian students. The enthusiasm seen by Finnish females is less than with their Egyptian counterparts, an outcome that is probably the result of their national culture.

The third research topic, the *study of EI and/or antecedents in relation with EE* covers eighteen articles. Only the articles which measured entrepreneurial intention directly or via its antecedents are discussed in this section (articles measuring other variables were discussed as part of the second research topic). This means that these studies are based on the theory of planned behavior or the entrepreneurial event model. Two different subcategories can be distinguished here: differences in EI among gender, and the effects of EE on EI.

A number of papers discuss the *differences among gender* concerning the level of EI. Kurczewska and Bialek (2014) found via paired t-tests in their survey of 232 bachelors and masters students at a faculty of economics and sociology that females show less EI, although entrepreneurial self-efficacy (ESE) is not the key driver. This means that educators should focus not only on ESE but look for other ways to increase EI as well. Yordanova and Tarrazon (2010) tested the moderating effects of gender on EI and its antecedents via binary logistic regression in a cross-sectional design. Women showed less EI here as well. Other papers with regression analyses arrived at the same result (Vukovic et al. 2015; Karhunen and Ledyaeva 2010). Joensuu et al. (2013) found via structural equation modeling that females have fewer initial entrepreneurial intentions. These results are in line with research that uses other methods (Shneor et al. 2013; Maresch et al. 2016; Schwarz et al. 2009; Teixeira et al. 2012). However, Dabic et al. (2012) found that men are more willing to start a company, although with EI itself, the differences are less distinctive. All in all, most of the articles conclude that females show initially lower EI scores than males. Most of these papers suggest that educators and policymakers should create effective EE programs that are customized to deal with specific gender needs.

A traditional approach of an entrepreneurial course should be supplemented by guest lecturers, including female entrepreneurs, to more intensively promote female students who have a lower initial level of EI.

When searching for the *effects of EE courses on the EI* of students, the conclusions are more diverse. In a 3-year longitudinal study, Joensuu et al. (2013) found that the EI of students decreased over time and education. This declining EI was even stronger for females. This conclusion is in line with the paper by Varamäki et al. (2015) where a path analysis measured active-based and lecture-based courses, revealing a decrease in female EI. Packham et al. (2010) also found that a single course where students create a business model has less effect on the entrepreneurial attitudes of females compared to males.

Several papers did in fact find that EE courses positively influence EI, while the differences in gender are not obvious (Küttim et al. 2014; Turker and Senem Sonmez 2009). Vukovic et al. (2015) observed that EE has a positive impact on students' attitudes and knowledge. Here EE is less successful in motivating students to actually start work as an entrepreneur. Shneor and Jenssen (2014) noticed that entrepreneurial experience, social norms, self-efficacy and age influence both genders, while the direct effect of EE and risk perceptions are only significant for female students. Maresch et al. (2016) also found that EE has a positive effect on EI in their cross-sectional study of 4548 Austrian students (64% female) taken from the 2011 GUESS project. Agapitou et al. (2010) found that initial differences in EI between male and female students who participated in EE courses diminishes over time.

All in all, measuring the effects of EE on EI shows a more diverse outcome. Researchers nevertheless agree that different types of and customized EE programs can help students more effectively. Here, a multidimensional approach can be effective in raising entrepreneurial intentions.

The fourth research topic *beliefs or attitudes of students about characteristics of entrepreneurs* comprises three articles which deal with the research questions of who the perfect entrepreneur is and what kinds of characteristics this person should have. Hytti and Heinonen (2013) analyzed the diaries of students to investigate the entrepreneurial identities that are acceptable and attractive to them. Male participants could identify themselves more with the *heroic* identity, while females relied on a *humane* identity of running a low-tech firm with modest business goals. With this in mind, EE courses should not only foresee business knowledge and skills but also pay attention to the role models entrepreneurs could use to effectively operate their business. The two other articles (Jones 2014, 2015) discuss the differences in EE from a *feministic discursive approach*. Jones suggests that entrepreneurship is more closely related to the traits of a masculine world. Gender is discussed as socially constructed, and is not based on the difference between being male or female, but by masculine and feminine characteristics. Analyzing diaries and interviewing students, she concludes that females believe that becoming an entrepreneur requires certain "masculinized" traits, i.e. they should perceive male entrepreneurship as natural and unquestionable. With the other five topics, "gender" is used as a synonym for "sex," while in the articles within this topic, gender is more based on the masculine and feminine characteristics of individuals. This gives rise to the question of what research could be performed when the effect of EE is measured on EI, not only with testing for the variable "sex" (being male or female) but also for the socially constructed "gender" (having masculine or feminine characteristics).

The fifth research topic covers the *beliefs or attitudes of students concerning entrepreneurship education*. Beynon et al. (2014) noticed that students will follow entrepreneurship programs when they want to obtain more knowledge or gain further skills. Females here sought more advice before starting the course. In terms of content, female students should be provided with a customized learning program (which could be gender-specific). Petridou et al. (2009) concluded via descriptive analysis that there is a higher enrollment of males than females in entrepreneurship courses. Female students are also more interested in acquiring knowledge, developing skills, and networking with local businesses than male students; here they state that a customized program is needed for these kinds of activities. Hytti et al. (2010) analyzed that educators should not take for granted that students are simply motivated to follow entrepreneurship courses, but that a differentiation in motivation can influence the learning outcomes of students. Different course formats could be the solution: team-based learning could have a positive effect where every individual can play their own role. This last approach is in line with the research of Hoogendoorn et al. (2013) who found that teams with an equal gender mix perform better in terms of sales and profits than male-dominated teams. The authors state that this is because men and women can complement each other's skills and knowledge.

The last research topic deals with the *beliefs or attitudes of students about starting up an entrepreneurial career*. Jones et al. (2011) performed a qualitative semi-structured data collection method of 122 Polish students who were taking an entrepreneurial course. They found that male and female students have different perceptions and attitudes towards an entrepreneurial career. Boissin et al. (2011) noted that the entrepreneurial aptitude of women is lower, and is related to risk aversion. However, female students are more positively stimulated than males when they meet entrepreneurial role models. Moreover, in a European comparison, Bergmann et al. (2016) concluded that significantly more male students become entrepreneurs compared to female students, which is in line with other papers (Staniewski and Szopinski 2015; Oehler et al. 2015). Still, they state that initiatives and programs that aim to encourage students to become entrepreneurs make a difference, which is also seen in other research (Castiglione et al. 2013). Again, interesting role models and customized EE programs could encourage female students to start companies and lower their risk aversion.

4 Discussion

This first aim of this literature review was to give an *overview of the recent state* of gender and EE in Europe. Recent years have seen a modest increase in work performed here, although the total amount of research remains scarce. In a first phase, 2104 articles were selected for further analysis. Only 43 articles address this topic with European samples. This small amount of relevant articles is in line with former research about the effects of EE (Rideout and Gray 2013) and with former research about women entrepreneurship and university education (Tegtmeier and Mitra 2015). Although some papers are conceptual or qualitative, the majority of the papers selected applied a quantitative method. This implies that more research is generally needed, and from a methodological point of view, more qualitative research or mixed methods would fill the current research gap. And from a quantitative perspective, additional research with more samples is needed to discover the similarities and differences between EE and gender in every European country. Path analyses and structural equation modeling in particular should be performed more to measure/identify the structural relationships between different variables that could strengthen the entrepreneurial intentions and aptitudes of women.

The second goal of this paper was to identify the general and gender-specific *main topics and key findings* to find implications for practitioners and policy. The first three topics discuss the impact of EE on women entrepreneurship, entrepreneurial competencies, and entrepreneurial intentions. The other three topics discuss the beliefs and attitudes of students towards the characteristics of entrepreneurs, entrepreneurial courses, and an entrepreneurial career. Analyzing the key findings provides interesting insights concerning the difference of entrepreneurial intentions or aptitude between men and women, and what kind of role entrepreneurship education can play to foster women entrepreneurs.

An overall conclusion is that women initially show fewer entrepreneurial intentions than men, have less interest in an entrepreneurial career compared to males, and that there are also fewer females pursuing entrepreneurial paths. These findings are in line with the current situation in Europe where fewer women have an entrepreneurial career compared to men (European Commission 2014). Since women are less present in the entrepreneurial world, the next question is whether entrepreneurship education can foster women entrepreneurship. If so, how should this specifically be done?

The conclusions of the analyzed papers regarding the capacity of entrepreneurship education to increase the entrepreneurial aptitude of women and the amount of female entrepreneurs in general are very diverse. In some studies EE positively influences the entrepreneurial intention of both genders, sometimes only more explicitly for males, sometimes more explicitly for females. The effect and duration can also vary: EI can be fostered by EE for a shorter or longer period, or the positive impact is only temporary, followed by a sharp decrease in self-efficacy after 6 months. In other studies, EE directly caused a decline in EI, especially for women.

All in all, there is no clear conclusion whether EE has a positive impact on entrepreneurial intentions or not. Because of this, many articles question whether entrepreneurship education is being offered correctly. EE could indeed stimulate (female) students to become self-employed if it were offered differently. The *implications for educators* here are twofold. Courses could be created in a more customized fashion, and also be more in tune with women/gender and their specific requirements.

A number of suggestions emerge from the *didactical perspective* to elaborate on courses addressing the specific needs of different student groups. Educators should refrain from creating one uniform educational program, and instead have different course formats. A team-based practical method could achieve better results than pure lectures, especially when a business plan needs to be created. Variation between lecture-based and activity-based courses can develop the entrepreneurial intention of students to even greater degrees. Along with specific, non-uniform courses, students prefer networking, tutoring and coaching activities instead of lectures and seminars. If possible, EE programs should consist of effective assessments and interesting stories from and about entrepreneurs offered in a more specialized contextual setting. This makes flexibility in courses that recognize the needs of specific student groups all the more important.

Translating these didactical needs especially when focusing on gender and female entrepreneurship, EE should provide a more *women-centered approach*. Customized entrepreneurship programs to respond to gender-specific needs will increase the entrepreneurial participation of women. More specifically, females need more individual coaching and networking events. Women entrepreneurs could here serve as role models by conveying their success stories. Furthermore, research on behavioral beliefs reveals that participation in entrepreneurship is lower than men's due to risk aversion (Boissin et al. 2011). Here too, the success stories of female entrepreneurs could help remove this feeling of insecurity.

This women-centered approach is a good basis to start upon, and could even be extended when educators not only look at the differences between sexes, but also at the students and their *diversity in general*. This kind of approach is related to the issues of socially constructed gender where a difference is made between masculine and feminine characteristics. More "feminine-focused" countries like Norway evaluate the virtues of masculine characteristics (e.g. entrepreneurship) differently than in more patriarchal societies such as Turkey (Shneor et al. 2013). EE programs should be implemented in a way specific to the gendered context, or could even differ per country based on the individual cultural context. More concretely, Shinnar et al. (2009) found that women from Belgium and the USA perceive fear of failure and lack of competencies as serious barriers, while Chinese women don't. This implies that EE should be adjusted to meet the specific needs of the country or culture in question. Indeed, educators must be aware of differences in gender, culture and national settings when creating EE courses.

Implications for European policymakers can be developed structurally. The government should create the blueprint for more entrepreneurial courses, allowing educators to organize them on a voluntary or compulsory basis to enhance entrepreneurial intentions and behavior in a more structured fashion. Policymakers could also better inform young people about the possibility of an entrepreneurial career. Fostering adequate knowledge will increase the aptitude to start a company, which is why policymakers should support universities and help students become entrepreneurs. Many women state that they feel a lack of support when it comes to this, so assistance via structural, institutional support providing diversified entrepreneurial courses to heighten and improve entrepreneurial skills is a good idea. Figure 1 gives an overview of the most interesting outcomes which could be used for further research.

Entrepreneurship Education and Gender in Europe

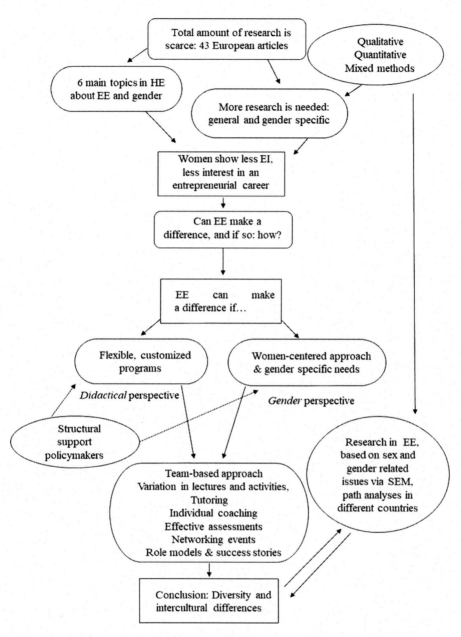

Fig. 1 Conceptual overview of how EE can play a role in stimulating student EI. Source: Own figure

5 Conclusion and Future Research Implications

The purpose of this paper was to create a topical map of research in EE and gender in an effort to identify implications for European educators and policymakers when fostering the female entrepreneurial ecosystem. This research was performed to understand why there is still a minority of women entrepreneurs in Europe, and to provide an answer on how FEI differences within European countries can be countered. Although the total amount of research on this topic is very limited, several conclusions were obtained. In many of the articles, women are seen as having initially lower entrepreneurial intentions and/or interest in an entrepreneurial career, which causes a lower amount of them to become entrepreneurs. Entrepreneurial education could reduce this gender gap in entrepreneurship if it is offered the right way. Customized, women-centered and diversified educational programs could allow female students to become more interested in an entrepreneurial career and have higher entrepreneurial intentions. Networking events, tutoring sessions, testimonials of successful women entrepreneurs and female role models from the educational realm, combined with structural support from European and national governments are the key to stimulating female entrepreneurship.

This review has several limitations. First, although the systematic method of Pickering and Byrne is used, it is still possible that not every single paper on EE and gender from the past 10 years was included in this research, especially since the search was performed in only four databases. A second limitation is the method used to include or exclude articles in the final database. Although the selection reliability was tested with three other coders besides the main researcher, there is still some subjectivity possible in the selection. A third limitation could be found in the setting of the main research topics. Since these were established by only one researcher, they could be biased as well. There are also limitations in the reviewed studies. The state of research on this topic is not as advanced as it could be because a number of the studies were done using non-equivalent, non-randomly-assigned groups.

Our study also includes *some implications for further research*. More research on a larger scale in more countries is needed, and when possible on a longitudinal basis. Secondly, non-economic or non-business students should also be tested. From a third perspective, and something that is of key importance for this review, more research is needed from a customized EE perspective. Research could be performed on the ideal learning style of individuals in an effort to achieve different pedagogical strategies. Personal and environmental factors should also be analyzed in greater depth. More research could be performed concerning intercultural differences and how they affect individuals from different European countries who want to become entrepreneurs. Finally, research on gender stereotypes and the differences in characteristics might offer indicators for explaining EI instead of simply looking at the differences between men and women. All in all, more qualitative and quantitative empirical research is needed to test what kind of EE will help female students become more motivated to start an entrepreneurial career in Europe.

Appendix

Author names	Year	Study design with measures	Sample characteristics	Method—analysis	Stimulus: what kind of EE is being reviewed?	Key findings	Key findings reg gender
Henry, Colette Treanor, Lorna	2010	How can entrepreneurship education benefit veterinary students	No sample	Conceptual paper—literature review	None	Entrepreneurship education has the potential to make a valuable contribution to veterinary medicine curricula	The inclusion of entrepreneurship within veterinary curricula will become increasingly important in the future since EE helps women to overcome gender-specific barriers
Treanor, Lorna	2012	Gender in entrepreneurship education	No sample	Qualitative case study	None	EE within veterinary curricula and more in general over in non-business disciplines is important	The need to positively impact upon entrepreneurial self-efficacy, especially among female students, was considered important
Tegtmeier, Silke Mitra, Jay	2015	Literature review about research in women's entrepreneurship with a focus on university education	No sample	Conceptual paper—literature review	No sample	Quantity of papers is still very limited although more and more attention is drawn to the subject	Most of the authors use either only gender (or search terms: women or females) as a control variable, or that they do not focus on education in their articles

(continued)

Author names	Year	Study design with measures	Sample characteristics	Method—analysis	Stimulus: what kind of EE is being reviewed?	Key findings	Key findings reg gender
Rae, David Martin, Lynn Antcliff, Valerie Hannon, Paul	2012	An overview of curricular and extra-curricular EE in UK	116 HEI are surveyed	Trend analyses	NA	HEI's have a major contribution to make to innovation and economic development. This can only be achieved through developing entrepreneurial people	More males are following more accredited programmes in enterprise than females
Petridou, Eugenia Sarri, Katerina	2011	Knowledge, skills and attitude of students following an EE-course	904 Greek students of business or science following EE-courses (47% fem)	Pre-post-analysis with paired samples and t-tests	2 different entrepreneurial programs focusing on business competences in 2 different institutions	The knowledge, skills and attitudes towards the undertaking of entrepreneurial activities are positively influenced	Men are more interested in entrepreneurship than women
Vilcov, Nicoleta Dimitrescu, Mihaela	2015	Entrepreneurial competences of students and partnership of schools with other stakeholders	171 students enrolled in several HEI 61% fem)	comparative and descriptive analysis	Entrepreneurial skills training concerning designing and implementing a product idea	Entrepreneurial training gives students more insights and competences	Gender seems to influence the career choice
Mirjana Radović-Marković, Carl Edwin Lindgren, Radmila Grozdanić, Dušan Marković, Aidin Salamzadeh	2012	Entrepreneurial abilities	95 respondents over 4 countries	Mixed method: regression analysis and in depth interviews	Not specified	Entrepreneurial abilities can be best fostered when there are multi-dimensional relationships between the course concepts and entrepreneurship experiences	The new entrepreneurship education strategy should provide a more women centred approach
Jones, Paul Miller, Christopher Jones, Amanda Packham, Gary	2011	Attitudes and motivations	122 Polish students (51% fem)	Qualitative semi-structured interviews	Course about starting a new enterprise	Male and female Polish students have different perceptions and attitudes towards an entrepreneurial career	There is a need to provide tailored provision to meet their gender-specific needs

Kriz, Willy C. Auchter, Eberhard	2016	Entrepreneurial competences and aptitude to start up	1217 Austrian and German students who followed a simulation business game (35% fem)	Regression analysis, correlation tables	Business games	Overall increase in the participants' entrepreneurial knowledge and business plan preparation skills	Males tend to have more entrepreneurial attitude but extended debriefing seem to reduce this decrease in the motivation of women
Kailer, Norbert	2009	Evalution of EE in Germany: literature review	Surveys of former researchers are analyzed	Conceptual paper—literature review	Not specified	The impact of diverse course designs should be re-evaluated	Female students express a special need on individual coaching and networking events
Tiago, Teresa Faria, Sandra Couto, João Pedro Tiago, Flávio	2015	What are the contextual factors influencing entrepreneurial propensity	734 students (46% fem) in 4 European universities	Multifactorial variance analysis	Not specified	EE seems to be an important indicator for entrepreneurial propensity	Sex and age are not key determinants for EI
Kurczewska, Agnieszka Kyrö, Paula Abbas, Amal	2014	Impact of EE programs + students understanding about the venture creation process	298 master students of Finland and Egypt (49% fem in Egypt, 22% fem in Finland)	Content and thematic analysis	More than half of the students followed a (not further specified) course in EE	The way that society and education systems are organized, has a strong impact on understanding of EE	Finnish females showed less enthusiasm and inclination towards venture creation
Kurczewska, A. Bialek, J.	2014	EI and entrepreneurial behavior are the depending variables	232 Economic students from Poland (59% fem)	χ^2 tests, two means t-test, coefficient of correlation test and Mann-Whitney U test	Students from the faculty of economics and sociology (no specification about EE-courses)	Males have substantially higher EI than females	Gender was not mediated by self-efficacy but directly affected entrepreneurial intentions

(continued)

Author names	Year	Study design with measures	Sample characteristics	Method—analysis	Stimulus: what kind of EE is being reviewed?	Key findings	Key findings reg gender
Yordanova, Desislava I. Tarrazon, Maria-Antonia	2010	EI and the antecedents of the TPB	366 Bulgarian university students in Economics (50% fem)	Binary logistic regression	1/3 of the respondents have taken compulsory or elective EE-courses	Women have lower EI than men	Gender effect on EI is fully mediated by perceived behavioral control and partially mediated by SN and ATB
Vukovic, K. Kedmenec, I. Korent, D.	2015	The effect of EE on EI and the 3 antecedents SN, ATB and PBC of the TPB of students in one of the 5 years of their study of Economics	347 Croatian students (71.6% females) of Economics of Entrepreneurship	Multiple Regression analysis on EI and antecedents, combined with Levene-test, ANOVA, Welch-test and Tukey Post hoc	Students get during their 5 years of study all kinds of finance and accounting courses, but also specifically entrepreneurship-orientated courses	EI do not increase due to exposure to entrepreneurship education, but the antecedents are significant in the model	Sex turned out to be a statistically significant variable: males have significant more EI than females
Karhunen, PÄIvi Ledyaeva, Svetlana	2010	Entrepreneurial interest/attitude and risk tolerance via the 3 antecedents of TPB: SN, ATB and PBC by perceived Self-efficay	200 Russian students of 3 economic and technical universities in their 3rd, 4th or 5th year of studes (52% fem)	Ordered logit regression	Economic students with business courses versus engineering students without business courses	Students with higher ESE are more risk tolerant and show more entrepreneurial interest.	Females, students of technical specialties, students without entrepreneurial experience and students with lower ESE tended to have a lower degree of risk tolerance
Joensuu, Sanna Viljamaa, Ammari Varamäki, Elina Tornikoski, Erno	2013	EI, ATB, SN, PBC and the change over years	192 Finnish students from 7 different universities of applied sciences (60% female)	Latent growth modeling and structural equation modeling	Students followed 7 different study fields with or without EE	EI decreases during the studies. Males show initially higher levels of EI. The initial level of intentionsdoes not affect the future development of intentions	Male students have a higher initial level of intentions, which do not decrease that much as their female counterparts

Authors	Year	Focus	Sample	Method	EE measure	Findings	Gender findings
Maresch, Daniela Harms, Rainer Kailer, Norbert Wimmer-Wurm, Birgit	2016	The effect of EE on EI and the 3 antecedents SN, ATB and PBC of the TPB in a cross-sectional design	4548 business and engineering students	Ordered logistic regression on EI and its antecedents	Entrepreneurial education was measured by the number of entrepreneurship courses that each student had taken; examples included Business Planning, Creativity, Entrepreneurial Marketing, and others	General support for a positive effect of EE on EI, but in a rather low way (improvement of EE is the key)	EE seems to positively affect EI when controlled for age, gender, and motivational drivers. Female students (control variable) however, have a lower degree of EI
Schwarz, Erich J. Wdowiak, Malgorzata A. Almer-Jarz, Daniela A. Breitenecker, Robert J.	2009	3 predicters of EI: general attitude, attitude toward entrepreneurship and the perception of university environment & start-up infrastructure	2124 students from 7 Austrian universities (53% fem)	Linear regression analysis and ANOVA's	Different study fields with and without business related items: medicine, law, technical,natural, social and business science	No significant differences in the predictors is discovered between the different fields of study	Male students students have more intention to start up
Shneor, Rotem Metin Camgöz, Selin Bayhan Karapinar, Pinar	2013	EI in interaction with culture and sex	401 Norway students (55% fem) and 292 Turkish student (52% fem) of business education	Non-parametric ANOVA	Not specified	Turkish students, regardless of sex, exhibit significantly higher levels of EI and ESE	Male students, regardless of national background, exhibit higher levels of entrepreneurial intentions, self-efficacy and social norms
Dabic, Marina Daim, Tugrul Bayraktaroglu, Elvan Novak, Ivan Basic, Maja	2012	EI measured by perceived feasiblity (PF) and perceived desirability (PD) (Entrepreneurial Event Model)	3420 university students in more than ten countries	Mann-Whitney Test	Different programs, according to the country or the university	Female students are less willing to start their own businesses compared to men	The gender differences appear less in terms of EI but more in terms of PF and PD

(continued)

Author names	Year	Study design with measures	Sample characteristics	Method—analysis	Stimulus: what kind of EE is being reviewed?	Key findings	Key findings reg gender
Varamäki, Elina Joensuu, Sanna Tornikoski, Erno Viljamaa, Anmari	2015	EI is measured together with entrepreneurial potential, and also the 3 predictors and the impact of EE in the change of EI	197 Finnish students of HE institutes (61% female)	Structural equation modeling and path analysis	The difference between lecture-based or active-based entrepreneurship education	EI of students decreased over time.	Intentions and attitude of female students decreased significantly compared to the male students
Küttim, Merle Kallaste, Marianne Venesaar, Urve Kiis, Aino	2014	ATB, SN, PBC in combination with age, gender and EE	55,781 European students from 17 countries (56% fem)	Binary logistic regression	Lectures, seminars, networking and coaching	Students want less lectures and seminars, but more networking and coaching activities. EE-courses influence positively EI	The difference in EI of both sexes is not that big. Women think they will be an entrepreneur within 5 years rather than right after their studies
Turker, Duygu Senem Sonmez, Selcuk	2009	EI measured with self-confidence, perceived level of education and perceived opportunities on entrepreneurial propensity	300 of 4 Turkish universities (49% fem)	Lineair regression	Students of natural and social sciences are tested in various years of studies	Educational and structural support strengthen the EI of students	No conclusions about gender are taken in this study
Shneor, Rotem Jenssen, Jan Inge	2014	EI is measured, based on the study of Kolvereid and adopted with 3 additional items. 12 independent variables are added	1782 students from all the departments and programs of the University of Agder (UiA) in Norway (58% fem)	Multiple regression and path analysis	Since students come from different departments, no discussion about the kind of EE is given (except the impact of the major Economics which is more general)	The effects of entrepreneurial experience, social norms, self-efficacy and age have a positive impact for both sexes	The direct effect of entrepreneurship education and risk perceptions are only evident among females. The direct effects of role models and taking an economics major are only evident among males

Entrepreneurship Education and Gender in Europe

Agapitou, Sofia Tampouri, Petros Bouchoris, Nikolaos Georgopoulos and Alexandros Kakouris	2010	Entrepreneurial intentions and beliefs	413 Greek students in science or economics of 2 universities (43% fem)	Correlation and ANOVA tests	Optionally offered courses in the format of case studies	Males tend to have more intention than females. EE courses are needed.	Gender differences disappear within the subgroup of those who have participated entrepreneurship education
Packham, Gary Jones, Paul Miller, Christopher Pickernell, David Brychan, Thomas	2010	Entrepreneurial attitude by impact of EE	237 undergraduate students in France, Poland and Germany (49% fem)	Two tailed t-tests and ordinal regression (pre-post test)	A single course given in all three universities about developing a viable business idea	EE has a positive impact on entrepreneurial attitude of French and Polish students, but not for German studetnts	The impact of enterprise education on entrepreneurial attitude is actually more significant for male students
Barakat, Shima Boddington, Monique Vyakarnam, Shailendra	2014	Self-efficacy as predictor to entrepreneurial activity (= starting up) with direct correlation to creativity and innovation by a self created and validated tool	Students and postgraduates of different universities mainly in UK, but also in Finland, Portugal, Greece and Ireland (45% fem)	Pre and post test, combined with a follow up after 6 months	Different entrepreneurial programs, some residential, some only for women programs	Different learning activities can lead to specific entrepreneurial programs to help students in becoming entrepreneurial in a more customized way	In the women's only group students had a sharper increase of ESE and then a drop off at 6 months after the course
Teixeira Dina, Simoes Jorge Simões, Silva Maria José Madeira	2012	ESE in relation with personality, level of education, gender, professional experience and propensity for risk	No sample	Conceptual paper—literature review	None	The relationship between Entrepreneurial Self-efficacy and Personality, Professional Experience, Level of Education, Gender and Propensity for Risk should be investigated	/

(continued)

Author names	Year	Study design with measures	Sample characteristics	Method—analysis	Stimulus: what kind of EE is being reviewed?	Key findings	Key findings reg gender
Shinnar, Rachel S. Giacomin, Olivier Janssen, Frank	2012	EI and entreprneurial perceptions in interaction with culture and sex	761 university students (45% fem) from 3 different nations (China, Belgium, USA), which give 3 different cultural backgrounds	Structural equation modeling	Not specified	There are significant differences in barrier perceptions	Women of USA and Belgium perceived fear of failure and lack of competency more important barriers than men
Hytti, Ulla Heinonen, Jarna	2013	Identities of entrepreneurs	Qualitative case study analysis of diaries of 7 students	Qualitative case study	Entrepreneurship program with business skills	Students should identify themselves with entepreneurs before becoming an entrepreneur	Male participants rely more to the heroic identity while females rely more to the humane identity who is running a low-tech firm with modest business goals
Jones, Sally	2015	Beliefs about entrepreneurs	2 UK female students and 1 educator	Qualitative case study	Entrepreneurship course with discussion about ethnic minorities	Students and staff misrecognize the masculinization of entrepreneurshipdiscourses that they encounter as natural and unquestionable	Students heard that entrepreneurship requires certain (masculinized) traits or you that you have to be special to become an entrepreneur

Jones, Sally	2014	Masculine and feminine characteristics of the entrepreneurship theory	No sample of student, only some documents and diaries were analyzed	Qualitative case study	None	Feminist concerns with social categorisation are important to analyze deeper	HE entrepreneurship education currently encourages students to develop a sense of fictive kinship with the entrepreneurs but since the foundations of entrepreneurship theory are masculinised, this could cause problems for those who do not accept this socially constructed form of masculinity
J. Beynon, Malcolm Jones, Paul Packham, Gary Pickernell, David	2014	Motivation to follow an EE-course	720 students in an undergraduate enterprise program (53% fem)	New data mining technique (CaRBS)	Undergraduate entreprise degree program	Students follow EE courses when they are motivated to acquire more knowledge or skills	Female students were more discerning in their responses regarding motivational characteristics than their male counterparts: EE-courses should be gender specific
Petridou, Eugenia Sarri, Aikaterini Kyrgidou, Lida P.	2009	Proportion of participants in EE (differences in gender and study field), attitude towards course	1639 Greek students following EE-courses (46% fem)	Descriptive analysis	An entrepreneurship course that varies from one till three semesters in different universities	Differences in participation rates, attitudes towards entrepreneurship education and perceptions about required skills between the two genders	Higher enrollment rates of males than females

(continued)

Author names	Year	Study design with measures	Sample characteristics	Method—analysis	Stimulus: what kind of EE is being reviewed?	Key findings	Key findings reg gender
Hytti, Ulla Stenholm, Pekka Heinonen, Jarna Seikkula-Leino, Jaana	2010	Perceived learning outcome, motivation, team behavior	117 students in EE-courses (47% fem)	Regression analysis, pre- post-analysis and follow up	Obligatory basic level entrepreneurship course where a viable business idea is developed	Extrinsic motivation has a positive influence on learning outcomes, intrinsic has a negative influence	Age nor gender are associated with the learning outcomes of the students
Hoogendoorn, Sander Oosterbeek, Hessel van Praag, Mirjam	2013	Need for achievement, need for power, perseverance, risk aversion, self-efficacy and social orientation among others	516 undergraduate students divided in 43 student teams	Analysis of team performances, regression	Starting up a venture as part of their curriculum	Teams with an equal gender mix perform better than male-dominated teams in terms of sales and profits	Men and women in mixed teams may complement each others' skills and knowledge
Jones, Paul Jones, Amanda Packham, Gary Miller, Christopher	2008	Attitude towards EE-course, impact of EE-course and future intent	50 Polish students (53% fem)	2-taled t-tests on a pre- and post design	An entrepreneurship course where students get knowledge and skills about business planning	Students had limited prior entrepreneurial experiences and expectations and welcomed the opportunity to undertake enterprise education	Male students show more entrepreneurial intent
Boissin, Jean-Pierre Branchet, Bénédicte Delanoë, Servane Velo, Veronica	2011	Behavioral beliefs affecting Attitude towards entrepreneurship (ATB)	941 French students (56% fem) of different universities	χ^2 tests	Not all students have the same courses of EE since they are enrolled in different universities	Female students show less aptitude to start as entrepreneur.	Women's attraction and participation in entrepreneurship are lower than men's due to risk aversion: this could be countered by stories of role models

Authors	Year	Topic	Sample	Method	Controlled pre-existing knowledge	Main findings concerning entrepreneurial education	Main findings concerning gender
Bergmann, Heiko Hundt, Christian Sternberg, Rolf	2016	Propensity to start up in relation with individual and contextual factors	Analysis of student entrepreneurs in 41 European countries via micro-data of the 2011 Global University Entrepreneurial Spirit Students' Survey (GUESSS)	Multi-level techniques	NA	Entrepreneurship education has a positive effect on nascent entrepreneurship behavior of students	On the individual level, age, being male, age, and parental self-employment have a consistent and significant positive impact on nascent and new entrepreneurial activity
Staniewski, M. W. Szopinski, T.	2015	Entrepreneurial attitude/readiness to start	253 Polish students of Finance, management and engineering	χ^2 tests	NA	Polish students exhibit a strong interest in establishing their own businesses, which is promising for the Polish economy	Men were found more eager to start as an entrepreneur than women
Oehler, A. Hofer, A. Schalkowski, H.	2015	Entrepreneurial knowledge, education and ambition of young bachelor students	386 undergraduate German students (49% females) without having entrepreneurial courses yet	Crosstab analysis, regression analysis and ordered logistic regression	Students knowledge and interest in entrepreneurship were measured before any entrepreneurial course	Students' age, their knowledge and ambition to become entrepreneurs substantially influence the gaps in knowledge and competences	Female students show less aspiration to become entrepreneurs
Castiglione, C. Licciardello, O. Sánchez, J. C.	2013	Entrepreneurship motivations and difficulty measures to start up, more related to family business	100 engineering students (50% fem)	ANOVA and student t-test	NA	Students who had a family business background show a stronger entrepreneurial orientation than who had not a family business background	Educational institutions should organize trainings in order to prepare new generations to the enterprise culture for both genders

References

Agapitou, C., Tampouri, S., Bouchoris, P., Georgopoulos, N., & Kakouris, A. (2010). Exploring underlying beliefs on youth entrepreneurship of higher education graduates in Greece. In A. Kakouris (Ed.), *Proceedings of the 5th European conference on innovation and entrepreneurship* (pp. 10–17).

Ahl, H. (2006). Why research on women entrepreneurs needs new directions. *Entrepreneurship Theory and Practice, 30*(5), 595–621.

Bergmann, H., Hundt, C., & Sternberg, R. (2016). What makes student entrepreneurs? On the relevance (and irrelevance) of the university and the regional context for student start-ups. *Small Business Economics, 47*(1), 53–76. https://doi.org/10.1007/s11187-016-9700-6

Beynon, M. J., Jones, P., Packham, G., & Pickernell, D. (2014). Investigating the motivation for enterprise education: A CaRBS based exposition. *International Journal of Entrepreneurial Behaviour & Research, 20*(6), 584.

Boissin, J.-P., Branchet, B., Delanoë, S., & Velo, V. (2011). Gender's perspective of role model influence on entrepreneurial behavioral beliefs. *International Journal of Business, 16*(2), 182–206.

Caliendo, M., Fossen, F. M., Kritikos, A., & Wetter, M. (2014). The gender gap in entrepreneurship: Not just a matter of personality. *CESifo Economic Studies, 61*(1), 202–238.

Castiglione, C., Licciardello, O., Sánchez, J. C., Rampullo, A., & Campione, C. (2013). Liquid modernity and entrepreneurship orientation in university students. *Procedia - Social and Behavioral Sciences, 84*, 1250–1254. https://doi.org/10.1016/j.sbspro.2013.06.738

Cheraghi, M., & Schøtt, T. (2015). Education and training benefiting a career as entrepreneur. *International Journal of Gender and Entrepreneurship, 7*(3), 321–343. https://doi.org/10.1073/pnas.1016733108

Dabic, M., Daim, T., Bayraktaroglu, E., Novak, I., & Basic, M. (2012). Exploring gender differences in attitudes of university students towards entrepreneurship. *International Journal of Gender and Entrepreneurship, 4*(3), 316–336. https://doi.org/10.1016/0883-9026(88)90018-3

Epstein, L., & Martin, A. (2005). Coding variables. In K. Kempf-Leonard (Ed.), *Encyclopedia of social measurement* (pp. 321–327). Amsterdam: Elsevier.

European Commission. (2013). *Entrepreneurship 2020 action plan: Reigniting the entrepreneurial spirit in Europe*.

European Commission. (2014). *Statistical data on women entrepreneurs in Europe*.

Frank, H., & Hatak, I. (2014). Doing a research literature review. In A. Fayolle & M. Wright (Eds.), *How to get published in the best entrepreneurship journals: A guide to steer your academic career* (pp. 94–117). Northampton: Edward Elgar.

Henry, C., & Treanor, L. (2010). Entrepreneurship education and veterinary medicine: Enhancing employable skills. *Education & Training, 52*(8/9), 607–623. https://doi.org/10.1108/00400911011088944

Hoogendoorn, S., Oosterbeek, H., & van Praag, M. (2013). The impact of gender diversity on the performance of business teams: Evidence from a field experiment. *Management Science, 59*(7), 1514–1528. https://doi.org/10.1287/mnsc.1120.1674

Hughes, K. D., Jennings, J. E., Brush, C., Carter, S., & Welter, F. (2012). Extending women's entrepreneurship research in new directions. *Entrepreneurship Theory and Practice, 36*(3), 429–442.

Hytti, U., & Heinonen, J. (2013). Heroic and humane entrepreneurs: Identity work in entrepreneurship education. *Education & Training, 55*(8/9), 886–898. https://doi.org/10.1108/ET-06-2013-0086.

Hytti, U., Stenholm, P., Heinonen, J., & Seikkula-Leino, J. (2010). Perceived learning outcomes in entrepreneurship education. *Education & Training, 52*(8/9), 587–606. https://doi.org/10.1108/00400911011088935.

Joensuu, S., Viljamaa, A., Varamäki, E., & Tornikoski, E. (2013). Development of entrepreneurial intention in higher education and the effect of gender - a latent growth curve analysis. *Education & Training, 55*(8/9), 781–803. https://doi.org/10.1108/ET-06-2013-0084.

Jones, S. (2014). Gendered discourses of entrepreneurship in UK higher education: The fictive entrepreneur and the fictive student. *International Small Business Journal, 32*(3), 237–258. https://doi.org/10.1177/0266242612453933

Jones, S. (2015). You would expect the successful person to be the man. *International Journal of Gender and Entrepreneurship, 7*(3), 303–320.

Jones, P., Jones, A., Packham, G., & Miller, C. (2008). Student attitudes towards enterprise education in Poland: A positive impact. *Education & Training, 50*(7), 597–614. https://doi.org/10.1108/00400910810909054

Jones, P., Miller, C., Jones, A., & Packham, G. (2011). Attitudes and motivations of Polish students towards entrepreneurial activity. *Education & Training, 53*(5), 416–432. https://doi.org/10.1108/00400911111147721

Kailer, N. (2009). Entrepreneurship education: Empirical findings and proposals for the design of entrepreneurship education concepts at universities in German-speaking countries. *Journal of Enterprising Culture, 17*(2), 201–231.

Karhunen, P., & Ledyaeva, S. (2010). Determinants of entrepreneurial interest and risk tolerance among Russian University students: Empirical study. *Journal of Enterprising Culture, 18*(3), 229–263.

Krippendorff, K. (2012). *Content analysis: An introduction to its methodology*. Thousand Oaks, CA: Sage.

Kriz, W. C., & Auchter, E. (2016). 10 Years of evaluation research into gaming simulation for german entrepreneurship and a new study on its long-term effects. *Simulation & Gaming, 47*(2), 179–205. https://doi.org/10.1177/1046878116633972

Kurczewska, A., & Bialek, J. (2014). Is the interplay between self-efficacy and entrepreneurial intentions gender-dependent? *Argumenta Oeconomica, 33*(2), 23–38.

Kurczewska, A., Kyrö, P., & Abbas, A. (2014). Transformative capacity of entrepreneurship education in two different cultural settings - morphogenetic analysis of Egypt and Finland. *Journal of Enterprising Culture, 22*(4), 401–435. https://doi.org/10.1142/S0218495814500174

Küttim, M., Kallaste, M., Venesaar, U., & Kiis, A. (2014). Entrepreneurship education at university level and students' entrepreneurial intentions. *Procedia - Social and Behavioral Sciences, 110*, 658–668. https://doi.org/10.1016/j.sbspro.2013.12.910

Lombard, M., Snyder-Duch, J., & Bracken, C. C. (2002). Content analysis in mass communication: Assessment and reporting of intercoder reliability. *Human Communication Research, 28*(4), 587–604.

Maresch, D., Harms, R., Kailer, N., & Wimmer-Wurm, B. (2016). The impact of entrepreneurship education on the entrepreneurial intention of students in science and engineering versus business studies university programs. *Technological Forecasting and Social Change, 104*, 172–179. https://doi.org/10.1016/j.techfore.2015.11.006

Oehler, A., Hofer, A., & Schalkowski, H. (2015). Entrepreneurial education and knowledge: Empirical evidence on a sample of German undergraduate students. *Journal of Technology Transfer, 40*(3), 536–557. https://doi.org/10.1007/s10961-014-9350-2

Packham, G., Jones, P., Miller, C., Pickernell, D., & Brychan, T. (2010). Attitudes towards entrepreneurship education: A comparative analysis. *Education & Training, 52*(8/9), 568–586. https://doi.org/10.1108/00400911011088926

Petridou, E., & Sarri, K. (2011). Developing "potential entrepreneurs" in higher education institutes. *Journal of Enterprising Culture, 19*(1), 79–99.

Petridou, E., Sarri, A., & Kyrgidou, L. P. (2009). Entrepreneurship education in higher educational institutions: The gender dimension. *Gender in Management, 24*(4), 286–309. https://doi.org/10.1108/17542410910961569

Pickering, C., & Byrne, J. (2014). The benefits of publishing systematic quantitative literature reviews for PhD candidates and other early-career researchers. *Higher Education Research & Development, 33*(3), 534–548.

Radovic-Markovic, M., Lindgren, C. E., Grozdanic, R., Markovic, D., & Salamzadeh, A. (2012). Freedom, individuality and women's entrepreneurship education. *Entrepreneurship education - a priority for the higher education institutions* (pp. 203–208).

Rae, D., Martin, L., Antcliff, V., & Hannon, P. (2012). Enterprise and entrepreneurship in english higher education: 2010 and beyond. *Journal of Small Business and Enterprise Development, 19* (3), 380–401. https://doi.org/10.1108/14626001211250090

Rideout, E. C., & Gray, D. O. (2013). Does entrepreneurship education really work? A review and methodological critique of the empirical literature on the effects of university-based entrepreneurship education. *Journal of Small Business Management, 51*(3), 329–351. https://doi.org/10.1111/jsbm.12021

Schwarz, E. J., Wdowiak, M. A., Almer-Jarz, D. A., & Breitenecker, R. J. (2009). The effects of attitudes and perceived environment conditions on students' entrepreneurial intent. *Education & Training, 51*(4), 272–291. https://doi.org/10.1108/00400910910964566

Shinnar, R., Pruett, M., & Toney, B. (2009). Entrepreneurship education: Attitudes across campus. *Journal of Education for Business, 84*(3), 151–159.

Shneor, R., & Jenssen, J. I. (2014). A comparison of factors influencing male and female students' entrepreneurial intentions. In D. Vrontis, Y. Weber, & E. Tsoukatos (Eds.), *5th Annual euromed conference of the euromed academy of business: Building new business models for success through competitiveness and responsibility* (pp. 1854–1858). Kristiansand: EuroMed Press.

Shneor, R., Metin Camgöz, S., & Bayhan Karapinar, P. (2013). The interaction between culture and sex in the formation of entrepreneurial intentions. *Entrepreneurship & Regional Development, 25*(9/10), 781–803. https://doi.org/10.1080/08985626.2013.862973

Staniewski, M. W., & Szopinski, T. (2015). Student readiness to start their own business. *Economic Research-Ekonomska Istrazivanja, 28*(1), 608–619. https://doi.org/10.1080/1331677x.2015.1085809

Tegtmeier, S., & Mitra, J. (2015). Gender perspectives on university education and entrepreneurship. *International Journal of Gender and Entrepreneurship, 7*(3), 254–271.

Teixeira, D., Simões, J., & Silva, M. J. M. (2012). *Self-efficacy of students attending higher education institutions.* Paper presented at the ECIE2012-7th European Conference on Innovation and Entrepreneurship, 20–21 September 2012, Santarem Portugal.

Terjesen, S. A., & Lloyd, A. (2015). *The female entrepreneurship index.* Washington, DC: The Global Entrepreneurship and Development Institute.

Tiago, T., Faria, S., Couto, J. P., & Tiago, F. (2015). Fostering innovation by promoting entrepreneurship: From education to intention. *Procedia - Social and Behavioral Sciences, 175*, 154–161. https://doi.org/10.1016/j.sbspro.2015.01.1186

Treanor, L. (2012). Entrepreneurship education: Exploring the gender dimension. *International Journal of Gender and Entrepreneurship, 4*(2), 206–210. https://doi.org/10.1108/17566261211234689

Turker, D., & Senem Sonmez, S. (2009). Which factors affect entrepreneurial intention of university students. *Journal of European Industrial Training, 33*(2), 142–159. https://doi.org/10.1108/03090590910939049

VanderBrug, J. (2013). The global rise of female entrepreneurs. *Harvard Business Review*. Retrieved August 21, 2017, from https://hbr.org/2013/09/global-rise-of-female-entrepreneurs

Varamäki, E., Joensuu, S., Tornikoski, E., & Viljamaa, A. (2015). The development of entrepreneurial potential among higher education students. *Journal of Small Business and Enterprise Development, 22*(3), 563–589.

Vilcov, N., & Dimitrescu, M. (2015). Management of entrepreneurship education: A challenge for a performant educational system in Romania. *Procedia - Social and Behavioral Sciences, 203*, 173–179. https://doi.org/10.1016/j.sbspro.2015.08.278

Vukovic, K., Kedmenec, I., & Korent, D. (2015). The impact of exposure to entrepreneurship education on student entrepreneurial intentions. *Croatian Journal of Education-Hrvatski Casopis Za Odgoj I Obrazovanje, 17*(4), 1009–1036.

Yordanova, D. I., & Tarrazon, M.-A. (2010). Gender differences in entrepreneurial intentions: Evidence from Bulgaria. *Journal of Developmental Entrepreneurship, 15*(3), 245–261.

Part II
Case Studies

Coming to Entrepreneurial Berlin and Making Their Way in Silicon Allee: The Ups and Downs of Two Women Entrepreneurs

Alexander Goebel and Sebastian G. M. Händschke

Abstract This case study examines the life stories of two female entrepreneurs, from their early childhood experiences to their more recent and strenuous experiences in their professional lives. We focus on the common arena of their life paths—Berlin—and their personal differences. Although both entrepreneurs hail from different locations and have different previous experiences, they also share similarities which will become clear when working through the case. The following recounts how they entered the German start-up scene in Berlin and how they have experienced and coped with failure. Our case focuses on their current failure. It also shows how this failure and the personal experiences, thoughts and emotions, as well as the reactions and coping strategies it triggered are nested in each individual's life. While the experience of failure is prominent in the case study, it also highlights key coping mechanisms. We additionally pay attention to the specificities of the Berlin start-up scene throughout the case.

A. Goebel
Industrial and Organizational Psychology, Friedrich Schiller University Jena, Jena, Germany
e-mail: alexander.goebel@uni-jena.de

S. G. M. Händschke (✉)
Organization, Leadership, and HRM, Friedrich Schiller University Jena, Jena, Germany

Jena Schumpeter Center for Research on Socio-Economic Change (JSEC), Friedrich Schiller University Jena, Jena, Germany
e-mail: sebastian.haendschke@uni-jena.de

© Springer International Publishing AG, part of Springer Nature 2018
S. Birkner et al. (eds.), *Women's Entrepreneurship in Europe*, FGF Studies in Small Business and Entrepreneurship, https://doi.org/10.1007/978-3-319-96373-0_8

Teaching Note—Coming to Entrepreneurial Berlin and Making Their Way in Silicon Allee: The Ups and Downs of Two Women Entrepreneurs

Target Group

- Interdisciplinary entrepreneurship seminars
- As supplementary material for a lecture on entrepreneurship (general)
- As supplementary material for a lecture on women/female entrepreneurship

Background Information

This case is based on the personal stories of two female entrepreneurs, Victoria and Paula. Their names, the places where they were born, the universities where they studied, and other information have all been altered to protect their anonymity. Both have worked and/or still work successfully and prominently in the Berlin start-up scene.

Main Learning Objectives/Key Issues

There are two key issues which can be learned when dealing with this case.

- On the one hand, students should develop a differentiated view of success and failure in the start-up process and what these two concepts really mean for female entrepreneurs.
- On the other hand, students should gain insight into how to cope with failure in the process of venture founding.

How to Use the Case (Teaching Strategy)

It is our belief that each teacher knows best how to use this case in his or her class. We do however provide the following suggestion for how to use it: First, allow the students to brainstorm their own ideas of success and failure. Then have them develop ideas about how to generally cope with failure and in particular what women would or could do in the case of failure. Then ask the students to discuss their ideas in class and critically examine each other with regard to how much they feel they are falling prey to their own stereotypes and prejudices. Follow this by reading the entire text and letting the students discuss it in small groups.

Afterwards, ask the students to complete the following task e.g. as part of a term paper (Master's level): do a literature search (Google Scholar, Web of Knowledge) on "coping" and "failure" in general and in the context of "entrepreneurship." Then the students should select a number of these papers and write a term paper/essay (4–5 pages) discussing how the experiences in the case are generalizable, i.e. to what extent research contradicts or confirms the experiences in the case description. Here the students should pay specific attention to the paradigmatic background of the literature used (in terms of the discipline in question, i.e. psychology, sociology, economics; as well as in terms of the level of analysis, i.e. individual (cognitive, emotional, behavioral),

(continued)

societal, etc.) as described in Händschke (2015). Note: this task can also be used for Bachelor's students. Simply skip the first part of the literature search, and have the instructor provide the students with a list of appropriate references to work with.

Questions/Topics for Discussion
Every lecturer is free to choose his/her own questions for discussion. We offer the following indicative questions as a starting point for personal reflection. (These can also guide the questions posed in the term paper task described above):

- What are individual ideas of success and failure?
- What are the positive and negative aspects of regional factors (Berlin)?
- Which role does the family background play in general?
- How do/did the two protagonists cope with failure? What are the similarities and differences in this regard?
- How do/did the two protagonists learn from failure and success? Do/Did they learn differently from them?

1 The Case—Coming to Entrepreneurial Berlin and Making Their Way in Silicon Allee: The Ups and Downs of Two Women Entrepreneurs[1]

1.1 The End of a Baby

VICTORIA Victoria shut Michael's door quietly. Then she slowly went back to her office. Sitting down at her desk, she was about to cry for a split second, but became calm again when her mind cleared as she went through what had just happened. She took a pen and started flipping it back and forth between her right thumb and forefinger—something she's always done since pre-school when she had to think about something.

Earlier that morning she had arrived at the office as usual at 8:30 AM sharp, carrying a paper cup of coffee that she picked up every morning from around the corner. When she came in, her co-founder Sarah bumped into her and she spilled some coffee on the new floor that had been put down in the office 1 week ago. They had just moved their office to this new, fancier location in Berlin 2 weeks ago. As she was about to say "Oh, Sarah, good morning! Everything OK? Normally you start at 9:30, right?", Sarah cut her off, "Hi! Michael called this morning. He said I should come in earlier. We need to talk. And, me and you, we need to be on stand-by this morning to come over to his office to talk." Michael was the main shareholder and a

---

[1]By Alexander Goebel and Sebastian G.M. Händschke

rather active investor of the start-up Victoria and Sarah had founded: GOODY SHOP, an online platform that sells fancy products.

After talking with Sarah about what the issue might be—the roll-out in Spain or some issues with the new building—Victoria went to her office, settled in at her desk and worked through the list she had prepared for that morning. This morning was even busier than usual for them, or even for a start-up of their size and age. There was excitement among everyone as things seemed to be moving forward better than planned over the past week, especially since the weeks before had been really slow. Finally, once Victoria entered her "workflow mode". Michael suddenly called her and Sarah into his office, everything became faster and then ... ground to a halt. After his usual brief hello-and-good-morning he let the bubble burst: "Sarah and Victoria, this morning the board and I decided to close GOODY SHOP. I'm sorry. You'll have 1 day, today, to inform everyone, and 4 weeks to shut down. Thank you for your passion. Your share in GOODY will be paid out to you plus 10%. We'd like you to stay with us in the headquarters or in another firm of ours. We look forward to getting other things moving together. Let's make a new appointment, let's say in 2 weeks, to talk about this in more detail." Victoria and Sarah were confused and stunned. A short and heated discussion started "Why? Why now? Why didn't you talk to us earlier?" The discussion became less heated as it continued and cooled off a little before Michael politely ordered them to "inform the team right now and come back to me afterwards. All the best to you!" There were no more questions to ask and, well, no potential answers. Victoria and Sarah left the office devastated.

Later at 11:00 AM they called the five executive managers and team leaders into Sarah's office for an extra-ordinary management team meeting. Normally, it was a brief meeting as they basically just informed the managers about the latest news. This time took longer. A short and a little less-heated discussion followed. This time, Victoria and Sarah found themselves on the other side of the table. At the end of the meeting, Sarah whispered, "Vicky, you tell everybody in the team 'I can't do it.' You need to do it. I've got your back." So, then at noon, when they normally had lunch together, Victoria stepped up onto a box of Bionade (a former hipster drink in Berlin) and said: "Sorry folks, I need to say something before we have lunch. Sarah and I need to tell you something. This morning we were called in by Michael who told us that GOODY SHOP will be closed and will go offline within the next week, and in 4 weeks will be fully shut down. We argued for a while with him—no chance. So, this is it. You'll get your dismissals tomorrow in the mail [...]." Then, a cacophony of shouting, crying, discussing burst out. No one wanted to eat the vegan burgers that had been delivered by the award-winning nearby vegan catering service.

At 1 PM, Victoria told Michael that the team had been informed. Michael seemed somewhere else with his thoughts and just nodded vacantly. Victoria closed his door quietly.

Now, as she reflected about that morning flipping her pen she thought, "2 days after I started, I went to China and bought goodies for 10 months and ten markets that didn't even exist at the time. And now, 2 months later, when the first countries are up and running, we close it down and let almost everyone go." On the surface, it was a failure and she thought she should feel empty. But was it really a failure? Had she lost money or her job? No. What dissatisfied her was something else: she couldn't finish the job. She stopped flipping the pen, stood up, packed her bag and with those thoughts, left the office. On her way home, she remembered how things had moved along in the past months and days with GOODY SHOP, how sad but happy she was, and how she had gotten where she was right now.

PAULA Without knowing it, 1 week earlier Paula, another woman in her 30s, and a distant acquaintance of Victoria's she knew from various events, had a very similar experience in another part of town. Paula was working for a company in which she held some equity. Holding equity in a company that she had not founded herself has always given her the odd feeling of being only "kind of" an entrepreneur. She was involved in this company as a minority owner and manager. They had been 90 people, although it was clear to Paula that this number would not be sustainable. And then, 1 week ago, they had to let half of their team go to allow the rest of the company to survive. It was up to her to tell everyone.

Paula had to stand up and speak in front of all these people. Although this meant facing one of her biggest fears, it had to be done. It seemed like someone was shoving her from behind. She just didn't want to do it. Her inner voice was telling her, "Paula, you're here now and everybody is watching you. Say something. There's no other way." This is how she always pushed herself into action to do these kinds of very unpleasant things. Afterwards she felt free, thinking that now she had got it behind her. And it really hadn't been as bad as she first thought. She actually felt liberated but weary and exhausted. She had spoken with many of her team members individually. "What do you want to do next? Can I help you get to where you want to go? Is there a company you would want to talk to and where I could put in a good word for you?"

In the evening on her way home, she reflected on the situation. "It was a tough moment, standing in front of these people and telling them that half of them would have to leave. And actually, I knew it was coming." She was questioning herself. "Why did I decide to run this company at all? Am I the Pied Piper of Hameln who just somehow led all of them into the river? I'm desperate. This is the biggest failure of my life."

1.2 Life Path

VICTORIA When Victoria went home the day the GOODY SHOP closing was announced, she reflected on how she had got where she was right now. All in all, she had a very good childhood. Intense to be sure, but also full of experiences that had enriched her life then and now. When she was young she had to move a lot (more or less every 3 years) because her father was a diplomat. This meant that everything was new for her over and over again, with the continual routine of new school mates, new friends at the riding stable, and of course, a new environment and language in general. This helped her learn how to meet new people and make friends easily in unfamiliar places. And Victoria learned to show a general openness towards new experiences. However, after all those years, when she had finished school, she wanted to study in Germany. She chose Cologne and business administration as her field of study. When the end of her studies drew nearer, the world called again, and she finalized her studies with an international internship at a German car company in Bangkok. There she was able to extend her stay to do her Master's thesis with the firm as well. Her first job straight out of university was in marketing with a major mobile phone company where she stayed for 2 years. She left after problems with the company culture and the bad business environment that the firm had entered into. Her next job was with the largest family-owned chain of coffee retailers in Germany, known for its weekly-changing range of non-food products as diverse as lingerie, stationary, and cutlery. Victoria was lucky to work there for a boss who gave her all the freedom she needed to succeed. Actually, to some extent she had already been an entrepreneur there—at least as an *intra*preneur. Her boss had always been supportive in nearly everything she did. But after 2 years, and upon telling him she was considering the idea of an additional Master's degree or an MBA, he was upset and disappointed. After cooling down however, he returned to "normal" mode with her, supporting her as before, and writing her a much-needed letter of recommendation. He took her word that she would rejoin the firm after her studies. Victoria was surprised a little by his anger and disappointment. For her, a Master's in business administration was nothing that she had dreamt of in particular. There was even a reason why she had not done one so far: one of the constants in her life as a child were the yearly stints to New York City where her father had studied for an additional Master's degree, later teaching a course at Columbia Business School on a regular basis. Victoria had spent time on campus and had been in regular contact with the business school as a child, basically growing up there during the summers and getting to know half of the faculty. For her, it was natural to have universities in her life. That's why an MBA did not seem to be such a big deal to her when she asked her boss for his letter of recommendation. In the end, he was positive and supportive too, and encouraged her to "go for it." There was now only one more obstacle—her boyfriend (he's now her husband) Daniel. Although he couldn't accompany her, they got engaged before she left and then later got married.

Personal affiliation was the main reason for Victoria to go for her Master studies to Columbia. Of course, she knew Columbia was Ivy League and in New York. This was great and to the envy of everybody who knew her. But Victoria went there because she is more of the family type. As a diplomat, her father had always been an "organization man", almost like a corporate manager. When teaching at Columbia, he got involved in teaching classes on entrepreneurship and on founding new international NGOs. This was where Victoria inhaled the entrepreneurial spirit. Maybe this was one reason why she always had had the idea to start a new company. This was always something that ignited her, not really pressing her into action, but lingering nevertheless.

Victoria finished her Master's degree at Columbia. After this, founding her own business was inevitable. Founding and becoming an entrepreneur had been part of the curriculum. Students were confronted with this every day. Also she had been involved in founding processes at the university. This made it much easier for her, and even helped her get over her fear of failure. Almost all of her classmates had become self-employed during their studies. And then there were entrepreneurship courses that were held by professors from all kinds of fields. Victoria took courses on venture capital, where the largest VC firms were brought into class. Every week they had to submit ideas that the VCs and professors would provide their feedback on. The VCs wanted students to exhibit grit when pursuing their ideas, even after they finished their studies. The VCs communicated this expectation clearly. Venturing was such an essential part of the culture there. And from her class, over half of them started a venture afterwards. There really was no way around it. She would have to start a company, too.

However, Victoria returned to Germany and her husband. And because of her great boss, she returned to her old employer, the coffee retailer. Unfortunately, a few things had changed since she left. Her old boss was still there, but not for long. He had previously announced that he was leaving without the option to take her with him, which he would have liked. So what followed was a 4-week-long in-house search for a new position for her. This process, although supported by the head of human resources, exposed the rigid HR structures and the corporate culture in other parts of the company. In one of her conversations for a new position within the firm, her HR representative criticized the bright color of her sophisticated Ralph Lauren cardigan, stating that it was a sign of her exuberant self-confidence and dominance. Those were tough weeks, and at the end of the fourth week, she knew this would not lead anywhere. Since the end of the MBA course she had stayed in close contact with her fellow alumni and other people at Columbia. Through the Columbia network, she received an offer to start as co-founder in an incubator-based venture in Berlin, then the hotspot of start-ups in Germany. The day had come! She happily agreed.

PAULA Paula had a somewhat different family background and life path. Her parents were both active entrepreneurs even into their 60s. Her father owned a few retail stores and her mother was the CEO of the family business. In some ways, they had a decisive influence on her because they actually encouraged her to be creative and implement ideas that generated income. Basically, as a young adult, she was offered the opportunity to test what it is like to be an entrepreneur herself with a sufficient safety net. Failure had already been cautiously taken into account by her mother: "If your idea is good, then you can do it. And if it's bad, we'll let it go." She then successfully convinced her mother and father of her idea to establish a new regional food concept. They financed the idea's implementation through a loan, which she had to pay back over the following years. Paula is grateful to this day for having had this opportunity because she knows that she was privileged to learn many lessons through it. She ran the business for a few years and then sold it when she moved on to study. Later, she founded another company in the regional food business. Although it was never launched, in fact, she had already lined up investors for this business. Here, Paula experienced for the first time in her professional life something that could be referred to as failure. Failure was prevalent in her private life as well, as her marriage suffered from the situation and ultimately came to an end.

1.3 Walking the Tightrope Between Success and Failure

VICTORIA On the evening after Victoria had to announce the end of GOODY SHOP, she was preparing dinner with her husband Daniel at home. While cutting leeks, peppers, onions, and the like she talked with him about what had happened during the day. This was one of their rituals: cooking together and reflecting on the day. Of course, Michael's decision and the closure of GOODY SHOP was the main topic. When they set the table, Daniel asked Victoria out of the blue, "Darling, mmh, actually, what is failure for you? Was today a failure?" It caught her off guard, and, still holding the plates that she was about to place on the table, she paused for a moment to think. Then, she started setting the table as she thought aloud, "Failure is, I believe at least, if I am personally really disappointed about what I've done. Like if I run something into the ground. A financial failure, debt, personally or the company. And certainly, and maybe that's the most important part, if I haven't done what I could have." Daniel wasn't going to let her off the hook that easily. They finished setting the table and after they had sat down and begun enjoying their meal, he asked her, "Darling, if this is your definition of failure, what is success for you then? Is it just the opposite of failure?" Victoria smirked briefly. She smiled at him and said, "Dan, you're a cruel man. That's a tough question too." That's what she loved about him. He said tough things warmly and friendly. "No, it's not just that simple. Of course, the business needs to be above break-even, but I believe above all, for me, the interpersonal component is also extremely important. Maybe this is seen as typical for women—but I don't care—somehow, I see as one of our biggest achievements that we've put together a great team and that we, as a team, pulled the thing off, supporting each other. I think this is not typical in bad times where people often start trying to do what's best for them and say: it was your fault, not mine, and all the success was thanks to me."

PAULA For Paula success has an economic component when it comes to various dimensions. It means creating a product or an idea that has a market, and creating something that people really want to have. At best it comprises the creation of a new market instead of just innovating within an existing one. For her, financial success means the creation of an idea and a company that is so good that it can generate profits, not just for the sake of being profitable, but in order to use that profitability to implement further ideas. If there's no profit in the long or medium term, a positive corporate culture and investments (e.g. in research and development) are simply not possible. And success for her is not to make a quick million, i.e. start a venture, sell it and then hop on to the next idea and do the same thing over and over again. Success for Paula would be if, much later in her life, e.g. at the age of 50 or 60, the companies she founded were still around. This would prove that the new ventures had worked sustainably. Failure, at least according to Paula's understanding, is a personal experience. Failure is not that something is not working. Failure instead is about situations where someone doesn't even try to implement his or her ideas. In her view, failure also involves situations where people do not act honestly and transparently.

For Paula, one example of failure is when someone acts opportunistically at the expense of others.

1.4 Coping with Failure: Learning, Personal Development, and Growth

VICTORIA Victoria and her husband had finished their meal. They were clearing the table when the phone rang. Daniel answered it and Peter, Victoria's brother, was on the line. Peter had just come back from a sailing trip on the Baltic Sea, and since Daniel was into sailing too, they started to talk about the trip for a while. Victoria continued loading the dishwasher, lost in her thoughts, recounting what she had just said to Daniel. She felt content with what she had done at GOODY SHOP. She had put together a great team and everybody had been working hard towards their goals. And whenever they have had issues with each other in the executive team at GOODY SHOP, they discussed them openly. These thoughts lifted her spirits while she overheard snippets of Daniel's and Peter's sailing discussion—"great winds", "some storms", "foresail torn"—when Daniel called her, "Hey Victoria, come over here. Peter called to talk to you." With a kiss on her cheek, he handed her the phone and sent her back into the living room on the other side of the kitchen counter, saying, "I can finish cleaning up the kitchen. Talk to him, I think you have a lot to talk about." Victoria has always been close to her two siblings, and they call each other regularly. They all appreciate how they are still so close. She took the phone from Daniel and opened the conversation with "Hey, Peter, how are you? How was the Baltic Sea?" because she simply did not want to go through the day again. The conversation would go into that direction early enough, she thought. So Peter told her about the trip too, but quickly changed the topic and asked her what was going on in her life, adding "You don't sound so good. Actually, you sound like...a little bit like back when we were children and Dad told us that we needed to move again. What's up?" Victoria smiled when she realized how well her brother knew her. She told him about the day that she had had and what happened. Peter listened patiently and when she had finished he asked her: "Wow, that's a lot for one day. How do you feel? You sound much better now. I've always been impressed by how well and fast you bounce back. When we were kids, you were sad when we needed to move again, but as soon as we had done it, you were always the first of us to feel at home in the new setting. How do you cope with all that?" Victoria had heard that before but had to pause for a moment before she answered. "Yeah, you're right. I can fall hard, but I can also get up quickly again. Yeah, it's bad. Something failed and went wrong, but there is still enough beauty in life. And I just think: let's try again. It's times like these that I appreciate the beautiful things in life. I know exactly what I have in life and what I don't. I make the choice that I want to see the beautiful things in life, and I appreciate them. Quite honestly, I have a good life. I have a husband I'm happily married, too. I have a great family with two siblings who call me all the time." She started laughing now. "Like you, Peter. It's so good to talk to you right now. And, I have many friends. In good and bad times, it's always my family and my friends who help me. They lift my spirits like you're doing right now. And the worst for me are the moments when I'm lonely. You know that, Peter!" She started laughing again and before Peter could say something, she added, "And that's exactly what I got out of it all. At the end of the day, get up and say: 'Get up and try again.' Whenever I've failed an exam or a pitch, or if I've somehow failed personally, sure that hurts, because no one wants to fail. Of course, I wanted it differently, but then I think, okay, try again. The next day you have to get up and in the case of an exam, register again, this time 3 months later. And do it again." Now Peter was laughing, too. "What a tough girl! Like . . ." But Victoria interrupted him as she felt a thought become clearer, something she had always felt but had never articulated. "I think you learn more from failure. That's where you're forced to deal with it. Successes are taken for granted. Because then you can always say, 'Great, it worked, but I already see the next challenge coming, so I now I have to focus on the new challenge.' Successes are easier to check off, because there's no real need to deal with them. When you fail and still want to succeed, you can't just wipe it away, you have to deal with it to be successful the next time. Sometimes you need the pressure of failures. It doesn't have to be a direct failure, but in order to optimize, you might need that kind of pressure to intensively deal the right way with failure."

PAULA Paula had to cope with failures as well. To her, problems were not only problems; they provided challenges. And her family has always provided important support and guidance for dealing with them. Her mother has always been especially helpful. When Paula's business and marriage failed, her mother said to her, "Paula, you have two options now. You can go on, which means get up again, dust yourself off and move on. Or from now on you stay at home and do nothing. But then it's not you anymore. And that's when others have managed to take your life. Is that what you want? I don't think so." Her children were also important in her decision to move on. At the time she had twins who were one and a half years old and, obviously, these toddlers needed her. There was no time and room to go into "out-of-order" mode and cry all day. Stopping was not an option. She thought the fact that the children were there helped the most to move on right away. This was supplemented by great friends and family who offered their help, too.

For Paula, however, failure had a specific connotation in two ways. She knows that it is seen as something negative to fail. But actually, for her the learning experience is more important, and therefore for her, the word has a rather positive connotation. She understands life in general and life as an entrepreneur in particular as the recurring interaction of action and reaction, which provides ample opportunity to learn from mistakes where stopping is only an option for reflection in order to move on afterwards. "Even if you fall on your face you're still moving forward." If you fall, get up and move on. In her view, it is even better to still make the same mistakes again rather than standing still. Consequently, in her perspective, in order to learn from mistakes, these mistakes have to be your own. She actually believes that you have to live through your own failures; you can't learn much from the failure of others, even though learning from the positive examples of others is different. In other words, she could learn a lot better when reading a book by an entrepreneur full of success stories than someone else who took 300 pages to describe what didn't work. Paula thinks that she would not feel the same way if she was the one doing the failing anyway, i.e. it would not prevent her from making the same mistakes.

So for Paula, failure is a stepping stone in a positive direction. She thinks that she would never have founded a new company if she hadn't failed before. If the first firms had not failed, she would never have founded the next companies. In her own words, "I totally believe in this, you have to make mistakes, and you also have to register an insolvency. You have to have the feeling of "wow", growing a company really is fun, but dismantling it, is really exhausting. So, next time I might want to think ahead. And think through whether it would have been much easier if I had done things differently and then do it differently right now. Someone can tell you all these things a hundred times, but it is much better if you experience them yourself."

Paula is clearly aware of the importance of reflection in this endeavor. "Yes, life is lived forward and understood backwards. This doesn't always mean immediate success, but this is somehow a very good piece of advice, because you often don't know where something leads you. You often don't know if you're doing it right when you do something for the first time. And only one thing is clear: if you do nothing at all, then nothing happens. It is more costly to stand still than to make mistakes (even repeated mistakes), because if I stand still here today, it is guaranteed that I will experience something negative and be moved to the back of the line as life moves on. If I move on and make more mistakes, okay, I have the chance to learn something along the way which I can do differently and better next time. I can then take the time to reflect on what happened, what worked and what didn't."

1.5 Berlin's Start-Up Scene

VICTORIA AND PAULA The next evening Victoria went to a small women entrepreneurs' "meet-n-drinks" socializer at one of the most established bars in former West-Berlin. She had already been asked to come by an old friend a few weeks before who also works in the Berlin start-up scene—Anna—and Victoria did not want to reschedule just because her company was going down the tubes. So she went. The bar was not at all as fancy as the places where they normally had their start-up events in the Berlin scene. A little run-down, the interior from the 1980s, back then when the city was still divided. The bar certainly exhibited the charm of old West-Berlin. She liked that as it reminded her partly of her youth in West Germany before the Berlin Wall came down.

It was a rather small and intimate event. It took a while until, after a round of introductions, hellos and hugs here and there, they sat down with their drinks at a Fabricius/Kastholm cocktail table. There were four of them, as Anna had brought along Paula, whom Anna had known better through their early days in the Berlin start-up scene. Sarah from GOODY SHOP was at the event, too.

First, Sarah told them about the new developments at GOODY SHOP. Then they were talking about their lives in general when Paula asked Victoria why she would not return to the corporate world. Victoria replied, "Maybe you're right. I was really happy there. I had a fantastic boss. I would stuck by him through thick and thin for him. He was extremely supportive. I had my own small start-up projects, for which I did basically everything as his right hand, developed most of the strategies for him. It was always up to me to handle everything from extremely strategic to extremely operational issues. Maybe that's something to think about." Ordering another mojito, for a moment, she really was thinking that this could be an option. But she still wanted to talk about something else. Taking the easy route, she smiled at Anna and asked, "So, what's going on with the guy you're dating? Getting serious?" To which Anna waved her hand and said, "No, we only had dinner last week. Nothing serious at all. Just another one of those buffs who's studied business administration, worked for a while and now has this great idea of a platform business model that'll change the world and—without admitting it—just wants to get rich fast. Well-mannered, can talk well but no character. A boy still, no guy, neither a man. Bad thing is, most likely I'll start seeing him regularly now. They'll move into our incubator. I even was the one to get him into touch with Springer." Victoria started a new topic. "So, what's going on with your new start-up plan? What did the VCs say?" Anna sat down her gin and tonic and said, "We haven't discussed the idea yet. I'm not there yet. Good thing was though, I learned that they are planning a new line of start-ups at Springer Ventures. It'll be headed by this guy who did his Master's at Stanford, founded a think tank in Berlin and ran for parliament for the Green party." Victoria nodded and said, "Interesting." With that they started to exchange the newest gossip in the start-up scene and Berlin. The longer they talked, the more they delved into the topic of Berlin; Paula was especially keen on the topic. The common denominator was that Berlin is a vibrant metropolis and great city that attracts a lot of talent, but is still as diversified in the start-up scene as it is as a city in general. In Victoria's view the founders in the U.S., especially in New York, are much more mixed and diverse. A lot more. She added, "They have a completely different exchange culture between corporates, start-up firms, law firms, etc. That is totally missing here in Berlin. And I also believe that this is one of the reasons why there are more successful firms in the US. This kind of exchange is extremely important. Besides, the scene is a lot bigger there." Paula on the other hand mainly believed in the advantages of the manageable number of relevant actors in Berlin's start-up scene. So she added, "I think it's great that everyone knows each other. Chains of communication are super-short, and if you need something, it's easy to get. I really like Berlin's start-up scene. We're all in the same industry, we all know that when you share knowledge, it helps a lot more than if you hold it back. And everyone who joins is an asset. There can't be enough. And anyone who dares to start up or come over into this industry will be welcomed with open arms. You get everything you need to know to get started right away. 'Go to this notary. Open your account here. Take care of your bookkeeping.' That's really helpful, isn't it? It saves you so much time. I like the extreme willingness to help. And then you feel safe. I mean, there's this certainty that we don't compete with each other, but see it instead as a cake that gets bigger with everyone who joins in. I've never had the feeling of competition. It's not like, 'Oh, my gosh, there's a new competitor, and I have to avoid any contact with them.' It's the opposite. I would probably want to meet them immediately to see what they're doing, and think about what we can do together. All in all, it's a great atmosphere at a breakneck speed."

The talk went on for hours, with the topics changing between a variety of past experiences, current obstacles, and future chances. As always, it was a vivid event—just a normal evening in Berlin.

1.6 How Things Unfolded Afterwards

VICTORIA After the business closure was completed, Victoria was offered to join a new venture within the same incubator, which she declined because she was pregnant. She was, however, now hooked on the start-up thing. During her pregnancy, her old boss called with a venture idea and asked her whether they could develop a concept together. So she developed the concept, wrote the business plan and even sacrificed her family vacation to meet the investors and pitch the idea. Unfortunately to no avail: the proposal was rejected. Victoria was very disappointed, and all the effort seemed wasted. This time, failure felt even worse. She had been working very intensively on it for 4 months, and the longer she worked on it, the more she really looked forward to it. That's when the company's supervisory board rejected the proposal. The bubble burst, the excitement was gone, and she wondered why this felt so painful. "Maybe it's the emotional anticipation that you have. You get wrapped up in things before they become a reality. You're happy when you're working towards a goal, you want it, and then it's such a miscarriage. The emotional expectation causes a lot of hurt."

But she also managed this setback successfully. Another friend in the start-up scene asked to join her to attend yet another women networking event in Berlin. Just a few days before the event Victoria's husband drew her attention to a job offer at an established company in the digital business. The job advert sounded good. By chance, the company's recruitment manager held a speech at the networking event. Victoria used the evening to get in contact and talk with the recruiting manager. She got the job offer 1 week later. Truth be told, she did not want to re-join the corporate world. But as a mother, it was an attractive option. Starting up again is always just a few steps away, so she accepted.

PAULA Paula started a new business a few months later. She learned from the past, did things differently, and built up a profitable company which operates internationally and plans to pay its employees from its cash flow. She also found a new love, got engaged and is now married to another entrepreneur. This is huge benefit for the mutual appreciation of how things are as an entrepreneur.

Further Reading About Berlin's Start-Up Scene

https://www.theatlantic.com/technology/archive/2017/05/european-tech-campuses/526359/

https://www.theguardian.com/small-business-network/2015/oct/22/berlins-startup-scene-is-knuckling-down-to-business

https://www.economist.com/news/business/21707599-rocket-internet-fizzles-other-startups-take-freaks-are-coming

http://www.nytimes.com/2011/09/17/world/europe/berlins-tech-scene-offers-hope-to-economy.html

https://www.bloomberg.com/news/articles/2016-07-28/berlin-s-startup-hub-wants-to-prove-it-s-more-than-just-a-scene

Reference

Händschke, S. G. M. (2015). Scholarly impact in the long run by teaching pluralism today. *Academy of Management Annual Meeting Proceedings, 2015*(1), 18933–18933. www.researchgate.net/publication/291377738_Scholarly_Impact_in_the_Long_Run_by_Teaching_Pluralism_Today

Allure and Reality in FemTec Entrepreneurship

A Case Study of a Female Entrepreneur Who Struggled in the Mechanical Engineering Entrepreneurial Ecosystem in Germany

Frauke Lange

Abstract The following case study describes the founding process of a female engineer who, frustrated and discouraged by her years of work experience, was attracted to the benefits of self-employment. Associating self-employment with being freed from the specific constraints she had experienced in her everyday working life, her notion of self-employment was based on role models from her private surroundings. Her dissatisfaction with her former working life was especially the cause of the decisions by her direct superior and the lack of opportunities to effectively participate at her job. In her self-evaluation, she saw the reasons for her company's failure most notably in the lack of competence and qualification when it came to e.g. customer acquisition. She was also frustrated by the wrong advice she had received by start-up consultants. She found helpful advice only from self-organized, private consultants and mentors, as they (unlike the "professional" start-up consultants) had specific knowledge and experience in their technical fields. The drama in this case lies especially in the fact that the female foundress' product idea was in fact implemented and capitalized upon by one of her clients when the market entry of her own company was delayed by a few months. As a result, she lost the promising starting point of her own founding, while unintentionally placing an experienced competitor onto the market. The interesting aspect of this case lies in the confrontation with the reality of entrepreneurship and the conscious experience of "walking the path" of entrepreneurial work, especially the organizational work of getting the own company up and running. In this instance, it ultimately represented the foundress' downfall.

F. Lange (✉)
Female Entrepreneurship, University of Oldenburg, Oldenburg, Germany
e-mail: frauke.lange@uni-oldenburg.de

© Springer International Publishing AG, part of Springer Nature 2018
S. Birkner et al. (eds.), *Women's Entrepreneurship in Europe*, FGF Studies in Small Business and Entrepreneurship, https://doi.org/10.1007/978-3-319-96373-0_9

Notes to Teachers—Allure and Reality in FemTec Entrepreneurship
Target Group

This case study examines the field of female engineering and is therefore located at the interface between gender studies and entrepreneurship. It is addressed primarily towards students in this scientific field. Because it discusses a founding process in mechanical engineering, it can additionally be used for career-related seminars or engineering sciences modules.

Recommended courses are—among others—Entrepreneurship, especially Female and/or Women Entrepreneurship; Intrapreneurship; Business Psychology; Career Management; Business Administration; Gender Studies.

Background Information

This case study is the result of a 1-hour qualitative interview and a personal description written by the foundress conducted and evaluated as part of a grounded theory study of female high-tech start-ups in 2016. It is written in the style of a retrospective narrative of the foundress, which was reconstructed by the author on the basis of the existing data. The story thus combines excerpts and information from different data.

The special character of this case is its focus on a failed startup idea. The failure was presented at the 2015 "Fuckup Night" in Bremen, Germany.[1] The main elements of the case study are the actions and decisions which led to the failure of the project and the consequences and evaluation of the failure itself by the foundress—all occurring in a country which still considers failure taboo. The original documents this paper is based on are available in German. A thorough examination of them was performed to minimize (if not fully eliminate) any translation errors.

This case study focuses on the gender role/social gender of the foundress while operating in a male-dominated field, something it identifies and considers a professional obstacle. Interestingly, the foundress described her being a woman as a greater obstacle in the field of start-up counseling than in her professional life as an engineer ("I was able to come across well and convincingly in the job. But with these people I came across like a stick in the mud"). She described her physical stature (petite and very young-looking) as an ever-present obstacle to her professional progress and in her professional reality. This however would disappear after a period of convincing professional performance.

(continued)

---

[1] "Fuckup Night is a global movement and event series that shares stories of professional failure. Each month, in events across the globe, we get three to four people to get up in front of a room full of strangers to share their own professional fuckup." Source: https://fuckupnights.com/ (retrieved on September 10, 2017).

Main Learning Objectives/Key Issues

Working with this case study, the students will obtain deeper insight into the possible causes and consequences of technical female entrepreneurship in Germany. As part of this insight, they will also learn how the foundress herself justified and evaluated her own founding process. The students will additionally gain knowledge about the following aspects of female entrepreneurship:

- The influence of entrepreneurial knowledge and/or entrepreneurial education.
- Motivational factors of self-employment in connection with the reality of the founding process (structural, personal and contextual prerequisites for a successful startup).
- Factors influencing the founding process in the case of the female foundress presented and the entrepreneurial ecosystem.
- The complexity of entrepreneurial decisions (far removed from funding), the assumption of risk in a technology-based start-up process and insight into possible consequences of major entrepreneurial decisions.

How to Use the Case/Teaching Strategy
Step I. Getting Started: The Failure of Businesses

Insight can be achieved by jointly developing the Global Failure Index (for example using Power Point slides). The Global Failure Index was developed against the background of a positive culture of failure. It allows an analysis based on real numbers (age, gender, sales figures, survival rate, region, etc.). This content evaluation can be complemented by the special characteristics of the German start-up culture. Examples here include failure as a taboo in German society, as well as the issue of gender relations in entrepreneurship based on current entrepreneurship research (e.g. the low proportion of women in technical start-ups).

Step II. Independent Examination of the Case

In Step II the students will first receive the graphic overview of the case study to get acquainted with the basic data of the case and facilitate its independent examination. This is followed by an examination of the self-description of the entrepreneur, which can be briefly presented as a real case.

Step III. Deepening and Reflecting the Case in Small Group Work

Reflection on the case in small groups is recommended for the third step to deepen the knowledge developed to this point.

Two aspects are of particular interest here:

- Reflection on failure (causes/background/influence factors, etc.).
- Reflection on the influence of the entrepreneur's gender and personality factors (as can be determined from the text).

(continued)

For this purpose, the small working groups receive the two supplementary texts on:

- The assessment of the process of failure by the foundress herself (interview-based text).
- The personality, motivation and the background of the foundress (also an interview-based text).

The small group work can also aim to develop solutions or aspects for an effective start-up consultation in this case. Exemplary task: Develop a consulting approach that corresponds to the foundress' clear consulting requirements and which provides helpful support for these obstacles in the founding process. The following questions can help to motivate the discussion:

- What are the main challenges of this start-up project? How do you assess this?
- What would an alternative founding process look like in a similar situation? What alternative measures and founding steps are conceivable here?
- Which statements regarding the motivation of the foundress can be identified?
- Which motivational causes are often determinants in female entrepreneurship?
- What is your own attitude towards failure in the context of entrepreneurship or professional activity in general?

Another good discussion starting point includes first asking the students about their own experiences with failures and barriers in life.

Step IV. Combine the Results (Plenary Session)

The foundress can first be located demographically and with regard to her founding field (technology, production) in the Global Failure Index. In a second step, the results of the small working groups can be introduced and discussed (deviations/similarities/possible assessment in the context of current entrepreneurship research).

The information listed in the appendix can be used to compare or contrast individual and specific aspects of the discussion with the personal perspective of the foundress. On the basis of this deepening information, further questions and group work are conceivable that are not directly related to the foundation process, but for example, to the connection between her company's failure and her motivational or biographical situation instead.

1 The Case—Allure and Reality in FemTec Entrepreneurship

1.1 The Adventure of Founding a GmbH (LLC) in the German Engineering Industry

I am a mechanical engineer specialized in process engineering. I am 40 years old and have 14 years of professional experience in plant engineering. I was permanently employed at a company until May 2014. Afterwards I worked as a freelancer for a period of time. In the autumn of 2014, this self-employment ended upon finishing the project I was working on at that time. This is when the business idea for a pipeline product emerged, for which I wanted to enter the market. I thought being self-employed would give me the chance to be a better boss than I had experienced from my former superiors: I wanted the opportunity to value the ideas of my employees. At that time I was very enthusiastic about being an entrepreneur.

In January 2015, I began to write a business plan for this, and contacted a well-known company and potential customers to introduce them to the idea. This customer received the idea very positively, which motivated me to actually pursue the idea of founding my company. That's when I should have seen the dark clouds on the horizon...

The start-up process, with all its hurdles and bureaucracy, took up so much of my time that I was only able to contact the potential customer after 2 months. He never replied. He had taken the ball and run with the idea himself—as I learned from a later trade fair visit. But I'm getting ahead of myself. I had registered as unemployed in November 2014 and was receiving unemployment benefits. At the time I had no tax consultant—maybe he could have helped me the best. Then I made two mistakes:

1. *I took part in a business education seminar.*
2. *I looked for a start-up adviser.*

1.1.1 The Consulting Experience

At the halfway point of the 3-day seminar in mid-January of 2015, I left after I had corrected the seminar director four times. After that, I just couldn't believe anything he was saying. He also was just not a motivating person.

The first consultant I talked to after that was from a public institution who gave free advice to start-up companies. This person gave me such helpful tips as "Buy a second mobile phone, so that you have separate private and business numbers." I felt like I wasn't being taken seriously at all.

He didn't give me real information such as that I wouldn't have to pay trade association fees as long as I didn't have any employees. Maybe he just didn't know. Anyway, I expected information from a consultant which would spare me the painstaking time-consuming detail work. I left that appointment feeling no better off than when I walked in.

I called the Chamber of Industry and Commerce (the IHK in Germany) for some information. The employee said I needed to do "this" before "that" and NOT "that" before "this." And with the establishment of the GmbH at the notary, I would in any case set the official starting date for my company.

So I thought feverishly about what I had to do before the founding date—the whole bureaucracy (business office, tax office, business account, etc.), I needed the entry in the commercial register, and I wanted to start in a timely fashion. I spoke before the actual foundation with a bank about a start-up loan and founded the GmbH after this. Then nothing happened.

The founding day was hardly ever inquired about or noticed. Why this is supposed to be some kind of a historical event is a mystery to me to this day. The only thing the staff of the Chamber of Industry and Commerce did was to make me more insecure.

Somehow, the whole week went like this. Everyone told me what would be easy and difficult, what was important and unimportant, urgent and not urgent. And honestly, no one was right. Really, everything was different from what I was told. No matter if it was consultants, the IHK, the citizens' office, or friends, everyone had something to say.

I felt as if I was doing something that no one had ever done before.

1.1.2 The Bureaucratic Hurdles

And then I started running around. What should I do first? Create a new business account? Business registration? Ask the tax office for the VAT identification number? Articles of association with the notary? Clarify the possibilities for funding? Apply for a business start-up subsidy at the employment office?

So I just got started—and was sent away everywhere. I couldn't open a business account as long as I had not finished the articles of association with the notary and didn't have an entry in the commercial register. For the business registration, I also needed the commercial register entry.

OK, then let's try the tax office. When I registered as a freelancer it went relatively quickly and easily. I thought, OK, I can manage filling in one or two forms.

Only then did I learn that as the foundress of a limited company, I was not a business start-up (Existenzgründer) at all. And that changed nearly everything.

Then I was sent on a wild goose chase across the German financial office (Finanzamt)—no one was responsible for my situation. Again, I felt like I was an alien. The founding of a GmbH seemed as rare and as extraordinary as a UFO landing. I felt like an idiot and frustrated because I really thought it was impossible for the consultants to have such a lack of information that, to add insult to injury, was also downright wrong.

A little later, my neighbor said something very decisive to me: "You should only be advised by people who are where you want to be, or have already been there."

That changed everything. No more consultants who had never founded or led a company and had never been active in the industry.

Luckily there is a senior service where I live. It's made up of people who have left the professional life and advise young companies. Ahhh—that did me good. Someone who understood me. Someone who could tell me the really important and right things. Someone with whom I could sort out my thoughts. Someone who would tell me that I have to ask for a down payment of 10,000 euros from customers. I knew this from my professional career only with contracts around 500,000 euros—but why not also with "smaller" orders? This would relax the liquidity in my business plan. Someone who would check my GTCs, who looked through my offers to see if I forgot something. Someone who looked at my homepage. Someone who told me that the "other costs" in the business plan are about 5% of the other total costs and could tell you what they are in black and white.

Weeks later, I submitted all of the documents. They filled up an entire folder—from the opening balance of the tax consultant to the manager's employment contract.

1.1.3 Financing

I needed money to create the homepage and brochure, to buy licenses for a construction program, etc. and to pre-finance the pipe components. At this time, several newspapers reported that loans had never been so favorable because the interest rate was extremely low and the banks would be more than willing to make them.

The banks I went to apparently didn't get this memo. They also didn't buy the argument that I could always go back to working as an engineer to pay off the loan if the GmbH didn't work out. My discussion with a development bank was unsuccessful. Further loan requests at other banks were equally unsuccessful—despite the presentation of a business plan. "These are just fictional numbers," *they said. How did I know when I would sell how many products? I was advised to address more potential customers. But I just couldn't imagine it at all.* "Would you buy my product if I entered the market with it?" *I just couldn't imagine getting binding commitments to this question. And a "maybe" wouldn't have brought me any further—it would have just become embarrassing.*

I was in fact set to receive funding from a regional development bank. But this didn't pan out because I would be making the pipe components in a locksmith shop, so I didn't need a workbench and a welding machine (these are what I would have gotten the loan for).

What really took the cake was an appointment I had after the spin-off at a local business promotion. I had read that they would support 50% of the cost of business creation. Great, I thought. But then... The business promotion guy berated me for an hour—only to tell me they wouldn't be helping me after all. Huh?

"Because you're a merchant," he said. *"No I'm not,"* I replied, *"I'm a 'quasi-manufacturer.' I design my products, specify them and do technical drawings." His answer?* "Anyway, for us, you're a merchant." *Damn that set me off!*

As a side note, for the insurance company I was, well, a manufacturer because insurance for a merchant would have been much cheaper. For the business development, I was a merchant. Everyone defined me the way it was best for them.

Anyway, to top it all off, when this guy was done, he said hoped he was able to help me. HELP me!? I had had a funny gut feeling about him from the start—I should have forgotten the whole thing in the first place. In the evening, I shared my frustration with a complete stranger at the launderette. I Had to talk to someone. Otherwise I would have just burst.

I had acquired customers for my previous employers and negotiated millions of contracts. I wasn't a newbie! So? This man had already been self-employed twice (he was a little older) and had had exactly the same experiences. At least this provided a little reassurance. I took a while to think about whether I presented myself so poorly or whether it was because I was a woman. I felt I was able to come across convincingly. But with these people I came across like a stick in the mud. A guy opened a cafe in my street and had similar experiences. That told me this was not a woman-specific thing.

Later, I told my counselor at the senior service about that appointment. He said, "You're not a merchant at all! If you were, then Apple and Microsoft and all the companies that make their products in Asia would also be merchants." Right. Gotcha.

When I used this argument the next time I called the business development organization, the person on the phone said, "I don't care if you are a merchant or not. You will not get any money from us anyway, because for us you are a start-up entrepreneur (Existenzgründer)." I told this to my senior consultant, who replied, "You're not a start-up entrepreneur! You founded your company in February!" I thought: that's true. But did I really want to call them again?

It had been a long time since someone pissed me off like that, and treated me as rudely as this local so-called business promoter. I ended up borrowing money from my family.

1.1.4 Foundation Phase

My company was founded in early February 2015 at the notary. Then I waited for the entry into the commercial register and searched for a tax consultant, with whom I then made the entry into the commercial register, opened a bank account, and finally registered the business. With the tax consultant, I gathered the documents for the tax office and worked on the pre-designed homepage. I then wrote my general terms and conditions with the notary.

Other funny things were on my "to do" list: Completion of compulsory liability insurance and registration of utility model protection. These were both projects that turned my GmbH into a "GmbHorror." I was with three insurance agents and three insurance brokers. It took until August to get a decent offer. Everyone said that his offer was the only "real" one, and that everyone else had no clue what he or she was talking about.

I didn't have the slightest idea and just had to believe what they told me. I wanted someone who clearly showed me the risks, what was insured and what wasn't. Just like with a car: comprehensive or partial liability? How much does it all cost? I ended up going to an independent insurance consultant I paid for to help me. Meanwhile, it was early April. Three months had passed and I had neither acquired a customer during this time nor produced my products. I'd been busy with bureaucracy, insurance, utilities, etc. the entire time. But the homepage was ready and the business cards too. So at last I was able to get started.

I started making phone calls. I had looked at a number of companies and phoned them to present my product. Some companies asked me for a brochure. But I didn't have one. So I gave them the homepage address instead and started to organize the creation of a brochure. This was done by a professional company, and some friends did the proofreading. Then the brochure came (500 copies). The lower bar on it was purple instead of blue. The business card was half in blue, and needed to match the brochure. More discussions with the printing house and the designer. Finally, the printing house reprinted it. The new brochure came. The lower bar was now blue, but all the other pictures had a yellow tint where previously there had been a red one. It looked like a big pile of crap. Now I was really about to go over the edge!

I went to a trade fair in Hamburg. I ran around talking to companies and distributed my lilac flyer with my blue business card. A day later, my sister came to visit and discovered two really bad spelling errors in the top heading. I could have cried at this point. And I did. After this I signed up at a boxing club. Since than I have been doing kick boxing once a week.

1.1.5 Market Reality

From April to June I got four inquiries. After that, not even one. Three hundred phone calls, and not a single request. Trade fair visits? Nothing. And not a single call from the brochures I handed out.

In August, my frustration and existential fear increased, so I started writing applications. This phase lasted until October 2015. Then I got a commitment for a job starting on January 1, 2016. Part-time jobs are very rare in the engineering sector. Otherwise, I might have tried to keep operating my GmbH. But anything other than a full-time job would have been unrealistic. My motivation to run my own company had also hit rock-bottom.

During the application phase, I finally realized that the foundation just wasn't my thing. I didn't want it anymore. Looking back, there were only stumbling blocks and dead ends. There was nothing smooth about it. It never took off, so I figured it was just time to surrender. And I thought, no, it wasn't meant to be. So I guess I had to do the experience once and get it out of my system. Perhaps I can now better appreciate being an employee with all of its certainties and stability again.

1.1.6 My Personal Conclusion

I read in the newspaper that only a few people in Germany actually take the step to start their own business. The most common reason for not doing this was a lack of courage. I held on to a few newspaper clippings on the topic of company foundations and hung them over my desk. Their main message is not to get discouraged. I am convinced my product would have been good. The customer reactions were positive. Starting a GmbH as a woman, alone, in the technical arena; investing private money; a private loan; having an uncertain future (what will my life be like in half a year? a year from now?). None of that got me down.

The only things that discouraged me were my experiences with the funding, the bad consultants, and the entrepreneur seminar. These were all groups that should really have helped and encouraged me. My advice to anyone who wants to start a company is to look for someone who has already been there (or still is). And look for a good tax consultant right from the start. As for all the other alleged "advisers": just give a friendly nod, and don't believe a word they say.

Appendix

I The Founding Process at a Glance

II Additional Information that Focuses on the Personality of the Foundress

The following aspects allow deeper insight and complement the self-presentation by providing additional personality factors taken from the interview transcript.

Professional Background/Employee Perspective

- The foundress studied mechanical engineering because she did not feel secure about "interpersonal factors." She was very surprised that the interpersonal factors in this field are as powerful as they are—not only when it comes to technology and technical issues.

- In her 14 years of experience working as a mechanical engineer for a company, she worked in a number of mostly smaller establishments. These companies tended to be more patriarchal (with the owner being the "king"). She in some ways felt she was the only "rebel" in the entire business. Another company she worked for expanded very quickly. No one gave her concrete feedback regarding her work performance until after 3 years of employment she received overall criticism about her job, leading her to leave the company at her own request.

Role Models/Founding Experience

- The foundress never planned or thought she would be self-employed.
- The foundress was told about two acquaintances who successfully founded a company together and continue to successfully run it. She stated that this however did not consciously motivate or encourage her to start her own company.
- Later in the interview, she told us that her mother had been an entrepreneur in the catering industry and had gone bankrupt. The foundress also remembered the considerable burden of her mother's endless working days.

Motivational Factors

- The main reason to become a foundress was her frustration with her specific situation as an engineer employed at her former company.
- In this context, she reported having particularly "bad" bosses and problems where no one provided her with the necessary support.
- With her own company, she wanted to be a better boss, and work with her team cooperatively while motivating people. She made it her goal to receive and appreciate the ideas and suggestions of her employees. She felt that she would enjoy having a leadership position.
- Among other things, being an entrepreneur allowed her the opportunity for a self-determined, free organization of her everyday work activities.

III Her Take on Failure

The Dilemma with the Start-Up Consultation

The foundation consultant upset her in particular (*"I felt incredibly badly advised"/ "He scared me without actually helping me"*). She named some reasons for this:

- The consultation gave her the impression that the founding of a GmbH was difficult and problematic.

- She received different answers to her questions everywhere she went, and got the impression that no one knew what to actually do (*"I ran from Pontius to Pilate and no one could really tell me the right way to do it"*).
- She had the impression that the so-called "experts" were not experts at all. They displayed no specific knowledge of their professional field, and in some cases never had their own founding experience.
- The expert advice (e.g. from the IHK on patents) was also bad. She also received answers which even turned out to be wrong and not even applicable to her case. On the other hand, she learned the right information about her specific case with regard to patent law from her circle of acquaintances.

Business Planning

- She was not aware of the fact that the founding process of the GmbH would actually take several months. In her opinion, this delayed the process so much that she lost customers she had already acquired.
- It was only during a later phase of the start-up process that the foundress looked for a consultant who had real entrepreneurial experience. In her opinion, this consultant gave her very competent advice and could help her in concrete terms. The time lost by this point however was vast.
- The foundress herself also reported difficulties with the business planning. *"I thought I would sell the more parts and with a bigger profit margin."*
- In retrospect, the foundress described it as "naive" to have asked the advice of only one single potential customer. It struck her as "embarrassing" to ask without having founded a company or offered any products.

Entrepreneurial Knowledge

From the foundress' point of view, various knowledge deficiencies were responsible for uncertainty and the ultimate failure of the project. She identified (among other things) the following factors:

- Loss of time due to lack of entrepreneurial knowledge.
- Self-conception (*"Who am I? An entrepreneur or a foundress? Do I trade or am I a manufacturer?"*). The ability to assess the proper "to do" list to be able to assess promotional possibilities.
- Knowledge about concrete bureaucratic steps and proper sequence of the company founding.
- Knowledge about what documents have to be submitted, in what order, and where (*"I was rejected at each office because I didn't have the right documents yet"*).
- Specific funding advice (counselling on her specific industry sector).
- Acquiring the right training (and feedback at an early stage about these kinds of training opportunities).

Resilience/Inner Pressure/Stress

- The foundress frequently reported an internal pressure or stress that was unbearable (also see the self-description). "Working more self-determined and more freely—during the founding process I noticed it just doesn't work. 'More freedom' just doesn't exist." "The internal stress was much, much greater than I thought it would be."
- The following aspects were particularly problematic for the founder:
  - The order situation.
  - The dwindling capital stock (she paid her wages with this): "I became so tense, I just couldn't stand it." "Then it was just pure existential fear. So I said, 'I'm gonna look for a job again.'"
  - Always being "on call."
  - No representation.
  - "Are the customers really going to pay their bills?"
  - Problems with third parties (e.g. brochure problems).

Further Reading

The Global Failure Index, which records and systematically evaluates data on failed business start-ups, is a good supplement to the case study. This index can be found at http://www.thefailureinstitute.com/global-failure-index/ (retrieved on September 10, 2017). Further publications on start-up failure are also available on the institute's website which might also be helpful (e.g. for seminar or dissertation work in this context).

The Female Hunting Instinct: Entrepreneurial Life in Germany

Juliane Mueller

Abstract The present case, FEMALE HUNTING INSTINCT, tells the true story of a German woman who founded a knowledge-intensive business service (in the German *GmbH* form, equivalent to the American LLC), after spending a few years in France. The case consists of an interview with the female founder which focuses on the establishment of her business and illustrates her occupational life. In addition, her diary account from past to present provides a closer look at the thoughts and attitudes of a *mompreneur*. Sabine Jotter, one of four founders of the business presented and a mother of two, wanted to push for big budgets for her company. After a few years of freelancing, her "hunting" instinct was aroused, causing her at times to feel like an uncaring mother. On most days however, she is satisfied with the flexibility, independence, and leadership role she enjoys as part of her work. Using the jigsaw approach, the teaching material below is divided into four "pieces" to help bring students and complementary data together. In doing so, different perspectives on entrepreneurial success are discussed, and light is shed on the role of the woman and mothers in France and Germany. Perceived motivational factors also play a key role.

> **Teaching Note—The Female Hunting Instinct**
> *Target Group*
>   This case primarily addresses undergraduate and graduate students in the humanities and social sciences who are currently enrolled in gender or entrepreneurship/business courses. The case can additionally be used to introduce students from other fields to lessons about entrepreneurship and economics.
>
> (continued)

J. Mueller (✉)
Martin Luther University Halle-Wittenberg, Halle (Saale), Germany
e-mail: juliane.mueller@wiwi.uni-halle.de

© Springer International Publishing AG, part of Springer Nature 2018
S. Birkner et al. (eds.), *Women's Entrepreneurship in Europe*, FGF Studies in Small Business and Entrepreneurship, https://doi.org/10.1007/978-3-319-96373-0_10

Background Information

FEMALE HUNTING INSTINCT refers to an actual business in the knowledge-intensive sector in western Germany. The information about the business development and entrepreneurial life of the founder comes from a personal interview in the summer of 2017. Although some of the interview content has been changed for the sake of anonymity, the important facts are real. The translated answers in the interview are taken from a portrait of the businesswoman published in Josten and Laux (2007). The cited literature in the learning material and the details from the founder's diary are based on real life, although the diary entries have been altered for the sake of anonymity, as is the case with all of the names presented.

Main Learning Objectives/Key Issues

This text will help students develop an understanding of a gender perspective in entrepreneurship and business. The participants will recognize the lack of representation of female entrepreneurs in this field. By answering questions, students will be able to critically reflect upon different concepts of success, especially the individual perspectives of women business owners in Germany. After attending the class, students will have the knowledge and ability to consider diverse parameters when it comes to measuring business success. They will note that the motives for women to become entrepreneurs differ from those of men. Another goal of the case is to encourage students to think about their entrepreneurial careers. Practitioners and researchers will recognize female academics (in the humanities and social sciences) as potential founders as well as research subjects.

How to Use the Case/Teaching Strategy

This case is suited for the jigsaw technique (see Section II). In addition, blended learning is possible for case analysis. Work in pairs or small/large groups is also a possibility. The teaching plan is divided into three sections (class opening, jigsaw method, closing the class).

Section I: Class Opening

The following task can be used to introduce the students to the subject:

- Do you know any successful entrepreneur from your own surroundings (circle of family, friends, acquaintances)? Otherwise, think of someone who is popularly known. Write a short, meaningful description that illustrates his or her success.

After working on the task, students form groups of 4 to 6 people and work on the following:

- Introduce your successful entrepreneur to your group, based on the description you prepared. Explain why *you* think he or she is a successful entrepreneur.

(continued)

Either one person from each working group or volunteers can present their example to the class. The instructor can ask how many of the students personally know at least one entrepreneur. As an added, interesting, and important detail, find out how many of the identified entrepreneurs are female.

The instructor can also ask the students to prepare the description before attending the class. Depending on the participants' previous knowledge, it may be necessary to give a short definition of the terms *entrepreneur* and *entrepreneurship*.

Section II: The Jigsaw

A cooperative learning approach, the *jigsaw technique* is an effective approach for entrepreneurship instructors teaching heterogeneous classes (Holloway et al. 2008). The learning material is divided into "puzzle pieces," making each student's part essential for a full understanding of the given topic. In general, this learning strategy follows three steps:

I. The lecturer arranges all learners into temporary groups (the so-called "expert" groups) where the learners are assigned to the same task (their "piece"). Participants are then given time to independently think about their own responses and discuss the main points of their piece within the expert group. All experts should prepare a brief presentation to explain their contribution to the overall jigsaw puzzle. The Female Hunting Instinct case material is divided into four pieces ("Success", "Performance Gap", "Motivation", "Roles in France & Germany"). So ideally, Step I will have four expert groups.

II. The instructor then puts all the participants into new jigsaw groups that are composed of one participant from each of the expert groups. Make sure each student presents her or his piece to the group. The Female Hunting Instinct case has four expert groups, meaning each jigsaw group is composed of at least four different experts.

III. At the end of the session, review and collect the results with the entire class. For example, each jigsaw group can summarize in one sentence what they have learned.

The teacher's role is to lead students through the tasks, give support if/where needed, and provide feedback. The teacher should also encourage students to help each other. This teaching plan is recommended for a class size of about 16 students. For larger classes, there could be more than one expert group for each piece (and, of course, more than one expert for each piece in the jigsaw group) to ensure a productive working atmosphere.

Female Hunting Instinct

After opening the class, all students receive the Female Hunting Instinct case. This consists of the interview and the diary account of the female founder

(continued)

(The Diary Part I). Every participant reads the case on their own while also doing the following:

I. Outline the business development.
II. Summarize the key points from the diary extract (Part I). While doing this, also try to create a timeline of Sabine's occupational life.

Step I: Expert Questions

The experts can answer the following questions after receiving their jigsaw pieces (Success, Performance Gap, Motivation, or Roles in France & Germany). The questions depend on the material given to the expert group the students belong to.

Piece "Success" (The Diary Part II)

I. What parameters are considered when measuring entrepreneurial success?
II. The case discloses different reasons that drove Sabine to choose entrepreneurship. Identify them and try to arrange them in a logical order.

Piece "Performance Gap" (The Diary Part III)

I. How is successful entrepreneurship defined in research?
II. Do you agree with Lewis's statement? Think of the ideas you had in the beginning of the class when you talked about entrepreneurs you personally know.

Piece "Motivation" (The Diary Part IV)

I. What advantages of entrepreneurship does Sabine see?
II. Summarize typical motives for choosing entrepreneurship and discuss the motives that drove Sabine to entrepreneurship. Do you think the motives for women to become entrepreneurs differ compared to men?

Pieces "Roles in France & Germany" (The Diary Part V)

I. Have a look at the diary entry about social roles and summarize the key points.
II. Entrepreneurial intention is influenced by different determinants. What entrepreneurial motives can you identify in your piece?

The lecturer is welcome to provide additional instructions if the class is not familiar with the jigsaw learning technique. The following questions can help students to prepare the first stage of the teaching process:

(continued)

I. How can you clearly explain the key message of your "piece" to your fellow students?
II. Will diagrams or examples help you?
III. What questions will you ask to make sure your jigsaw group understands what you're presenting?

Step II: Jigsaw Questions

After becoming experts in Step I, the students combine what they have learned. The following questions can be helpful after presenting and arguing their pieces in their jigsaw group. The level of discussion within the groups will vary, so the lecturer has to decide when additional impulses or advice are necessary (e.g. a question or information that directs the discussion).

I. Do you think Sabine is a successful entrepreneur? Why or why not? Think of your answers in Step I and discuss.
II. What would Sabine's answer to Lewis's statement be?
III. After considering Sabine's individual goals, would you answer question I. differently?
IV. After considering the first three questions, how would you now define entrepreneurial success to the person sitting next to you?

Step III: Evaluation

After finishing Step II, the teacher then evaluates the jigsaw groups. Shuffle the students again to compare and contrast their results. A final class discussion is recommended at this point to allow participants to learn from the other groups and clarify crucial issues. To start the discussion, each group can e.g. provide their key findings.

Section III: Closing the Class

Once the lecturer has evaluated the jigsaw method, take a few final minutes for reflection. The following questions could help guide a closing conversation:

- What do you know about the vocational intention of the founder Sabine when she was younger?
- If you were Sabine, what would you have done differently (in respect to her entrepreneurial career)? Which decisions were good?
- Do you have a clear idea of your career path?
- Have you ever thought about choosing entrepreneurship? Are there any conditions under which entrepreneurship would be an option for you?

1 The Case: The Female Hunting Instinct[1]

1.1 The Female Hunting Instinct: Entrepreneurial Life in Germany

Interview with Sabine Jotter, founder of a German knowledge-intensive business service

In the Name of Science: A Knowledge-intensive Business Service

My blog introduces a successful businesswoman every month. Today I talked with Sabine Jotter, the managing partner and one of four founders of a knowledge-intensive business service in western Germany.

Since 1999, Sabine and her team have faced the challenge of making scientific content accessible to whoever is interested in the wider public. They publish and communicate in the name of science. Their customers are mainly research institutions such as universities and foundations or publishers. Their business now includes corporate publishing, campaign building and launching, consulting, media trainings, and work in public relations.

Interviewer (I): Thanks for your time Sabine. In 2004, you established the limited liability company (GmbH) 'In the name of science'. I read in an article that you originally had the dream of being a lecturer or professor.

Sabine (S): That's right. When I was a child, I was regarded as 'cheeky' at school. That sounds negative, but in reality, it was great fun for me to communicate and take responsibility. My personality was also positively influenced by my grandfather. In my childhood, we visited the traditional weekly markets because he was a market trader: He was loud and lively. That inspired me early on. The responsibilities I had within my family were also formative. When I imagined my future back then, I had a clear vision of myself in an independent, leading role.

After school, I graduated with a degree in history from the University of Hamburg, where I later also received my doctorate. On completion of my master's degree, I decided to go to France with my future spouse. There, I worked at the Paris-Sorbonne as a lecturer for the German Academic Exchange Service (DAAD) and taught German language, literature, and cultural studies. I also advised on Germany as a study and research destination. I had a great time!

I: So why did you leave France? Had you ever thought about staying there as a lecturer?

S: Yes and no. I loved the idea of working as a permanent lecturer in France, but it was not an option for our family, unfortunately. Unlimited job contracts were assigned centrally in France, and I hadn't received my doctorate at the time. Instead, we decided to return to Germany, where my husband was the first to secure a permanent job. I got a 2-year grant for finalizing my doctorate in Berlin. At that time, the arrival of our second child was close, and I continued freelancing.

---

[1] By Juliane Mueller

I: Can you tell us about the daily life and circumstances in France compared to German living? What is your experience?

S: I want to focus on one big difference: There [in France], no one would ever think to criticize me as a mother for my decision to continue working. It is completely normal and natural to balance the two [a job and a family]. Here [in Germany] however, I struggled with the usual 'bad mother' reproaches. To leave children in the care of others outside the home in Germany isn't always met with the best reaction.

I: Let's talk about your entrepreneurial life. How did you meet your cofounders?

S: After our return to Germany, I temporarily worked as an exhibition assistant at the House of History in Bonn and subsequently took over the editing of the DAAD magazine *Letter*. It was through my work for the DAAD that I first met the Germanist and accomplished journalist, Christin. A little later, I met Charlotte, who had studied history, politics, and English at the universities of Bonn, Vienna, and Cologne. We all worked for many years as freelancers, which is why we had well-established networks. While meeting up and speaking about our current freelance projects, we developed a desire for independent and self-reliant publishing work. This led us to the idea of founding our own company in 1999.

In 2004, another entrepreneur, the daily newspaper editor and interim chief editor of a research service agency for scientific information joined the company. Today, our business is managed by four women with proven science-oriented profiles.

I: Did you see any other reasons to become self-employed?

S: You bet. On the one hand, we knew the field in which we wanted to establish ourselves. I was seized by a real hunting instinct to make more out of my initial freelance work for publishers and to push for bigger projects for my own company. On the other hand, I was in my mid-thirties and wanted to combine my ever-present desire for an independent and leading role and my abilities and interests with a career and a family. As it turned out, a foundation of my own was the best route for *me*.

I: Sabine, why don't you tell our readers about the important decisions in respect to the growth of your business.

S: In the beginning, we ran the company from home and had no real entrepreneurial strategy. Over time, we realized that all of us (as mothers) needed structured separation between our private lives and work. I want to be able to get lost in my thoughts if I work on demanding projects. We found nice rooms in a female business park—an office building that had been developed as a private investment place by women, for women—in a big city in western Germany. This decision was advantageous because our synergies with female consultants and other business-oriented services in the building were easy to achieve and intensively used. In my mind, a strong female network is important for our success.

In 2004, we decided to establish a limited liability company (the German GmbH), which could also be relevant to our liability by including printing technology. Especially in regard to public venders, it is much better to compete with a GmbH. However, we can use the GbR (private partnership) form for journalistic tasks. Back then, we sometimes heard people questioning whether the 'lady trio' could push for big budgets. I doubt men are asked that question.

So far, our growth has been organic and without major financial risks. Financing the company has also not posed a problem so far, and because the investments were very manageable, no critical banking discussions or meetings were required.

I: In your opinion, what can women learn from men, and vice versa?

S: In general, women have to negotiate tougher when it comes to money and their demands until they are respected. In this area, we can learn from men how to 'perform'; that is, how to stay tough and not let ourselves be duped. Order calculations, such as those for our business in which research, moderation, and knowledge have to be included, are rich in soft factors and are therefore more difficult to quantify than the purely material calculations. It's extremely important for women to learn what our work is really worth, to raise higher fees, and to refrain from self-exploitation. On the other hand, I'm convinced that women have many benefits due to their female features in the business world: We can actively listen, we're more sensitive to the other person, we're more communicative, and we are queens of smart diplomacy in negotiations.

I: How about business plans for the future?

S: In the near future, another permanent employee with experience in the free economy and with clear PR skills will complete our team. We also need to think strategically in the long term. A new colleague should not only complement our competencies but be a bit younger. In any case, a lot will be done in the areas of control and business management to make us stronger.

Overall, it's too risky to rely only on one or a few contractors. The more support [we have], the lower the risk, so it's worth competing in the market.

I: What was your attitude towards entrepreneurship when you were younger?

S: Honestly, I had no idea about the entrepreneurial life. I first became aware of entrepreneurial independence as a possible way of life during my studies through the parents of a friend. Soon after that, thanks to the rather random and sudden takeover of the position of chief editor and publisher at a German-speaking women's press service, I experienced entrepreneurial responsibility for myself. Despite the enormous pressure I experienced at the time, my memory of this phase is positive. This is completely in contrast with my work with national newspapers, where I was put off by the dominant hierarchical conditions.

In my mind, at least on the subject of entrepreneurship, it's important to be able to fall back on role models who successfully and harmoniously live this lifestyle and to even become this kind of role model yourself. I believe that many qualified young women would be encouraged if they had personal contact with these kinds of people. They have to be able to see for themselves that it can be done and how to do it. The image of women entrepreneurs in the public is defined only by exceptions. Mostly, the men in suits are in charge.

I: What can we do to change this picture in the public's eyes?

S: My team members are doing their bit for early education by organizing for example Girls' Days to introduce girls to careers in science. What I would like to say to young women in particular is that they shouldn't just study their favorite subjects but seek a healthy mixture of topics. This way, they can both play out their preferences and maintain a realistic view of the future of their careers. I studied history without a reliable sense of perspective, and if I had known then what I know today, I would have definitely chosen a combination of subjects that apply to the business economy.

I: What do you want to tell our readers about entrepreneurship?

S: It's worth it, because it's good to be able to make new, independent decisions every day about what to put your life energy into. There's no spoon-feeding and no alienation—for me, that's the most important thing about this way of living.

1.2 The Diary Part I

Sabine's diary entries

Hamburg, 05/1985
Yesterday at the family party, a friend of my mother asked me my favorite question again: "And how do you want to earn a living after your studies?" Argh... Of course, I was as quick as ever and didn't let my feelings show. But this topic still bothers me even though after a lot of deliberation I decided against changing the subject. Good thing I didn't tell anyone important about my thoughts on changing my major to become a history teacher! I'm now curious to see if this university event on career perspectives this coming Thursday helps.

Paris, 06/1996
Our time here is coming to an end. Herbert had an interview in Berlin which went well. It seems we really will be moving back to Germany. What's in store for me? In the meantime, I've spent so many years in academia, and I like working in it, especially the flexibility and the fact that I'm doing what I'm interested in. All too vivid are my memories from my time in Hamburg. Those days I wrote for various newspapers but could never choose a subject! Other journalists may be happy, but the established procedures, old-fashioned structures, and irrefutable pecking order—not for me! I would never consider this kind of a position again. At most as a stop-gap thing to get by. Because of the kids, I need maximum free time. I really am grateful to "Professor Go-for-it" that he gave me the courage to do my doctorate. So I could discover how much I liked the sweet smell of research, of freedom.

But if I'm honest, I don't see a real career option in science. Even if I had already finished my doctoral thesis, I've been away from German universities for too long. Wasn't "Professor Oddball" in fact quite right when he impressed upon me, my stomach as round as a ball, the saying that "motherhood and science don't mix"?!

Paris, 07/1996
Today was a good day. I bought some children's clothes at a flea market. The little one is growing faster than I can keep up with. And the attic is filling up with clothes which he's grown out of. Actually, I wanted to leave the children's clothing till after our move. But apart from currently working on the doctoral thesis, there's also a reorientation on my to-do list. I'll address it at the latest when I've completed my dissertation. I want domestic help. As soon as the budget allows it?

Bonn, 04/1999
Today I felt it again, the evil two words in illuminated letters on my forehead: BAD MOTHER. I had a busy day. As usual, I had to sprint after work to pick up Frederik from kindergarten. (it's really time I quit!). Anyway, the sun was shining, so I decided to take the little one to the playground. There I would also be able to edit a text that is due tomorrow. In any case, Frederik played the whole time with the sand toys of the other children, whose supermoms were of course prepared and had brought toys with them. Unlike me. Basically, I'm on the other side. And yet it eats me up emotionally. I miss the time in France so much. There the society had so much more understanding for working mothers. Having said that, I have to take better care of my balance between work and free time in the future.

Bonn, 09/2001
We did it! We just signed! From now on, we can work in our own office every day and no longer have to move meetings with our clients to the cafe. Much more professional. But what exactly does our business do?? Oh, at least I love this independence, this flexibility!

Bonn, 2002
Today I know how unobtrusively I approached the university career back then. Looking back in hindsight, it's really naive. But how could I have known? I was only young. And none of my family had a college degree. That might even make me an educational pioneer. At least I can give my children a lot. I'm really curious to see which path they take later on.

Bonn, 03/2002
I am so happy with my decision to be self-employed! The order situation at our publishing house is growing slowly but steadily. Yesterday I ran into an old friend from school. We hadn't seen each other for a long time, so we quickly exchanged the most important questions: "Are you married?" "How many kids have you got?" "What do you do for a living?" These are moments in which I notice again and again that the decision for self-employment was the right one. I can divide my time the way I want, can go to the doctor in the morning, and at the same time deal with the daily business topics that I enjoy.

Bonn, 2003

A hard week is now behind me. I had suspected as much. I was in Hamburg with a customer at the beginning of the week and presented our concept (fortunately, they liked it!). I also had to stick to two deadlines. There was a lot going on at home as well—my eldest was having his birthday and wanted to celebrate it with his friends at our home with games and sleep-overs. So yesterday was the family party with all the preparations, and I also watched the little ones with their karate group in the morning. Ugh... There was so much else. I got a tip from the Millers about my search for a cleaning lady.

Bonn, 09/2011

A dark day for our business. I'm having real concerns about the continuation of our company. Our biggest customer has jumped ship. I never expected that. What's next? What could possible strategies look like? Ugh, what a blow. Now we have to make active acquisitions for the first time. We can't avoid it. I'm trying to see this development as an opportunity. But what if we don't find a solution—or have to become employees again? No, none of that. In any case, I can expand my work as a moderator of university events and panel discussions. I'm sure everything will be ok.

Bonn, 2014

Our company is celebrating its ten-year anniversary! This week we celebrated with a small party. Later that evening, I sat with Charlotte and Christine and reminisced about the early days of 'In the Name of Science'. How fitting that I had just been interviewed for a journal about our founding story. Some memories came back to life. Charlotte and Christine said they felt the same way I did, and that they too had at first seen the benefits of time flexibility in their self-employment. Both also perceived increases in flexibility and greater ability to balance the rewards and demands of career and family.

The conditions for potential founders have, in my opinion, improved. This is especially true for university members. As I learned in an interview, many universities now offer various start-up grants for students and scholars. Back in my day, we received integration support at the Women Business Park. Beyond that, apart from legal and tax advice on the arrangement of the company, we didn't really get any other external support. In retrospect, we could have put someone who could tell us about a business plan or business model canvas to good use. That may have spared us some hard lessons.

Bonn, 07/2017

We organized a Women Science Slam. What a success! Yesterday, seven scientists stood on the stage who were very keen about their research. That could have been me back then. Well, maybe I'll go to a Fempreneur Slam. I would have a lot to tell. Although I'm not sure where to fit that in my calendar... Business and family are enough. I wanted to see my girls again. It's now urgently time to plan the annual women's holiday. And to focus more on life and less on work again. So that I remain efficient ☺

Bonn, 07/2017
What an evening! I have to let it sink in first... Today was our class reunion. Lanky Lewis from the parallel class was also there. He works in the financial sector and looks just like I remember him from the 10-year reunion. Back then, we were really nice to one another. In any case, today he whined about start-ups and the importance of business plans. What he finally concluded about women's entrepreneurship and success was something like this: "It's clear that men are the better entrepreneurs. So why all the programs to foster women? Female entrepreneurs are less successful because their businesses are often smaller. It's no wonder that women's business ventures are often short-lived."

I couldn't give any real response to this. I was actually speechless for a moment. I'd never had to have a conversation like this before.

Bonn, 07/2017
So, now I've picked out some numbers from our business. I can't get the conversation from yesterday out of my head. I cannot and will not agree with Lewis on this point so easily. Maybe I will find some insights in research, someone has certainly already dealt with this topic. But now I have to ask myself—What about my venture? Are we or am I successful? I've looked at the turnover development of the GmbH to date. Primarily due to the loss of our biggest customer, sales declined by 27% compared to 2011.

In terms of employee development, we have in fact steadily increased. We started with the three of us. In the middle of 2011, we took on the first trainee, and since then every two years a new one after the other. We currently have an online editor (working as part of an unlimited contract), and two volunteers (one focusing on print, the other on events). But I'm not sure if I'm successful based on this data. So far, we've secured the survival of the business, and we've always been able to make payroll. And this year on Mother's Day we even joined in a new initiative at the employment agency here in Bonn to support female job seekers. That counts, doesn't it?

2 Teaching Material

2.1 The Diary Part II

August 2017
I found an interesting article about a qualitative study on women entrepreneurs and success in Germany. Ettl and Welter (2012, p. 85) report: "[...] in relation to success, motivations appear to resemble the strategic, long-term orientation of the

entrepreneur, while goals reflect the operative background for entrepreneurial actions and behaviour. Success, on the other hand, has a pronounced link to personal life issues: 'satisfaction', 'work-life balance', and 'reconciling employment and family' are the key concepts used by our respondents to describe success."

That's exactly how I see it! The authors also give a nice literature overview that I think is really useful. I wrote down some quotations: "In this perspective, we assume that making one's living could be one of the goals of an entrepreneurial person" (Ettl and Welter 2012, p. 75). And "To sum up, we propose that entrepreneurial success has to be understood from a perspective, which includes economic, societal and individual aspects" (Ettl and Welter 2012, p. 75).

Rosa et al. (1996) reports that gender is a significant determinant of small business performance, and women are seen as less successful compared to their male colleagues. Hemer et al. (2006) summarizes common indicators of success, including the survival of the company, profit level and growth, the period to reach the break-even point, employment growth, sales growth, market share, equity ratio, sales productivity, labor productivity, cash flow and cash flow growth, shareholder value and return on equity, return on investment (ROI) and Internal Rate of Return (IRR).

What I've learned from my quick and dirty research is that (1) relevant instruments being used in entrepreneurship research were developed and tested on male entrepreneurs (Greene et al. 2003), hence male businesses and attitudes are taken as the norm for both sexes; and (2) studies about entrepreneurial success "usually use a few or even a single of these indicators. They ignore that the assessment of the success of such a complex and multidimensional entity as a (new) business can hardly be based on just a few dimensions" (Ettl and Welter 2012, p. 74). "With regard to objectives, several studies have drawn attention to the fact that women entrepreneurs aim at combining both business and family responsibilities, reflecting a more intrinsic goal setting, while men tend to concentrate more on economic objectives" (e.g. Rosa et al. 1996; Ettl and Welter 2012, p. 76).

August 2017
In addition to the facts mentioned above, I identified some quotes from interviews with businesswomen in Germany (Ettl 2010, p. IX). I really like these statements. Some of them express my opinion to a T!
"A successful female entrepreneur . . ."
". . . must also be a happy entrepreneur!"
". . . keeps her feet on the ground!"
". . . needs courage, self-confidence and a family that stands behind her!"
". . . has a company that runs well and is recommended by word of mouth!"
". . . is well and happy"
". . . has to prove herself every day!"
". . . am I. If I did not believe it, it would not work. Something inside me knows that what I do is right!"
". . . is happy and satisfied with her life!"
". . . has a self-confident appearance, with which she is quite recognized by men!"

"... has perseverance and is ready for continuous learning!"
"... is fully committed to what she is doing!"
"... is still less noticed than a successful entrepreneur!"
"... is a happy entrepreneur!"
"... is pure with herself!"
"... must be in high gear and flexible. Nothing can be created out of nothing. Without flexibility nothing works!"
"... leads a company exactly like a man, only with feminine social competence and intuition!"
"... gets on with all her roles as a woman, as a mother, as a manager and as a human being. And she can remain authentic and true to herself!"
"... believes in herself and knows what she wants!"
"... listens to her heart!"
"... that's what I will be! But you need courage!"
"... will not be so easy!"
"... has personality!"
"... must be like my girlfriend and me. Independent, dedicated, purposeful, enjoy life, be satisfied, have fun at work and laugh!"
"... should be authentic!"
"... is totally herself!"
"... has a househusband at home!"

2.2 The Diary Part III

August 2017
After the talk with Lewis, I did a quick and dirty analysis and identified some articles about entrepreneurial success. The existing literature found that female-owned firms underperform when comparing performance indicators on an aggregate level. Here are some insights from an empirical study that focused on the gender gap in business success: Gottschalk and Niefert (2011) tracked the performance of approximately 4700 German start-up firms using data from the German KfW/ZEW Start-Up Panel. The authors report that female-founded firms perform worse for all considered performance indicators (sales, two measures of employment growth, and return on sales). In addition, the data indicates that female entrepreneurs, compared to their male counterparts, have a lower level of formal education, less professional experience, are part of smaller start-up teams, are more often driven by necessity, and are overrepresented in the retail and service industries, and in lower-tech industries in general. The authors state that these differences can explain parts of female entrepreneurial underperformance, although their contribution to the performance gap depends largely on the performance indicator considered. Data analysis shows that gender differences in founders' resources (human capital, business partners) partly explain the performance gaps in growth and sales. Furthermore, although the investigation does not confirm gender

differences in profit orientation, female entrepreneurs are in fact affirmed as less growth-oriented.

Furthermore, I found the following information in the literature: "Growth of the firm has been an extremely important issue in the study of entrepreneurship, yet the relationship between gender and growth has rarely been studied in the field" (Greene et al. 2003, p. 13). Du Rietz and Henrekson (2000) provide support for several previous studies that female entrepreneurs tend to underperform relative to their male counterparts on the aggregate level. "Existing literature has established that most firms do not grow at all and that average growth in employment in firms is driven by a few firms growing very rapidly" (Minniti and Naudé 2010, p. 283). Robb and Wolken (2002, p. 15) found that "female owned firms were smaller, younger, more concentrated in retail sales and services, and more likely to be organized as proprietorships than were male-owned firms". In addition, women's ventures tend to be less profitable than those of men.

"The exit rate of new firms (or rate of firm turnover) is high in all countries" (Minniti and Naudé 2010, p. 283), whereas the survival rates of female-owned micro and small enterprises were lower compared to their male-owned counterparts (Mead and Liedholm 1998). "Females are more likely than males to voluntarily leave their firms" (Justo and deTienne 2008, p. 14). Justo and deTienne (2008, p. 13) found that "marriage is [...] an important predictor of voluntary exit, and this effect was reinforced in the presence of children".

2.3 The Diary Part IV

Summer 2017
An old friend told me that the Global Entrepreneurship Monitor (GEM) 2016/17 report was published recently, so I scanned it for the first time. Among other things, I read about the Total Early-stage Entrepreneurial Act (TEA), the central indicator of GEM. In fact, "Germany [...] and France report the lowest female TEA rates in the GEM sample, with around 3% of the adult female population engaged in entrepreneurial activity" (GEM Consortium 2017, p. 28).

The low activity rate grabbed my attention. So I searched for some more information about women's entrepreneurship and found this interesting paper: Lawton Smith et al. (2015, p. 2) point out that women "comprise very few academic entrepreneurs" and commercialize their research less frequently than their male colleagues. Because female academics have high levels of human capital, Ahl (2006) indicates that women often lack the knowledge and skills necessary to commercialize their research and start a business.

August 2017
What a rainy week! Yesterday I spent some time researching entrepreneurial motives. Here are some of my results:

Kirkwood (2009) analyzed 75 semi-structured interviews with 28 female and 47 male entrepreneurs. The findings suggest that both women and men appeared similarly motivated by a combination of push and pull factors. Three gender differences were found in the motivations: women were more influenced by a desire for independence; women considered their children as motivators more than men; and men were influenced more by job dissatisfaction than women (Kirkwood 2009).

Existing literature found gender differences in reasons for starting a new business venture. "Men stressed the desire to be their own bosses and women reported being concerned with personal challenge and satisfaction" (Scott 1986, in Greene et al. 2003, p. 7).

Rey-Martí et al. (2015) investigated female entrepreneurs' motivation (their propensity for risk, their desire to find a work-life balance and develop business skills, their need to seek self-employment, and their desire to earn more than in paid employment) to achieve business survival. A crisp set qualitative comparative analysis shows that female entrepreneurs whose motive is to pursue a better work-life balance are less likely to succeed, whereas women with a propensity for risk are more likely to succeed.

2.4 The Diary Part V

August 2013
Today I learned a new term: mompreneur—the neologism of 'mom' and 'entrepreneur'. I'm not sure if I want to be labelled a 'mompreneur'. I think motherhood doesn't define me in my career nor predict the success of my venture—my vision and courage do.

Although I am very sure that there are more similarities than differences between male and female entrepreneurs, I see one main difference: the need to balance two major social roles.

March 2016
During breakfast, I heard an interesting report about a new trend on the book market. It started with Pamela Druckerman's *French Children Don't Throw Food* (Druckerman, 2012) and has continued with the recently published book *Vive la Famille* by Annika Joeres (2015). In recent years, parenting books telling us why French kids are superior and what we could learn from French families (e.g. how to avoid tantrums) have become popular.

My kids are now grown, but I still often have debates with friends about the differences between motherhood in Germany and France. Last time the starting point was the German metaphor *Rabenmutter*, which means "bad mother" or literally a "raven mother." Most Germans don't know that there is no French equivalent of this pejorative. *Duden* (the quintessential German dictionary) explains the word's origin: It's a popular German misconception that parents don't care very well for their young "ravens" and might even "kick them out of the nest." In reality, the young birds leave the parental nest on their own even though they are not yet able to fly, and therefore look helpless. But after this happens, the bird is still protected and fed by his or her parents for a number of weeks. So in spite of these preconceived notions, these parents do in fact bring up their babies with an acceptable level of care.

Consistent with this notion, I read in Wiegel (2016) that in France, the notion of an uncaring mother is unknown, and the term *mère-poule* (to be a mother hen) is considered negative. Wiegel writes that French parents are more selfish, and their focus, unlike that in Germany, is to a lesser extent on the child. She mentions that German women want to be perfect mothers, whereas French mothers see themselves primarily as women with their own needs who focus on "femaleness." The population researcher Norbert Schneider (2013) explained that there is in fact an exaggerated ideal regarding parents in Germany.

As far as I can see, the main differences lie in the culture. I've always observed that French moms *believe* they are doing everything right, whereas German moms *want* to do everything right.

April 2016
I read an interesting article on the Internet today. Once again, it's about the role of the mother in France. In an interview, the journalist Annika Joeres talks about much lower expectations and demands of mothers in French society, so that they would never have to adapt to a guilty conscience or feelings. In this way, French women have more time for themselves, while in Germany, babies are showered with attention and young mothers are neglected. I was not aware that French women breast feed less than the global average. Joeres believes that this attitude is linked, inter alia, to French family policy which makes sure that mothers return to the labor market as quickly as possible. She says (polemically) "When German mothers sign up for Pekip courses [baby development activity classes], many French women are already back to work and are starting to optimize their bodies again."

Come to think of it, raising children in France is also a state matter. Since schools are all-day schools there, mothers with school-age children can more easily work full-time than in Germany. It goes without saying that the children are also taken care of in French schools when the lessons are cancelled (which isn't always the case in Germany).

As I read a while back in Wiegel (2016), in France, the working mother is seen as a "normal case," where French women stay on the job while caring for their first and second children. This is what I later became aware of: whoever takes a longer break, contrary to the French mainstream model, garners a lot of ridicule. A colleague in Paris at that time (who had put her daughters in day care after a year and had breastfed for the first six months) had to listen to critical comments like, "What do you do all day long? Don't you get bored with your children?"

In any case, in the course of this article I came across another recent article by Calla (2016). I agree when she writes that maternity is not automatically linked to a career break or a turnaround in France. According to her research, women work there full-time more often than in the rest of Europe. And yet (or perhaps because of this), France leads in birth rates, with an average of two children per woman, compared to 1.4 children per woman in Germany in 2014.

References

Ahl, H. (2006). Why research on women entrepreneurs needs new directions. *Entrepreneurship Theory and Practice, 30*(5), 595–621.
Calla, C. (2016). Das Wort "Rabenmutter" gibt es auf Französisch nicht. *Die Zeit Online*. Retrieved from http://www.zeit.de/kultur/2016-04/regretting-motherhood-mutterschaft-debatte-frankreich-10nach8
Druckerman, P. (2012). *French children don't throw food*. Random House.
Du Rietz, A., & Henrekson, M. (2000). Testing the female underperformance hypothesis. *Small Business Economics, 14*(1), 1–10.
Ettl, K. (2010). *Unternehmerinnen und Erfolg aus individueller und kontextueller Perspektive*. Peter Lang.
Ettl, K., & Welter, F. (2012). Women entrepreneurs and success. In M.-Á. Galindo & D. Ribeiro (Eds.), *Women's entrepreneurship and economics* (pp. 73–88). New York: Springer.
GEM Consortium. (2017). *Global entrepreneurship monitor global report* 2016/17. Retrieved from http://www.gemconsortium.org/report/49812
Gottschalk, S., & Niefert, M. (2011). Gender differences in business success of German start-up firms. ZEW Discussion Paper No. 11–019. *International Journal of Entrepreneurship and Small Business, 18*(1), 15–46. Mannheim.
Greene, P. G., Hart, M. M., Gatewood, E. J., Brush, C. G., & Carter, N. M. (2003). *Women entrepreneurs: Moving front and center: An overview of research and theory*. Florida: Coleman Foundation.
Hemer, J., Berteit, H., Walter, G., & Göthner, M. (2006). *Erfolgsfaktoren für Unternehmensausgründungen aus der Wissenschaft. Studien zum deutschen Innovationssystem 05–2006*. Karlsruhe: Fraunhofer-Institut für System- und Innovationsforschung.
Holloway, S. S., Tilleman, S. G., Macy, R., Parkman, I. D., & Krause, A. J. (2008, January). *Active learning in entrepreneurship: Applying the jigsaw method to entrepreneurship instruction*. In United States Association for Small Business and Entrepreneurship. Conference Proceedings, p. 1.
Joeres, A. (2015). *Vive la famille: was wir von den Franzosen übers Familienglück lernen können*. Freiburg: Verlag Herder GmbH.
Josten, M., & Laux, J. (2007). Erfolgreich die eigene Chefin. Portrait 04, Dr. Isabell Lisberg-Haag Die Brückenbauerin zwischen Wissenschaft und Wirklichkeit. *Inmit*, 38–43. Retrieved from http://www.vdg-forum.de/files/erfolgreich_die_eigene_chefin.pdf
Justo, R., & DeTienne, D. R. (2008). *Gender, family situation and the exit event: Reassessing the opportunity-cost of business ownership* (Working Paper WP08–26). Madrid: IE Business School, Instituto de Empresa, Area of Economic Environment.
Kirkwood, J. (2009). Motivational factors in a push-pull theory of entrepreneurship. *Gender in Management: An International Journal, 24*(5), 346–364.
Lawton Smith, H., Etzkowitz, H., Meschitti, V., Poulovassilis, A., Henry, C., Nelson, T., & Lewis, K. (2015). *Female academic entrepreneurship and commercialisation: Reviewing the evidence and identifying the challenge* (Trigger Research Working Paper Series Working Paper No. 1). Birkbeck: University of London. Retrieved from http://www.bbk.ac.uk/trigger/docs/TRIGGER_WP_01.pdf
Mead, D. C., & Liedholm, C. (1998). The dynamics of micro and small enterprises in developing countries. *World Development, 26*(1), 61–74.

Minniti, M., & Naudé, W. (2010). What do we know about the patterns and determinants of female entrepreneurship across countries? *The European Journal of Development Research, 22*(277). https://doi.org/10.1057/ejdr.2010.17

Rey-Martí, A., Porcar, A. T., & Mas-Tur, A. (2015). Linking female entrepreneurs' motivation to business survival. *Journal of Business Research, 68*(4), 810–814.

Robb, A., & Wolken, J. D. (2002). *Firm, owner, and financing characteristics: Differences between female- and male-owned small businesses* (FRBG working paper).

Rosa, P., Carter, S., & Hamilton, D. (1996). Gender as a determinant of small business performance: Insights from a British study. *Small Business Economics, 8*(6), 463–478.

Schneider, N. (2013, June 20). Elternideal schlecht für Kindersegen. *Frankfurter Allgemeine Zeitung*. Retrieved from http://www.faz.net/-gux-7aal4

Wiegel, M. (2016). *Deutsche Supermami und französische Rabenmutter- Der Blick auf die Frauen- und Mutterrollen der Nachbarinnen*. Retrieved from https://doi.org/10.5771/9783845272061-177